International Futures

DILEMMAS IN WORLD POLITICS

Series Editor

George A. Lopez, University of Notre Dame

Dilemmas in World Politics offers teachers and students of international relations a series of quality books on critical issues, trends, and regions in international politics. Each text examines a "real world" dilemma and is structured to cover the historical, theoretical, practical, and projected dimensions of its subject.

FORTHCOMING TITLES

David S. Mason
**Revolution and Transition in East-Central Europe,
Second Edition**

□   □   □

Thomas G. Weiss and Cindy Collins
**Humanitarian Challenges and Intervention:
World Politics and the Dilemmas of Help**

□   □   □

James A. Caporaso
Challenges and Dilemmas of European Union

□   □   □

Janice Love
**Southern Africa
in World Politics**

SECOND EDITION

INTERNATIONAL FUTURES

■ ■ ■

Choices in the Creation of a New World Order

Barry B. Hughes

UNIVERSITY OF DENVER

WestviewPress

A Division of HarperCollins*Publishers*

To Mihajlo D. Mesarovic,
who introduced me to world modeling
and to much of the world

Copyright © 1996 by Barry B. Hughes

Published in 1996 in the United States of America by Westview Press, 5500 Central Avenue, Boulder, Colorado 80301–2877, and in the United Kingdom by Westview Press, 12 Hid's Copse Road, Cumnor Hill, Oxford OX2 9JJ

Library of Congress Cataloging-in-Publication Data
Hughes, Barry, 1945–
  International futures : choices in the creation of a new world
order / Barry B. Hughes. — 2nd ed.
    p. cm. — (Dilemmas in world politics)
  Includes bibliographical references (p.   ) and index.
  ISBN 0-8133-3023-8
  1. Forecasting. 2. Policy sciences. 3. Forecasting—Mathematical
models. 4. Forcasting—Data processing. I. Title II. Series.
H61.4.H828 1996
003'.2—dc20   96-8405
                                                                  CIP

The paper used in this publication meets the requirements of the American National Standard for Permanence of Paper for Printed Library Materials Z39.48-1984.

10   9   8   7   6   5   4   3   2   1

□ □ □

Contents

□ □ □

Tables and Figures

□ □ □

Preface

This book will immerse you in thinking about global futures. It is not a book for passive readers. Unlike most books on the future, it does *not* communicate a specific vision of global developments. Instead it asks you to participate in the development of your own understanding and vision.

The book involves you in investigating the future in two ways. The first is via traditional text. Chapter 1 argues that we understand the future (1) through extrapolation of trends and (2) through causal understandings of the world. Chapter 2 assists you in the exploration of trends, and Chapters 4–8 help you to investigate competing causal understandings of global systems. Because you will combine your analysis of trends and causal relationships with your own values to create prescriptions, the text also helps you to identify common value orientations and to think about your own.

The second method, which will involve you even more actively in exploration of the future, is a computer simulation model called International Futures (IFs).[1] IFs is a global model that simulates population, food, energy, environmental, economic, and political developments from a base year of 1992, allowing forecasts extending as far into the future as the year 2050. It divides the world into 14 geographic regions—seven are individual countries (the United States, Canada, Mexico, Russia, China, India, and Japan), one is the increasingly close-knit grouping of countries in the European Union (EU), and six are broad groupings of countries (other economically developed countries, members of OPEC, other Latin American countries, other African countries, other South and East Asian countries, and the remaining countries of the world, mostly poorer Central European countries or former Soviet republics).

A few design features make the book more readable and the computer model easier to use. First, boxes highlight "Important Notes," attention to which should reward the reader. Second, indentation and an arrow symbol set off more technical computer information and tips so that the reader can more easily return to them later. Third, each of the chapters that focus on IFs includes "Research Questions" to help the reader begin explorations with IFs.

I hope you will find this book of considerable use in thinking about the future whether or not you use the IFs model. If you do not use IFs, it is reasonable that you skip portions of the text that focus on it (especially Chapter 3 and the last section in each of Chapters 5–8).

Although this book and the IFs model are fully self-contained, they can also usefully serve as supplements to the study of world politics presented in Barry B. Hughes, *Continuity and Change in World Politics*, 3rd edition, Prentice-Hall, 1997. The approaches in the two books are complementary.

Barry B. Hughes

□ □ □

Acknowledgments

This book and the IFs model it describes build upon the work of so many people over a period of so many years that it is impossible to acknowledge those individuals fully. I am grateful for the long-term, generous support and encouragement of Harold Guetzkow and Karl Deutsch. It is especially important to recognize the modeling debts this effort owes to Mihajlo D. Mesarovic, Thomas Shook, John Richardson, Patricia Strauch, Aldo Barsotti, Juan Huerta, and other members of the team that developed the World Integrated Model, and to recognize Stuart Bremer, Peter Brecke, Thomas Cusack, Wolf-Dieter Eberwein, Brian Pollins, and Dale Smith of the GLOBUS modeling project. Over the years, individuals who have used or tested earlier versions of the model, including Gerald Barney, Donald Borock, Richard Chadwick, and Jonathan Wilkenfeld, have contributed much to its continued development. Peter Brecke, Phil Schrodt, and Douglas Stuart provided very useful reviews of this volume. Michael Niemann, Terrance Peet-Lukes, and Douglas McClure assisted in the process of developing earlier microcomputer adaptations of IFs. Jennifer Knerr of Westview Press and George Lopez, the series editor of the Dilemmas in World Politics series, have been staunch supporters with consistently good advice. Many, many others have helped in the production of a model and a text that inevitably have more remaining flaws than the author would care to admit, but that would have been impossible without their ideas and encouragement.

B. B. H.

□ □ □

Acronyms

AIDS	Acquired Immune Deficiency Syndrome
CFCs	chlorofluorocarbons
CFE	Conventional Forces in Europe
EU	European Union
G-77	Group of 77
GATT	General Agreement on Tariffs and Trade
GDP	gross domestic product
GNP	gross national product
IBRD	International Bank for Reconstruction and Development
IEA	International Energy Agency
IFI	international financial institution
IFs	International Futures
IGOs	intergovernmental organizations
IMF	International Monetary Fund
INGOs	international nongovernmental organizations
ITO	International Trade Organization
LDCs	less developed countries
NACC	North Atlantic Cooperation Council
NAFTA	North American Free Trade Agreement
NATO	North Atlantic Treaty Organization
NICs	newly industrialized countries
NIEO	new international economic order
OECD	Organization for Economic Cooperation and Development
OPEC	Organization of Petroleum Exporting Countries
OSCE	Organization of Security and Cooperation in Europe
R&D	Research and Development
UNCED	United Nations Conference on Environment and Development
UNCTAD	United Nations Conference on Trade and Development
WEU	Western European Union
WIM	World Integrated Model
WTO	World Trade Organization

ONE

□ □ □

Action in the Face of Uncertainty

Contrary to some renditions of history, most early European naval explorers believed the earth to be round, so that one could eventually return to Europe by sailing far enough to the West. Successive expeditions chose to push further and further to the West in the search for a route around the world, a search that others viewed as foolhardy and dangerous. In 1519 Ferdinand Magellan sailed west from Europe with 5 ships and 265 men. In 1522 one ship returned to Spain from the east with 18 men, completing the first voyage around the world. Magellan himself died in the Philippines. His expedition and those of others in that era established new contacts among the peoples of the globe, the consequences of which we are still watching evolve.

We now confront a future as uncertain as that facing Magellan in 1519. We devote about 5 percent of total global economic output to the pursuit of military security, and we simultaneously have created an insecure world with nearly 60,000 nuclear weapons in the hands of a growing number of separate political entities. The economic product of the average human has attained levels surpassing any in history, though the economic performance of most of the world's economies in the past decade was weak and income disparities are growing in most of them. The technological sophistication of our scientists and engineers has created new marvels in electronics, biology, and other fields, but many aspects of our shared environment are deteriorating. Some of the choices that we make in the next decade on these issues will have consequences as important as the decisions made by Magellan. We will never be able fully to anticipate their consequences. We will act in the face of uncertainty. Yet we will make choices; collectively we will continue to reshape the world order.

What will be the future of human environmental, economic, and political-social systems? That is the central question of this book. The easy and correct answer is that no one knows. If we were so fatalistic as to believe that we had no control over the future, we might simply accept that response and return our attention to daily life. Most of us believe, however, that our actions substantially shape our own future and the futures of our descendents. Many of us fear that misguided action, whether it be environmental despoliation or nuclear war, could lead to catastrophe. Many hope that thoughtful behavior can instead assure a peaceful and prosperous world. We therefore find ourselves in *a very real dilemma: We cannot know the future, but it is important to act in the face of that uncertainty.*

The question that motivates this book takes on special importance today because many features of the world order defined in the late 1940s have changed dramatically in the past few years. It is clear that we face critically important political, economic, and environmental issues, and it is also clear that the structures and institutions with which we will address them are in great flux. A new world order will come into focus over the next decade. Any established world order constrains many choices and makes the consequences of action somewhat predictable. In contrast, a period of new world order creation requires that we reconsider even the most fundamental of choices, and it simultaneously reduces predictability. We must now act in the face of the greatest uncertainty.

In order to reduce the dilemma to manageable proportions, we must make at least reasonable estimates about what the future holds, with or without our action. In order to make such estimates, we can decompose our general question about the future into three more specific ones. First, *where do current changes appear to be taking us?* Second, *what kind of future would we prefer?* Third, *how much leverage do we have to bring about the future we prefer?* Each of these questions is more manageable than our central question (although hardly simple) and collectively they help us grapple with the necessity of choice in the face of incomplete knowledge. The task of this book is to assist you in investigating these three questions and thereby to address the dilemma we collectively face. In the process you will organize your own thoughts about the new world order.

THE EXAMINATION OF CHANGE

Where do current changes appear to be taking us? The two standard techniques for studying change are **extrapolation** and **causal analysis**. Extrapolation is trend projection. If global population is growing at 1.5 percent this year, a simple extrapolation of the future assumes that it will grow at 1.5 percent each year in the future. A more sophisticated extrapolation might recognize that the annual population growth rate has declined from 2 percent each year in the late 1960s to 1.5 percent now. Therefore, the rate of growth may decline further in the next few decades. An even more sophisticated analysis might recognize cyclical behavior in a phenomenon (such as business cycles in the economy) and extrapolate the cycles into the future.

Extrapolation might allow its user to make a fortune on the stock market ("technical" analysts or "chartists" rely on it heavily) and might also provide some very good guesses about global futures. It has, however, significant limitations. There is an old story about a person falling from the top of the Empire State Building. As she passes the 51st floor, a friend at a window asks how it is going. The response is "so far, so good." The reason that most of us see a little black humor in this is that we automatically supplement extrapolative reasoning with causal analysis, a consideration of cause-and-effect relations. We know the effect on the human body of hitting the ground at high speed.

In theory, causal analysis is much superior to extrapolation. In the stock market, for instance, "fundamentalists" direct their attention to the presence or absence of underlying strengths of companies that might eventually cause their earnings and stock prices to rise. Weather forecasting provides another example of how causal analysis differs from and may improve upon extrapolation. If it has been raining for four days, simple extrapolative analysis tells us to predict rain tomorrow; that forecast might indeed be a reasonably good one. In contrast, however, a meteorologist who knows that the low pressure area over us now will give way to high pressure by midnight, and that high pressure areas generally provide (cause) clear skies, will predict sunshine. Similarly, extrapolative analysis might lead us to predict that the world will use ever larger amounts of oil in supplying its energy needs. Causal analysis might consider estimates of the amount of oil in the earth's crust and predict that the oil use will peak and then decline.

In practice, however, causal analysis is difficult and complex and may not always be superior to extrapolation. The central problem is one of specification of the appropriate causal relationship(s). Students of international politics face this problem with respect to war. Extrapolations of the amount or intensity of warfare, even those that attempt to look at cycles of war, provide a weak basis for forecasting, because past patterns of warfare exhibit substantial irregularity. Instead, most scholars search for the causes of war: power differentials among countries, incompatible interests, ethnic rivalries, economic difficulties, the nature of government decision-making mechanisms, miscalculations by leaders, human aggressiveness, and so on. Among the problems with causal analysis of war, however, are that there seem to be a very large number of causes, and they often interact with one another in extremely complex ways.

To make forecasting of warfare even more difficult, it is a discrete variable. Like pregnancy, and unlike the amount of oil produced in the world, it either occurs or does not, with rather sudden breaks between the two conditions. Frequently with discrete variables (such as warfare, pregnancy, or rain) analysts replace specific forecasts with probabilities and seek to understand when probabilities increase or decrease.

In much causal analysis, the specification of the causal variables becomes rather complex. It can become difficult for analysts to calculate all of the relationships and to produce a forecast. They therefore sometimes turn to a computer representation (computer simulation) of the relationships that allows them to make experimental changes in the **independent variables** or causes and to recalculate quickly the implications for an interesting **dependent variable** or effect. For instance, with a computer model our student of warfare could change the value of ethnic tension and compute the implications for the outbreak of war. This book will analyze global change using both extrapolation and causal analysis.

VALUES AND THE FUTURE

What kind of future would we prefer? The second of our two questions is also not a simple one. There is a saying that the only thing worse than not getting your heart's desire is getting it. We probably have all had the experience of wanting something desperately and then finding that obtaining it did not make us happy. Often the problem is a failure to clarify our own values in advance.

Let us consider three value issues. These correspond to three complexes of issues: the broad environment (issues of human-environment relationship); the economy (issues of material well-being); and the international political system (issues of physical security). With respect to the broad environment there is a general and partly value-based debate between those who see the key to survival of humans over time in their mastery of the environment and those who see it in building sustainable relationships with the environment. The former value **progress** and are likely to desire ever-improving technology. They often see that progress as providing a cushion against the vagaries of nature. The latter value **sustainability**; they frequently propose accepting a basic standard of living compatible with human health and focusing further efforts on greater spiritual or cultural achievement. They often argue that humans are part of nature rather than superior to it and that humanity must recognize the limits that nature sets.

With respect to the economy and issues of material well-being, one group tends to emphasize **economic growth**. "A rising tide lifts all boats" could be their rallying cry; economic growth will improve the condition of all. They seek greater investment and improvements in economic efficiency. A second group may also desire economic growth but places greater importance than the first on **equality** (sometimes greater equality is seen as part of a broader phenomenon called **development,** involving widespread improvements in the quality of life, not simply increases in income). They often argue that individuals or even entire countries are at a relative disadvantage in reaping the benefits of growth because of their starting position in the economic system. They therefore prefer futures in which some compensation or even restructuring occurs to redress imbalances. The poor need not always be with us, at least not in such large numbers. And poverty is not simply a matter of absolute condition, but also of relative deprivation.

When we turn to the international political system and issues of physical security we find similar value-based disagreements. Some emphasize the virtue of protecting one's own **security** because, they argue, no one else will value it equally or sacrifice on our behalf. In some cases, war will be a necessary instrument of policy in that search for security. The price of security and peace is eternal vigilance. Others argue that our greatest attention should be to the preservation of **peace** and that only collective efforts in the world will ultimately provide both peace and security. Eternal vigilance gives rise not to peace, but to arms races and periodic wars. Therefore, we should collectively beat our swords into plowshares.

This discussion reminds us that our effort to understand the future must also incorporate an exercise in value clarification. Although this book will provide some assistance in that exercise, the burden of doing it lies overwhelmingly with the reader.

HUMAN LEVERAGE

How much leverage do we have to bring about the future we prefer? Competing value orientations often interact with different causal understandings of the world. Those who value progress and mastery of the environment understand the relationship between humanity and the environment as one that allows humanity to rise above the environment and to improve the condition of each succeeding generation. This view of the modern world originated in Europe within the past few centuries and gradually spread around the world; we will call those who hold it **modernists.** Those who advocate sustainability argue that what the modernists see as progress is often only unsustainable overexploitation of the environment. It relies upon using resources such as fossil fuels that are not replaceable and upon dumping pollutants onto the land and into the air and water faster than these environments can cleanse themselves. Technology may support that overexploitation in the short and even mid-term, but ultimately the economic systems based upon it are built on sand and will collapse. These individuals are **eco-wholists** (see Pirages, 1983; Hughes, 1985c; Haas, 1990) and look for leverage in population control and more careful husbandry of resources.

Many of those who value growth have a strong faith in the market. They generally believe that if governments let it function as unfettered as possible, it will generate growth of value to all participants. Traditionally (and still today in Europe) those who value free or liberated markets and who believe in their benefits were called liberals, and we will call them liberals or **commercial liberals**. Many commercial liberals also value some measure of equality. They often believe, however, that active participation in the market is the best mechanism for improving the lot of the poor. In contrast, those who focus our attention sharply on equality frequently believe that so-called free markets reward those who enter them with the strongest position. Those who control capital have a stronger bargaining position than those who can offer only their labor. Moreover, those who control capital often also have the means to influence the political system and can use it to reinforce their market position. **Structuralists** argue that these structural characteristics of the market environment make it very difficult for the disadvantaged to redress the inequalities of initial positions in the economic system and that society must act consciously to do so.

Those who value security often look to the traditional state (country) as the most reliable guarantor of that security. States use police to maintain order internally and rely upon military forces to pursue it externally. **Realists** recognize that the system is imperfect but argue that a world without central government is fundamentally a world of anarchy. In such an environment, protecting the power of states remains our best hope. Critics of that understanding, especially **political liberals,** point out that the security of the state system has always come at the cost of intermittent warfare. The weapons of the modern era, especially nuclear weapons, have raised that cost far too much. Moreover, the pressures for interstate cooperation on environmental, economic, and security issues have grown at the same time that communications and transportation technology make such global cooperation increasingly possible. Finally, and very important, the transformation of many states in the global system to democracies and the rapid growth in trade and other transactions among them have created a much stronger base for international cooperation than ever before. Liberals therefore understand the fundamentals of world politics very differently from realists and conclude that we should pursue cooperation and peace rather than the balance of power.

We thus face a complicated task in addressing the second and third of our three questions, those asking what future we would prefer and what leverage we have. Value orientations and understandings of the world tend to shape and reinforce one another. In fact, values tend to shape discussions even of our first question, concerning where current changes appear to be taking us. We will see that the different value-understanding orientations (we call them **worldviews**) emphasize different trends or can interpret the same trend in quite different ways.

HOW THIS STUDY PROCEEDS

To repeat, our central dilemma is that *we cannot know the future, but we must act as if we can.* A good place to begin our assault on that dilemma is with an attempt to extrapolate trends and to investigate with fairly simple tools where the future may be taking us. Chapter 2 provides information concerning major global trends. It draws attention to trends of interest to each of the worldviews and will note some differences of interpretation. In addition, it will provide a more extensive discussion of different extrapolative techniques. In short, the primary purpose of Chapter 2 is to make a preliminary effort to answer the first of our questions of decomposition, Where is global change taking us?

Chapters 4 through 7 will shift our attention fully to causal analysis and enhance our ability to address that question. Even more important, these chapters extend the brief discussion in this chapter of the understandings of the global system incorporated in the various worldviews. They therefore begin also to address the questions, What future do we want? and What leverage do we have?

As the causal discussion of global change in those chapters deepens, however, the question of human leverage will become quite complex. The issue of secondary and tertiary, or third-order, consequences of actions will become critical. There are, for instance, considerable disputes over the implications of giving food and other aid to less developed countries. Often those disputes do not center on the primary impact of aid on recipients but instead on the secondary implications of the aid for changes in their economic and political systems and the tertiary implications for their long-term well-being.

Such consequences make it very difficult to study issues in isolation. Everything becomes connected to everything else, and tracing through consequences of action becomes messy for any analyst. One approach to overcoming that difficulty is to use computers. If we can represent these complex interactions in a computer simulation or model, we can then let the computer trace through their implications.

Such a computer simulation accompanies this book. The International Futures (IFs) model will allow you to engage in your own experimentation with human intervention and to undertake your own assessment of the extent of human leverage (and of secondary and tertiary consequences). Chapter 3 presents that model and introduces you to its use. If you will not be using the model, you can skip that chapter.

Although the IFs model will assist you in better addressing our three questions, it is no panacea. Even with the best of computer simulations, the future remains essentially unpredictable. Some bold predictions will inevitably be correct, whether based on astrology or on computer simulation. A few of those based on computer simulation may even be correct for the right reasons—they will reflect an accurate causal understanding of the way the world works. As the Danish physicist Niels Bohr put it, however, "Prediction is very difficult, especially about the future" (Watkins, 1990: 152).

TWO

□ □ □

Global Change

Where do current changes appear to be taking us? Chapter 1 proposed that we address that question before asking what futures we prefer and what leverage we have in shaping our future.

At what specific trends should we look? Some general thoughts about human activity might help. We begin with demographics, because it is fundamental to know how many of us there are, how fast we are growing, and how many of us there might be in the future. We move next to our ability to feed ourselves. Is the food supply keeping up with our growth in numbers? Then we turn to energy. Energy is the "master resource"—it has been said that with sufficient energy, we can grow food on the top of Mount Everest and extract all necessary raw materials from sea water. What are the patterns in our use of energy and what can we say about its long-term availability? Next we move to the environment. We know that our impact on the environment has increased: How great is that impact? Technology greatly influences our patterns of resource extraction, waste creation, and interaction with each other. Are there recognizable patterns of technological innovation? Our economic system brings together humans as both producers and consumers, uses energy, and creates pressures on the environment. Changes in the economic structure therefore suggest much about the interaction of demographics, food and energy supply, the broader environment, and technology. Can we identify such restructuring? Finally, our political and social structures stand at the peak of this **human development system** (Mesarovic and Pestel, 1974: 29). What political-social trends and transformations can we recognize?

9

TYPES OF CHANGE

Before turning to an examination of specific trends, it is important to understand that there are several common patterns of change. The first is **linear**. A linear growth process adds equal increments year after year. If a relative gave you $100 for your birthday each year and you hid it away, your funds would grow linearly and at the end of 10 years you would have $1,000. If loggers, ranchers, and homesteaders in the Amazonian rain forest cleared 4,286 square miles each year, the forest size would decline linearly.[1]

Many processes grow **exponentially** rather than linearly. Instead of growing by a fixed amount in each period, they grow by a fixed percentage. For instance, if you received a onetime gift of $100 from your relative, put it in a savings account earning 7 percent annual interest, and left the account undisturbed, your money would grow exponentially. Your money would earn $7 the first year and produce a balance of $107. In the second year your money would earn 7 percent of the new balance, a total of $7.49, and you would have a balance of $114.49. At the end of 10 years your money would have grown to $196.72. Because the interest that you leave in your account also earns interest, an exponential growth process of this kind produces an upward sloping curve (see Figure 2.1). If the United States were to increase its nuclear arsenal by 14 percent each year (roughly the rate of increase between 1950 and 1990), that arsenal would exhibit the same type of upward-sloping growth curve.

In the example of a bank account growing at 7 percent, an initial investment nearly doubled in 10 years. We often characterize exponential

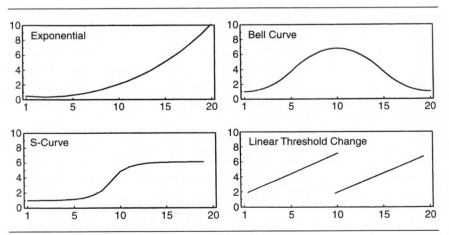

FIGURE 2.1 Types of growth.

growth processes by their **doubling time** (the number of years or other periods over which a growth process doubles an initial value). The **Rule of 72** provides an easy way of estimating that doubling time. Dividing 72 by a percentage growth rate provides a quite good estimate of the number of periods required for doubling. Money at 7 percent interest will double in just a little over 10 years. A nuclear arsenal growing at 14 percent will double in just a little over 5 years.

Sometimes the growth rate of a process accelerates. If the United States became ever more proficient at producing nuclear weapons, so that at the beginning of a decade the growth of its arsenal was 10 percent annually, and at the end it was 18 percent, the curve representing the stockpile would grow even more sharply, in a **superexponential** process.

Both linear and exponential growth implicitly assume that a process goes on indefinitely. We know, however, that there are often limits that constrain growth processes. Sometimes those limits cause an abrupt cessation of growth. For instance, your relative may decide that, when you reach a certain age, you no longer require financial assistance. Similarly, the end of the Cold War has caused the United States to reverse the trend of growth in its nuclear arsenal.

Very often, growth processes do not simply reach a limit and then abruptly cease. Instead, they often follow one of two patterns with respect to limits. The first is an **S-curve,** a pattern of exponential (or even superexponential) growth up to a turning point, and then a pattern of slowing growth up to a limit. The growth of most organisms traces such an S-curve. When a sapling is very small, it grows only a few inches in a year. As it grows, it adds a greater increment each year throughout its early life. Eventually, however, that growth increment declines and then ceases, following an S-curve like that shown in Figure 2.1. Whereas the bottom half of the S-curve is exponential growth, the top half is called **saturating exponential growth**—the process eventually reaches a saturation or cessation point.

The second growth pattern involving a limit also traces an S-curve, but it extends the upward growth by tracing another S-curve back down. The overall pattern becomes a **bell-shaped curve** and may indicate the phenomenon of **overshoot and collapse.** For instance, population growth in many historic empires followed approximately an S-curve pattern to a maximum value and then tracked an inverted S-curve back down. Some of those empires probably outgrew the ability of the environment to supply food or energy and then collapsed. If the United States and Russia avoid rekindling the mutual fears that stoked the Cold War, their nuclear arsenals may well decline over time in much the same way that they earlier grew.

A final basic pattern of growth involves **threshold change.** Instead of continuous change, some processes exhibit abrupt increases or decreases to new levels. The earlier example of an annual gift by a relative can illustrate this type of growth. If we tracked the bank account of a thrifty recipient on a daily basis rather than an annual one, we would see a pattern of large jumps annually (the birthday gifts) combined with smaller and smoother increases from the reinvestment of daily interest. Interstate war is another threshold event. Because of its irregularity, threshold change is probably the most difficult type on which to build forecasts.

These five basic growth and decline patterns (linear, exponential, S-curve, bell-shaped, and threshold change) can combine in complex ways. For instance, the repetition of bell-shaped growth over time can create a cyclical pattern (consider the repeated growth and collapse of an empire). Or a cyclical pattern might combine with an underlying pattern of long-term linear or exponential growth. For instance, the U.S. economy has exhibited exponential long-term growth, but roughly four-year-long business cycles have snaked around that underlying trend.

The complexity of possible patterns is, of course, what makes forecasting with extrapolation (projecting a growth pattern beyond the period for which we have data) dangerous. As obvious as it is, the most common error in forecasting is simple extrapolation of linear or exponential growth without considering the possibility of changes in the pattern.

For instance, Chapter 1 noted the forecasting flaw of the individual falling from a building and declaring halfway down, "So far, so good." Consider a similar story about exponential growth. An airplane with four engines departs Hawaii for an 8-hour trip to Los Angeles. When the plane loses power in one engine, the captain announces that there is no problem, but the flight will last 9 hours. When it loses another engine, the captain extends the forecast of flight time to 11 hours. After the third engine burns, a more nervous captain reassures passengers of the crew's continuing ability to fly and to land, but forecasts a total trip duration of 14 hours. One passenger turns to another and says, "You know, if that fourth engine goes out, we could be up here all night!"

Many people have lost fortunes in the stock market by investing in the belief that the market was following a pattern of exponential growth, only to discover that it was at the top of a curve (or about to undergo a threshold change). A linear extrapolation of the growth in earnings of Arnold Schwarzenegger between 1988 and 1989 would forecast an income for him of $360 million in 2000. An exponential extrapolation of the growth in the national debt of the United States from 1981 to 1991 would put that debt at $8 trillion in 2000, about twice the size of the economy in that year.[2] Mark Twain poked fun at such extrapolation:

In the space of 176 years the Lower Mississippi has shortened itself 242 miles. That is an average of a trifle over one mile and a third per year.

Therefore, any calm person, who is not blind or idiotic, can see that in the old oölitic Silurian period, just a million years ago next November, the Lower Mississippi River was upward of one million three hundred thousand miles long, and stuck out over the Gulf of Mexico like a fishing-rod. And by the same token any person can see that 742 years from now the Lower Mississippi will be only a mile and three-quarters long, and Cairo and New Orleans will have joined their streets together, and be plodding comfortably along under a single mayor and a mutual board of aldermen. There is something fascinating about science. One gets such wholesale returns of conjecture out of such a trifling investment in fact (Buchanan, 1974: 17).

How are we to know when extrapolation is useful and when it is ludicrous (or dangerous)? Linear extrapolation of the percentage of its economy that the United States spends on health care (about 7 percent in 1970 and 11 percent in 1990) would lead to a forecast of 13 percent in 2000. That might be a good forecast. Continued linear extrapolation would provide a forecast of 17 percent in 2020 and 21 percent in 2040. Even those might be good forecasts, but the longer time horizon makes them riskier. None of us would be so foolish as to extend that horizon to 2450 and produce a forecast of 103 percent.

Forecast risk obviously increases with length of time horizon; it also generally increases with the rate at which a process is growing or declining, and it often decreases somewhat with the length of the base period from which we are forecasting. The best rule is to combine extrapolation with at least a rudimentary consideration of the causal dynamics of the system in question. That strategy helps us to identify the existence of limits on a process and can even help us to spot likely turning points. We will try to keep these rules in mind as we turn to historical data and forecasts.

DEMOGRAPHIC CHANGE

Global population has grown exponentially, in fact superexponentially, over a very long period of time (see Figure 2.2). Humanity populated most of the globe by 8000 B.C. and numbered about 5 million (Ehrlich and Ehrlich, 1972: 12). By A.D. 1000, the human population had reached approximately 250 million, and by roughly A.D. 1600 it had attained a level of 500 million. The growth rate over that nearly 10,000-year period was less than 0.05 percent annually. By the end of the eighteenth century, however, the population growth rate had accelerated substantially (to about 0.5 percent), and in the nineteenth and twentieth centuries the rate rose quite steadily.

Simple exponential extrapolations of world population growth made in the mid-1960s began to create considerable anxiety. Were global popu-

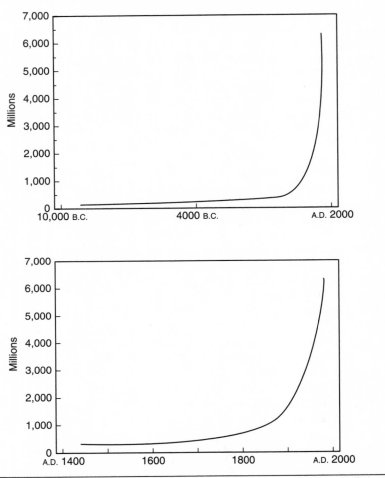

FIGURE 2.2 Global population growth. *Sources:* Paul R. Ehrlich and Anne H. Ehrlich, *Population, Resources, Environment* (San Francisco: W. H. Freeman, 1972), 12; Population Reference Bureau, *World Population Growth and Response* (Washington, D.C.: Population Reference Bureau, 1976), 4.

lation to continue growing at the 2 percent annual rate of that decade, it would double from 3 billion to 6 billion people by the year 1995, rise to 12 billion by 2030, and reach 24 billion in 2065 (the law of 72 makes such estimates easy).

In fact, the level probably will reach 6 billion shortly before 2000. Most forecasters believe, however, that population growth will increasingly exhibit the pattern of an S-shaped curve rather than continuing in superexponential form. Moreover, it appears that we passed the turning point of that S-shaped curve in the late 1960s and that the global population growth rate has since declined somewhat (see Table 2.1). Thus, instead of a steady climb to 12 billion, 24 billion, and even higher levels, global population will perhaps level off at about 10–12 billion people near the end of the twenty-first century.

In addition to indicating the probable leveling of growth in world population, Figure 2.3 shows the substantial differences in population growth patterns of economically more and less developed regions of the globe. The latter regions are growing much more rapidly. Population growth rates began declining in the more developed regions about a decade before they began slowing in the less developed regions. More significantly, annual rates in developing countries average about 1 percent more than rates in the developed countries. In Africa, annual population growth rates are a full 2.7 percent higher than those in Europe and are only now passing their peak. Table 2.2 shows the pattern of regional population increase over time.

Population forecasts, at least over a period of 20–30 years, tend to be more accurate than predictions in the other issue areas that we will

TABLE 2.1   Global Population and Population Growth Rate

Year	Population (millions)	Growth Rate (preceding period)
1750	791	
1800	910	0.4
1860	1,262	0.5
1900	1,600	0.5
1920	1,800	0.6
1930	2,000	1.0
1940	2,250	1.1
1950	2,510	1.0
1960	3,008	1.8
1970	3,683	2.0
1980	4,433	1.9
1990	5,321	1.8
1995	5,702	1.4

Sources: 1750–1900 values from John D. Durand, "The Modern Expansion of World Population," *Proceedings of the American Philosophical Society* 111 (1967):137; 1900–1950 values from United Nations, *Demographic Yearbook* (New York: UN, 1961); 1960–1980 values from Ruth Leger Sivard, *World Military and Social Expenditures* 1991, 14th ed. (Washington, D.C.:World Priorities, 1991), 50; 1990–1995 values from Population Reference Bureau, *World Population Data Sheet* (Washington, D.C.: Population Reference Bureau, 1990, 1995).

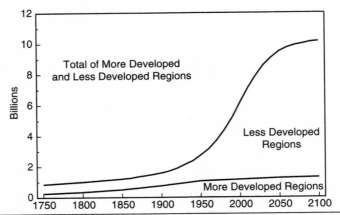

FIGURE 2.3 World population growth by development level. *Source:* Thomas W. Merrick, "World Population in Transition," *Population Bulletin* 41, no. 2 (April 1986):4.

review here. Most of the humans who will have children in the next 20 years have already been born, and fertility and mortality generally do not change rapidly. Nonetheless, there are great uncertainties about population forecasts, particularly over the longer term. Some argue, for instance, that the human population has reached or exceeded the ultimate limits

TABLE 2.2   Regional Population, 1750–2025

	Population (millions)					Growth Rate (1995)
	1750	*1850*	*1950*	*1995*	*2021*	
Asia	498	801	1,381	3,451	4,939	1.7
Africa	106	111	222	720	1,510	2.8
Latin America	16	38	162	481	706	1.9
Europe	125	208	292	729	743	−0.1
North America	2	26	166	293	375	0.7
Former USSR	42	76	180			
Oceania	2	2	13	28	39	1.2
Total	791	1,262	2,515	5,702	8,312	1.5

Sources: 1750–1950 values from John D. Durand, "The Modern Expansion of World Population," *Proceedings of the American Philosophical Society* 111 (1967):137; 1995–2025 values from Population Reference Bureau. World Population Data Sheet (Washington, D.C.: Population Reference Bureau, 1995).

imposed by its food and energy supplies (Brown, 1981; Meadows et al., 1972). If so, population growth might unfortunately be more likely to follow the pattern of a bell-shaped curve (overshoot and collapse) than that of an S-shaped curve. Such debates correctly take us beyond extrapolation, however, and into causal analysis. We will turn to such analysis in subsequent chapters.

CHANGE IN AGRICULTURE AND FOOD

There is a great deal of confusion about the growth of global food supplies relative to the growth in population. Repeated famines in Africa and regular expressions of concern about long-term food availability elsewhere have convinced many people that food production has not kept up with population growth. The reality is that in the 40 years between 1950 and 1990 global food production per capita grew by approximately 38 percent. That is, the amount of food available to the average human increased by almost 1 percent annually. Figure 2.4 shows that phenomenal record of achievement. Moreover, many regions of the world have shared in that achievement. Europe, Asia, and the United States have reported the most substantial advances, increasing production per capita by 79, 37, and 22 percent, respectively. In contrast, Latin American gains have been modest and African production per capita is 15 percent less than in 1950.

As always, there are dangers in simple extrapolation. The most significant is that the rate of global increase may be slowing or even stopping. Despite a global per capita increase of 10 percent in the 1970s, per capita grain production in the 1980s increased only 3 percent, and there were no gains between the mid-1980s and mid-1990s. One interpretation of this statistic is that we have reached the top of a bell-shaped curve and that forecasts of population growth eventually outstripping ability to increase food supplies have finally come true. Another interpretation is that the slowdown since the mid-1980s is a cyclical downturn around a long-term upward trend. Reasons might include stagnant economies in many less-developed countries during the 1980s, the disruption of the former Soviet Union, a number of bad harvest years in the United States, and ongoing efforts by both the United States and Europe to solve long-term problems of overproduction.

Figure 2.5 draws our attention further to the possibility that food production per capita is peaking by looking at the global production per capita of specific biological resources. It appears that we may have already reached or passed per capita production peaks in some.

The debate over the relative growth of population and food has deep historical roots. For example, at the end of the eighteenth century, the Reverend Thomas Malthus argued that population, left unchecked,

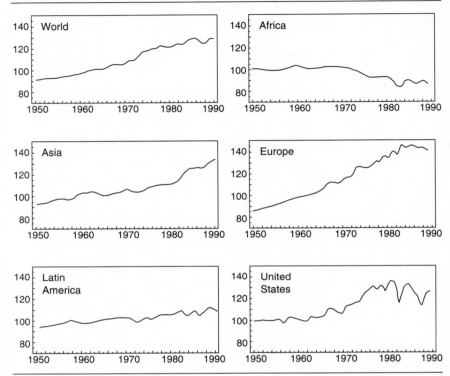

FIGURE 2.4   Food production per capita: Percent of 1961–1965. *Source:* United Nations FAO, *FAO Production Yearbook* (Rome: United Nations Food and Agriculture Organization, 1965, 1975, 1981, 1985, 1987, 1991).

grows geometrically (exponentially) and that food supply increases only arithmetically (linearly). He therefore concluded that it was inevitable that population would outstrip food production and that starvation would ravish humanity. Similarly, at the beginning of the twentieth century, Sir William Crookes made the following report in his Presidential Address to the British Association of Science:

> There remains no uncultivated prairie land in the United States suitable for wheat growing. The virgin land has been rapidly absorbed, until at present there is no land left for wheat without reducing the area for maize, hay, and other necessary crops. It is almost certain that within a generation the ever increasing population of the United States will consume all the wheat growing within its borders and will be driven to import and . . . scramble for a lion's share of the wheat crop of the world (Wortman and Cummings, 1978: 86).

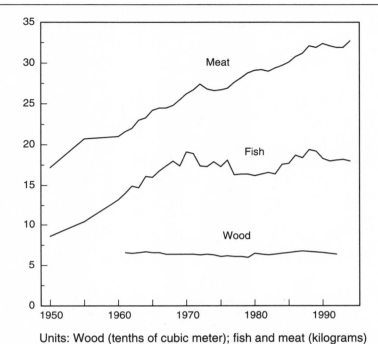

Units: Wood (tenths of cubic meter); fish and meat (kilograms)

FIGURE 2.5   Global production per capita of biological resources. *Sources:* Barry B. Hughes, *World Futures* (Baltimore: Johns Hopkins University Press, 1985), 180; Lester R. Brown, Hal Kane, and David Malin Roodman, *Vital Signs 1994* (New York: W. W. Norton, 1994), 81; Lester R. Brown, Nicholas Lenssen, and Hal Kane, *Vital Signs 1995* (New York: W. W. Norton, 1995), 31 and 33.

In light of so many incorrect predictions of food shortages, it is not surprising that many contemporary analysts voice suspicions of negative forecasts and interpret recent stagnation of food supply per capita as a temporary phenomenon.

Moving from the global to the local level, there are major differences in the amount of food available to humans in different world regions. Figure 2.6 illustrates these differences by showing per capita caloric consumption for various regions. Whereas citizens of the United States consumed an average of 3,671 calories per capita daily in 1989 (World Bank, 1992: 273), caloric consumption in the poorest countries of the world ranged generally between 1,700 and 2,600. It is obvious from these figures that global production per capita will need to increase a great deal more if the poor of the world are to have diets comparable to those of the rich.

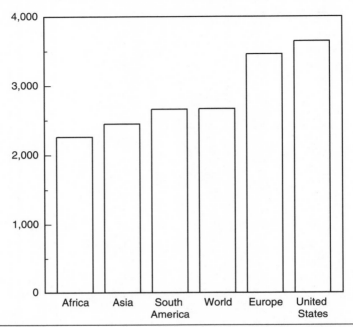

FIGURE 2.6 Per capita daily calorie consumption. *Source:* United Nations FAO, *FAO Production Yearbook 1989* (Rome: Food and Agricultural Organization, 1990), 289–290.

The differences in caloric consumption across regions would be even greater were it not for increases in the trade of grain. There was little trade of this type in the first half of the century. In contrast, substantial volumes of grain now flow from regions of surplus (primarily North America and Western Europe) to the rest of the world. Table 2.3 traces those flows.

The historical pattern of food production, consumption, and trade provides a less ready base for extrapolation than did that of population size. In fact, most forecasts quickly abandon the historical patterns and move to causal analysis. Some analysts are pessimistic. They point to the unavailability of additional land for the expansion of production, relative to historical eras, and to environmental degradation (for example, deforestation and desertification) of land already under production. Others are optimistic. They direct our attention to new technologies for manipulating plant and animal life. We will return to these issues of causal analysis in subsequent discussion.

TABLE 2.3   Annual World Grain Trade (in millions of metric tons)

	1934–1938	1950	1960	1970	1980	1990
North America	5	23	42	54	131	(103)
Latin America	2	1	(1)	4	(10)	2
Western Europe	(10)	(22)	(25)	(22)	(16)	23
Eastern Europe/ U.S.S.R.	1	0	1	(1)	(46)	(35)
Africa	0	0	(5)	(4)	(15)	(26)
Asia	(1)	(6)	(19)	(37)	(63)	(79)
Oceania	3	3	6	8	19	14

Note: Parentheses indicate imports.
Sources: Barry B. Hughes, *World Futures* (Baltimore, Md.: Johns Hopkins University, 1985), 133; Lester R. Brown, "Reexamining the World Food Prospect," in *State of the World 1989*, ed. Lester R. Brown (New York: W. W. Norton, 1989), 45; World Resources Institute, *World Resources 1994–95* (New York: Oxford University Press, 1994), 298.

CHANGE IN ENERGY

As food is energy for the human body, physical energy feeds the human economy. The amount of physical energy available to the average human has increased dramatically in the past 200 years. James Watt's steam engine generated 40 horsepower in 1800, a dramatic advance over earlier models and over water mills and windmills. A modern electric generating plant delivers 1.5 million horsepower (Cook, 1976: 29). Figure 2.7 shows an almost tenfold increase in per capita energy use since 1850. That figure, like others we have seen, could be extrapolated in more than one way. To some it may look clearly like an exponential, even super-exponential, curve that promises to continue sharply upward. To others it may appear that there is a turning point at the end of the curve that portends slower growth in years ahead and converts the overall form to an S-shape. To still others, it could be one side of a bell-shaped curve that is poised near the top and threatens to begin a descent as we exhaust fossil fuels.

Those who are less optimistic about future growth often direct our attention to oil, the largest single contributor of primary energy to the economy. Figure 2.8 shows that global oil production increased very sharply and quite steadily from negligible amounts in the 1920s to a peak of nearly 3.3 billion metric tons in 1979. It stabilized near that peak in the 1980s as a result of substantial increases in prices by the Organization of Petroleum Exporting Countries (OPEC) and other producers. As those who drew that figure correctly foresaw in 1982, global oil production ended the decade with little change (British Petroleum Company, 1991: 4).

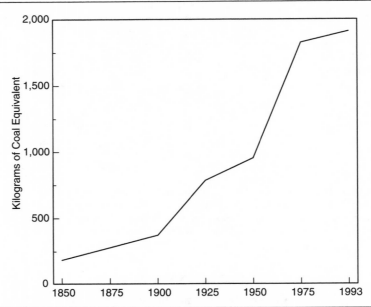

FIGURE 2.7   Energy consumption per capita. *Sources:* Joel Darmstadter, *Energy in the World Economy* (Baltimore: Johns Hopkins University Press, 1971), 10; United Nations, *Energy Statistics Yearbook* (New York: United Nations, 1986); British Petroleum, *BP Statistical Review of World Energy* (London: Ashdown Press Ltd., 1995), 34 and 37.

The forecast illustrated in Figure 2.8 by the Organization of Economic Cooperation and Development (OECD) assumes that there is a fixed amount of oil in the earth available to humans and therefore that oil production and consumption will eventually decline and almost cease. By estimating that limited amount, analysts have been able to match the area under the curve to this figure (a total of 327 billion metric tons) and draw a bell-shaped curve that forecasts the life cycle of global oil production. This procedure moves well beyond simple extrapolation and into causal analysis; we will return to this approach.

It should be obvious that the estimate of available oil, shown in the area under the curve, is critical. It should also be obvious, however, that larger and smaller estimates will only shift the peak and will not change the overall shape of the curve. M. King Hubbert made one of the most successful forecasts ever produced on the energy issue in the late 1950s using the same approach, matching the area under a bell-shaped curve to an estimate of ultimate oil resources within the United States. He forecast

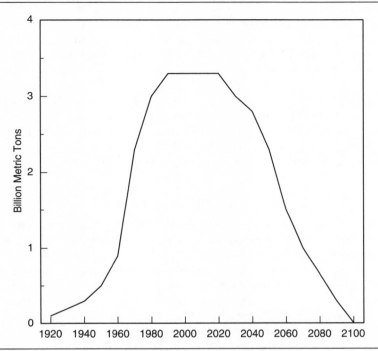

FIGURE 2.8   Hypothetical oil production and resource depletion profile. *Source:* International Energy Agency, *World Energy Outlook* (Paris: Organization of Economic Cooperation and Development, 1982), 215.

that U.S. oil production would peak about 1970 and begin a long, slow decline (Wildavsky and Tenenbaum, 1981: 233). U.S. oil production did, in fact, begin a decline in 1970, and the decline continues. Geologists have explored most of the world for oil much less thoroughly than they have the United States, however, so there is less basis for estimating the precise peak of the curve representing global production. We should remember that in 1891 the U.S. Geological Survey estimated the chance of finding oil in Kansas or Texas at near zero and that in 1939 the Interior Department declared that U.S. oil supplies would last only thirteen years (Kahn, Brown, and Martel, 1976: 94–95).

We generally refer to the projected decline of global oil production as an energy transition, because most observers expect other energy forms to replace oil and natural gas, much as oil earlier replaced coal. Table 2.4 shows the pattern of actual transition though 1990 and provides a forecast for the year 2000. It is, however, with the availability and use of other energy forms that energy forecasts become particularly murky (note that the forecast does not even include solar energy). In the 1950s, the Atomic Energy Agency forecast installed nuclear capacity in the United States alone at 2,000 gigawatts by 2000 (Hughes, 1985c: 104)—an amount that would require approximately 2,000 very large nuclear generating plants; in 1990 the country had approximately 100 gigawatts of capacity (World Almanac, 1992: 196).

This discussion has already touched upon some of the debates to which we will return in our discussion of causal logic. These include the resource base of fossil fuels and the promise (and cost) of alternative energy technologies. They also include the prospects for economic growth and the relationship between economic growth and energy demand.

ENVIRONMENTAL CHANGE

Humans have long had an impact on their biological and physical environments, exhausting local forests, overhunting nearby animals, depleting regional supplies of minerals, and destroying the productivity of plots of soil. We have also sometimes drained swamps (for better or worse), planted trees, and improved soil quality. It is only in this century, however, that we have begun to broaden the scope of our impact from particular watersheds, valleys, and coastal plains to the globe.

It is almost impossible to touch on all of the environmental concerns that have emerged in the past two decades; therefore, this discussion will single out three issues of large-scale, potentially global importance: the release of greenhouse gases into the atmosphere, the buildup of ozone-depleting gases, and the destruction of tropical forests. It is very difficult to simply present environmental trends without some comment on issues of causal linkage (such as the impact of changes in the scope of human ac-

TABLE 2.4 World Energy Supply by Energy Type

Energy Type	Percentage Contribution to Global Supply				
	1965	1980	1990	1994	2000
Oil	42	47	38	40	37
Coal	37	26	27	27	25
Gas	15	19	22	23	25
Hydroelectric	6	6	7	3	5
Nuclear	0	2	6	7	8

Sources: British Petroleum, BP Statistical Review of World Energy (June) (London: Ashdown Press, 1991), 34; British Petroleum, BP Statistical Review of World Energy (June) (London: Ashdown Press, 1995), 34. Forecast by author.

tivity); we have encountered that difficulty in our earlier discussions as well. In the case of our environmental discussion, however, we will more consistently cross the line between extrapolation and causal analysis.

Figure 2.9 shows atmospheric measurements of the primary greenhouse gas, carbon dioxide (CO_2), over the past 30 years. Note the clear exponential trend surrounded by annual cycles. The cycles correspond to seasons and the ability of vegetation to take some carbon dioxide from the atmosphere. The basic reason for the underlying trend is the increased burning of fossil fuels: The oxidization (burning) of carbon-based fuels generates carbon dioxide. The reason for concern about increased carbon dioxide is that the gas allows sunlight to pass through relatively easily but reflects a substantial amount of heat radiation back toward the earth. It thus acts much like the glass in a greenhouse.

We have noted before the danger of utilizing too short a baseline for forecasting. Figure 2.10 extends the time period shown in Figure 2.9 dramatically. It draws upon data from ice cores to construct a record of

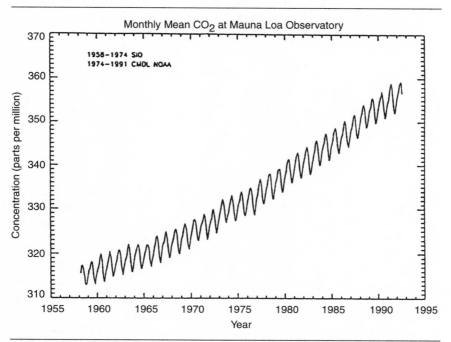

FIGURE 2.9   Increase in atmospheric carbon dioxide: Monthly mean CO_2 at Mauna Loa Observatory. *Source:* Carbon Cycle Group, Climate Monitoring and Diagnostics Laboratory, National Oceanic and Atmospheric Administration, Boulder, Colorado.

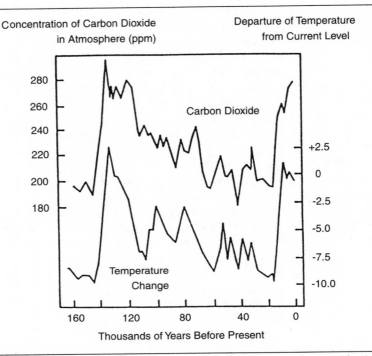

FIGURE 2.10   Long-term variations of global temperature and atmospheric carbon dioxide. *Source:* J. M. Barnola et al., "Vostok Ice Core Provides 160,000-year Record of Atmospheric CO_2." Reprinted with permission from *Nature* 329, no. 6138 (October 1–7, 1987):410. Copyright 1987 Macmillan Magazines Limited.

atmospheric carbon dioxide over a period of 160,000 years. Note that there are clear cycles in the concentration of carbon dioxide (and perturbations within cycles). Note also that the levels of contemporary carbon dioxide shown in Figure 2.9 exceed considerably even the highest levels in the entire 160,000-year-long period shown in Figure 2.10.

Figure 2.10 provides more information than simply carbon dioxide levels. It also reconstructs global temperatures over the long term. Note the very close relationship between movements in levels of carbon dioxide and those of temperature. As the authors of the World Resources Institute volume point out, "Showing clear links between carbon dioxide levels and temperature, the Vostok ice core has been recognized as irrefutable evidence for a fundamental link between the global climate system and the carbon cycle. However, it is still not clear whether rising carbon dioxide levels caused or followed rising temperatures" (World Resources Institute, 1988: 197). As that analysis suggests, parallel behavior does not prove causality. These two graphs make it easy to understand, however, why many scientists are forecasting a 1.5- to 2.5-degree Centigrade increase in global surface temperatures over the next 50 years.

A set of chemicals called chlorofluorocarbons (CFCs) serve as aerosol propellants, refrigerant fluids, foam-blowing agents (hence they appear in Styrofoam), and solvents. Like CO_2, CFCs act as a greenhouse gas, but scientists have a more substantial concern with their increase in the atmosphere. Specifically, the chemicals interact with ozone in the upper stratosphere and reduce its prevalence. Because atmospheric ozone protects life on the earth's surface from ultraviolet (UV-B) radiation, the entire process threatens humans via an increase in skin cancer, and also indirectly through damage to the plants and animals on which we depend.

Figure 2.11 shows the annual release of atmospheric chlorine in recent years. Its presence in the atmosphere roughly doubled between 1975 and 1985 (World Resources Institute, 1988: 170). A substantial hole in the ozone layer now appears annually over Antarctica, and measurements in both hemispheres indicate an ongoing decrease in ozone levels. A forecast of continued exponential growth in atmospheric chlorine would have

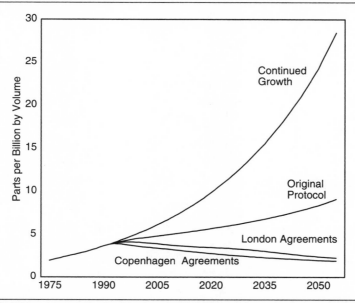

FIGURE 2.11 Atmospheric chlorine, 1975–1993, with projections to 2055 under four scenarios. *Source:* Worldwatch Institute, Worldwatch Database Diskette (Washington, D.C.: Worldwatch Institute, 1995). *Original Source:* E. I. Du Pont De Nemours, Wilmington, Del., private communication, March 9, 1994.

been reasonable had scientists not convinced policymakers to restrict the production and use of CFCs. New agreements have progressively reduced production that governments will allow.

Loggers, farmers, and ranchers clear approximately 0.9 percent of the world's tropical rain forest annually (World Resources Institute, 1992: 118). Table 2.5 shows some of the countries in which the rate of deforestation is especially great or that are important because of the extent of forest

TABLE 2.5   Deforestation: Worst Cases of the 1980s

Regions and Countries	Natural Forest Area (thousand hectares)	Annual Deforestation 1981–1990 (thousand hectares)	Percent Deforestation per Year
Africa			
Cote d'Ivoire	10,904	119	1.0
Ghana	9,555	138	1.3
Guinea-Bissau	2,021	16	0.7
Liberia	4,633	25	0.5
Malawi	3,486	53	1.3
Nigeria	15,634	119	0.7
Togo	1,353	22	1.4
Zaire	113,275	732	0.6
Latin America			
Brazil	561,107	3,671	0.6
Colombia	54,064	367	0.6
Costa Rica	1,428	50	2.6
Ecuador	11,962	238	1.7
Guatemala	4,225	81	1.6
Honduras	4,605	112	1.9
Mexico	48,586	678	1.2
Nicaragua	6,013	124	1.7
Paraguay	12,859	403	2.4
Peru	67,906	271	0.4
Venezuela	45,690	599	1.2
Asia			
Indonesia	109,549	1,212	1.0
Malaysia	17,583	396	1.8
Nepal	5,023	58	1.0
Sri Lanka	1,746	27	1.3
Thailand	12,735	515	2.9

Source: World Resources Institute, World Resources 1994–95 (New York: Basic Books, 1994), 306–307.

in the country (such as Brazil and Zaire). At current rates, Costa Rica, Malaysia, and Thailand are at risk of losing all of their forests early in the twenty-first century.

The condition of rain forests is less obviously a global problem than are emissions of CO_2 and CFCs. Scientists do worry, however, that substantial reductions in the extent of those forests can also contribute to global warming (by releasing the carbon that forests "bank") and will reduce the capacity of the earth to tolerate other changes. The forests also serve as habitat for large numbers of species that exist nowhere else and whose loss the entire world would bear. By one estimate, between 4 and 8 percent of species in rain forests will become extinct by 2015, and 17 to 35 percent will disappear by 2040 (World Resources Institute, 1992: 128).

There are uncertainties concerning environmental forecasts. One involves the degree to which human-induced effects will be gradual; another concerns whether, under certain conditions, the equilibrium state of the global physical and biological systems might "tip" quite dramatically into another state. Our earlier discussion of forecasting mentioned threshold changes—a sudden change in the level of one or more variables. It is possible that the earth's living systems have a capacity to absorb and dampen much insult to them, but that at some point the damage will become too great and fundamental patterns of temperature and living matter interaction will change.

TECHNOLOGICAL CHANGE

Technological change often exhibits exponential patterns. Most of us probably have greatest familiarity with this phenomenon in the area of computing power. Figure 2.12 traces the growth in functions per chip, beginning with the invention of the transistor. It indicates also the growth in the storage capacity of those chips over time. That figure uses a semilogarithmic scale; that is, each unit on the scale at the left is actually a multiple of 10 relative to the unit below it. Were that graph to use traditional arithmetic scaling, the curve would appear as an exponential one with an exceptionally steep rate of increase.

You may also have seen graphs that show the exponential drop in the cost of computing. It is obvious that there must be some limits on such drops (and on the increases in computing power). Therefore the curves will eventually flatten. We do not know when such leveling will begin—the turning points are not yet apparent.

Consider also the growth of transportation speeds. Figure 2.13 traces the speeds of human conveyances historically, from fast horses through chemical-fueled rockets, and projects them into the future. It uses a device called an **envelope curve,** a curve connecting the tops of other curves.

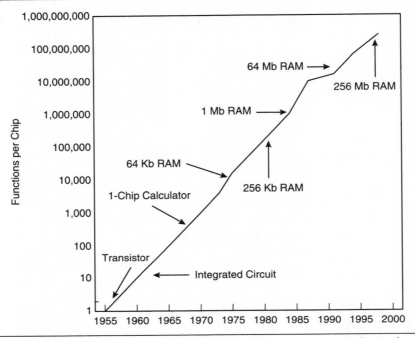

FIGURE 2.12   The evolution of integrated circuits. *Sources:* James A. Cuningham, "Using the Learning Curve as a Management Tool," *IEEE Spectrum* 17 (June 1980): 48; *Economist*, February 23, 1991:66; *Business Week*, December 10, 1990:185; *Business Week*, June 8, 1992:110.

The particular envelope curve of Figure 2.13 is an exponential line that traces the upper boundaries of the speeds attained by various individual transportation technologies, including trains and autos.

As we have seen with other issues, the historical record of transportation speeds does not provide a clear basis for forecasts. Some might be tempted to extrapolate transportation speeds ever upward in continued exponential growth; those familiar with "Star Trek" episodes know that the "warp speeds" of the Enterprise are vastly greater than the "impulse speeds" that it obtains from more traditional rocket engines. In a note of caution, however, one author argued that exponential extrapolation of earlier trends would have led to the following technological forecasts (Ayres, 1969: 20):

- Vehicles will attain the speed of light by 1982.
- Humans will achieve immortality by the year 2000.
- A single person will control the power of the sun by 1981.

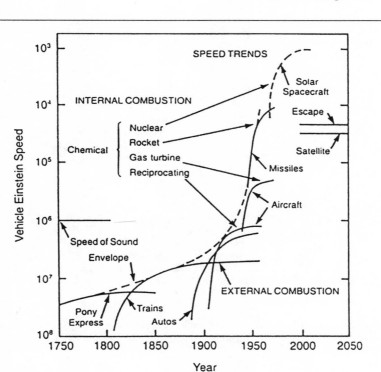

FIGURE 2.13 Trends in transportation speed. *Source:* Robert U. Ayres, Hudson Institute, Indianapolis, Indiana. Reprinted by permission of Hudson Institute.

Others therefore look to Einstein's theory for an argument that speed has an upper limit—as a body approaches the speed of light, the body gains mass and it therefore becomes ever harder to accelerate the object to still higher velocity. We may have already reached a turning point such that future gains in the speed of human conveyances will come ever more slowly.

With transportation speeds and computing power, the turning points (or the tops of the bell-shaped curves) are difficult to determine. The technological limits for some processes are more easily defined, and we are increasingly approaching them. For instance, clear limits bound the efficiency of energy conversion from the burning of fossil fuel (only 100 percent of the energy in the fire is potentially available for transfer to electricity generation or other use). Figure 2.14 shows the historical record of capturing the energy in fossil fuels; it strongly suggests that we have reached the turning point and will achieve lesser gains in the future.

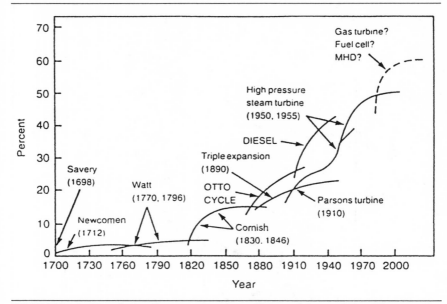

FIGURE 2.14 Trends in energy conversion efficiency. *Source:* Hans Thirring, *Energy for Man* (Bloomington: Indiana University Press, 1958). Reprinted with permission.

Even such limits, however, may be deceiving. As we approach them, we are discovering other ways of getting energy from matter, including the splitting and fusion of atoms. We may wish to avoid the pessimism with respect to future breakthroughs of Robert A. Millikan, a Nobel Prize winner and founder of the California Institute of Technology. In response to concerns expressed by science writer Frederick Soddy about the potential of nuclear power, Millikan wrote (prior to 1945):

> Since Mr. Soddy raised the hobgoblin of dangerous quantities of available subatomic energy, [science] has brought to light good evidence that this particular hobgoblin—like most of the hobgoblins that crowd in on the mind of ignorance—was a myth. . . . The new evidence born of further scientific study is to the effect that it is highly improbable that there is any appreciable amount of available subatomic energy to tap (Sinsheimer, 1980: 148).

Technology obviously brings tremendous benefits to humanity. In addition to the provision of computing power, transportation, and communication capabilities, and energy for the satisfaction of a wide range of needs and wants, technology has allowed the extension of life expectancy, has helped food producers keep pace with the growth in our numbers, and assists in the protection of our environment (for instance, via recycling). Technology also has a dark side, however, that we can see in human development of advanced military technology at the pace of other breakthroughs. Table 2.6 traces the development of explosive power over time and indicates the years in which countries have openly or most probably become nuclear powers. There has been exponential growth in destructive capability.

More generally, technology has contributed to the massive increase in human impact on the environment. That impact has not just controlled disease and produced food; it has also destroyed forests and threatens the global oceans and atmosphere. Often the secondary effects of new

TABLE 2.6   Milestones in Military Potential

Year	Equivalent Power (tons of TNT equivalent)	Weapon
1500	.001	Gunpowder "bombs"
1914	1.000	Large cannon
1940	10.000	Blockbuster bomb
1946	20,000.000	Hiroshima atomic bomb
1961	50,000,000.000	Largest hydrogen bomb

Year of Test or Probable Acquisition	Approximate Number of Current Warheads	Declared* and Probable Nuclear States
1945	12,100	United States*
1949	11,320	Soviet Union*
1952	96	United Kingdom*
1960	372	France*
1964	284	China*
1974	Unknown	India
Early 1980s	Unknown	Israel
Early 1980s	0	South Africa
Early 1980s	Unknown	Pakistan

Sources: Robert U. Ayres, *Technological Forecasting and Long-Range Planning* (New York: McGraw-Hill, 1969), 22; *The Columbia Desk Encyclopedia*, 3rd ed. (New York: Columbia University Press, 1963); Harold Sprout and Margaret Sprout, *Toward a Politics of the Planet Earth* (New York: Van Nostrand Reinhold, 1971), 403; Stockholm International Peace Research Institute, *SIPRI Yearbook 1990* (Stockholm: SIPRI, 1990), 23; Leonard S. Spector with Jacqueline R. Smith, *Nuclear Ambitions* (Boulder: Westview Press, 1990).

technologies are largely unpredictable, even when organizations like the former U.S. Office of Technology Assessment try to foresee them.

This discussion should have made clear the difficulties in extrapolating technological advance (or its implications). Progress sometimes appears exponential and at other times very much bounded. In addition, there is no clear understanding of the degree to which technology advances regularly over time. In fact, a common argument is that such advance occurs in long cycles. We return later to some of these uncertainties.

ECONOMIC CHANGE

In spite of periodic economic downturns (recessions and depressions), global economic growth has characterized almost all of the past 200 years. Figure 2.15 traces the growth of gross world product, the total production of goods and services, since 1960. After removing the effects of inflation, the global economy tripled in 30 years. During that same period, popula-

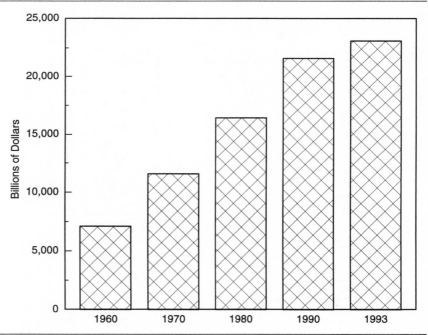

FIGURE 2.15   Gross world product. *Source:* Central Intelligence Agency, *Handbook of Economic Statistics 1991* (Washington, D.C.: Central Intelligence Agency, 1991), 26; World Bank, *World Development Report 1995* (New York: Oxford University Press, 1995), 167.

tion grew by about two-thirds, suggesting that the global per capita GNP nearly doubled.

Although the 1980s were a decade of relatively slow increase, global economic growth generally exhibits an exponential pattern and has done so since the beginning of the industrial revolution late in the 1700s. In fact, while we do not have data on gross national or world product before the twentieth century (the concept was not developed until the 1930s), data on industrial production trace that long-term growth curve. Figure 2.16 shows industrial production over the past 200 years on a semilogarithmic scale. The slight upward slope on that scale indicates a superexponential pattern in the curve—the twentieth century claims higher rates of growth than the nineteenth, in part because a greater and greater portion of the world has experienced industrialization.

We should supplement such an aggregated view of the global economy with two types of disaggregation: by geographic region and by economic sector. The industrial revolution began in England, spread to France, Germany, and elsewhere in Europe, and then moved around the world to the United States, Japan, and a considerable number of economies in Latin America and Asia. In the process, the world became generally divided into rich industrial countries and poor preindustrial countries. The industrial economies developed primarily in the northern half of the globe, whereas most of the preindustrial countries populate the

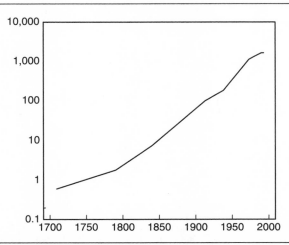

FIGURE 2.16 World industrial production index. *Sources:* W. W. Rostow, *The World Economy: History and Prospect* (Austin: University of Texas Press, 1978), 49, 662; United Nations, *Statistical Yearbook 1983/84* (New York: United Nations, 1986); United Nations, *Monthly Bulletin of Statistics,* December 1994:254.

southern half. Figure 2.17 sketches the ratio of per capita incomes in the two sets of countries (industrialized versus preindustrialized) and shows the fairly steady increase in that gap until the 1970s. The data for that graph are, at best, skimpy, but it is useful to have even a crude image of the long-term pattern. There is an active debate as to whether the gap has now stabilized and may even be poised for decline. Again we see how difficult it is to recognize turning points.

The second disaggregation we need to consider is one that a focus on industrialization already suggests, namely the division of the global economy into sectors. Prior to industrialization, the agricultural sector of an economy dominates it. At the time of the American Revolution, about 80 percent of the U.S. population was engaged in producing food. Over time the industrial sector became dominant and the agricultural sector experienced a very long relative decline (it generally continued to increase its overall production but used less labor and became less important in the

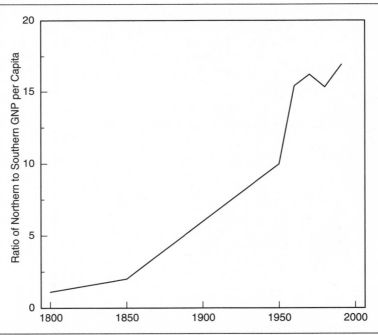

FIGURE 2.17   Ratio of GNP per capita in global North and South. *Source:* Constructed from estimates collected by Barry B. Hughes in *Continuity and Change in World Politics,* 3rd ed. (Englewood Cliffs, N.J.: Prentice-Hall, forthcoming). Recent estimates from Ruth Leger Sivard, *World Military and Social Expenditures 1993* (Washington, D.C.: World Priorities, 1993), 42.

total economy). The third large portion of an economy is the service sector. Figure 2.18 shows the relative size of these three sectors in four different groupings of countries.

Note in Figure 2.18 that even in what the World Bank calls "low-income countries," the industrial sector is large and the agricultural sector is shrinking quite rapidly. In fact, within what the bank calls "high-income countries," the industrial sector is actually smaller than it is in the low-income group. The high-income countries, which the World Bank called "industrial economies" until 1990, have clearly become predominantly service economies.

Even more important, the nature of service economies is changing. For example, between 1945 and 1991, service workers in the United States increased overall by 271 percent, but workers in finance, insurance, and real estate increased by 347 percent (Information Please Almanac, 1992: 59). We should explicitly identify a fourth sector of the economy and category of workers that most data sources now misleadingly lump with the service sector. That category, the information sector, may now be the largest sector in the most economically advanced countries. Figure 2.19 supports

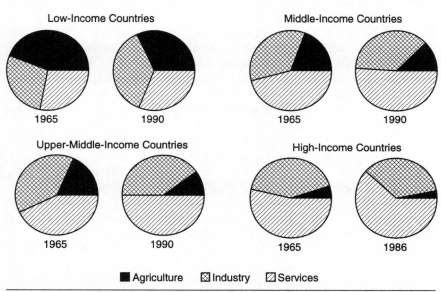

FIGURE 2.18 Distribution of GNP by development level. *Sources:* World Bank, *World Development Report 1992* (New York: Oxford University Press, 1992), 222–223; also *World Development Report 1988* (New York: Oxford University Press, 1988).

that claim for the United States. Readers should be aware, however, that in spite of the importance of the information economy, statisticians have not yet begun confidently to evaluate its size. Although the activities of teachers, scientists, and librarians belong obviously to the information sector, those of many other individuals prove harder to classify. Thus Figure 2.19 provides only a crude estimate.

There are many uncertainties in forecasting the global economy. Many countries progressed rapidly from industrialization to service and information economies. To what extent has this transformation affected our ability to adequately measure economic size, rate of growth, or productivity of workers? Will the less industrialized countries of the world automatically follow in the path of the first to industrialize, or has the widespread industrialization of the globe and the steady march of technology created new patterns for growth? Such questions will later move us into causal analysis and beyond the initial extrapolative exploration of this discussion.

SOCIAL-POLITICAL CHANGE

Social and political change is tightly interwoven with the other changes that this chapter has reviewed. It gives rise to many of those changes and is in turn shaped by them. Summarizing quickly the major trends in the social and political spheres is difficult. To simplify the task somewhat, we will divide it into two: changes that affect the lives of individuals and changes in social organization. In reality, of course, this division is artificial and the two sets of changes interact strongly.

The lives of individuals have changed and continue to change in several important respects. Most fundamentally, perhaps, is that people live longer. The pace of that change has been dramatic. In 1900 an astute observer of change, John Elfreth Watkins, wrote in the *Ladies' Home Journal* that by the year 2000 the average American would "live fifty years instead of thirty-five as at present" (Shane and Sojka, 1990: 150). He thereby forecast a 15-year increase in life expectancy; the reality was a 40-year increase by 1991. In fact, the average human (across the globe) had a life expectancy of 65 in 1991, only 10 years less than Americans at that time and 30 years more than Americans at the beginning of the century.[3]

Second, in spite of continued widespread poverty in many parts of the globe, the average human is also much richer than in any previous era. The global GNP per capita advanced from $2,331 in 1960 to $4,053 in 1990 (constant 1990 dollars; CIA, 1991b: 216).

Third, the average human is increasingly well-educated. Statistics on education of primary school–aged children in the poorest countries of the world suggest that the portion of those children actually in school

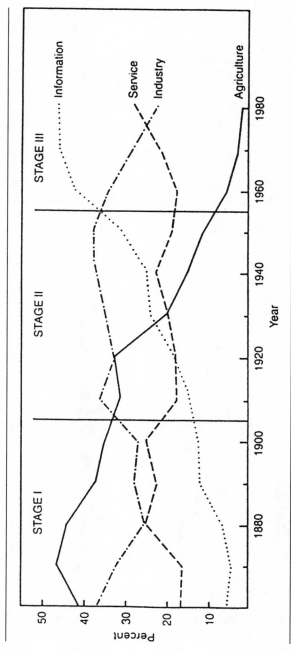

FIGURE 2.19 Four-sector breakdown of the U.S. work force, 1860–1980 (in percentages). Note: Median estimates of information workers are used. *Source:* Marc Porat, *The Information Economy: Definition and Measurement* (Washington, D.C.: U.S. Department of Commerce, Office of Telecommunications, 1977).

climbed from 37 percent in 1950 to 99 percent in 1990 (Hughes, 1991a: 27). Figure 2.20 shows the increase in adult literacy since 1960. It has been estimated that a majority of the world's adult population was literate in 1955 for the first time in history (Deutsch, 1988: 313).[4] Now even a majority of adults in the world's poorest countries are literate.

Fourth, the extent of inter-human contact has increased sharply. Rapid urbanization provides one reason for this. Whereas in 1950 28 percent of the world's population lived in urban areas (Council on Environmental Quality, 1981b: 300), in 1991 43 percent of humanity was urban (Population Reference Bureau, 1991). This statistic suggests an increase in urbanization of about 4 percent per decade; at this rate, a majority of humanity may live in cities by 2010.

Other avenues for increased contact also exist. The written word obviously reaches a much higher percentage of people as literacy increases. Televisions and radios supply more people with outside contact each year. In 1989 there were 155 televisions and 375 radios per 1,000 people in

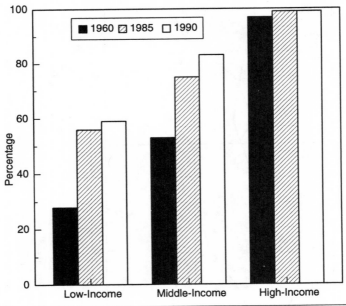

FIGURE 2.20　Adult literacy rate by development level. *Sources:* World Bank, *World Development Report 1982* (Washington, D.C.: World Bank, 1982), 110–111; World Bank, *World Development Report 1991* (New York: Oxford University Press, 1991), 204–205; World Bank, *World Development Report 1995* (New York: Oxford University Press, 1995), 162–163.

the world. Similarly, the option of "reaching out and touching someone" via telephone is spreading with incredible speed. Figure 2.21 traces the number of telephones per 1,000 population since 1930. Note the exponential rate of increase.

All of these trends, and arguably the increase in human contact in particular, have an impact on social organization. People now have the time, the money, the ability, and the instruments by which to become involved in social structures beyond their immediate families and villages. Alvin Toffler writes therefore of the "global village." Moreover, there is much evidence that large numbers wish further to extend their social contacts.

We can see the effect of these individual-level changes on the types and structures of social organization. With respect to the types of organization, one of the most dramatic trends has been the spread of European-style states (like England, France, and Spain) around the globe. In the contemporary era, the entire world is characterized by such states, and almost all of the multi-ethnic empires that ushered in the century, including

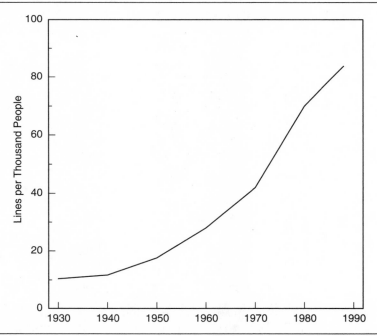

FIGURE 2.21 Global telephone lines. *Sources:* AT&T, *The World's Telephones* (Morris Plains, N.J.: AT&T, 1982), 14; AT&T, *The World's Telephones* (Whippany, N.J.: AT&T, 1989), 11.

the former Soviet Union, have given way to states built more closely around ethnic-cultural units.

Figure 2.22 indicates the even more rapid growth of two other forms of social organizations: intergovernmental organizations (IGOs), based on state membership, and international nongovernmental organizations (INGOs), based on individual membership. Intergovernmental organizations, such as the United Nations (UN), the North Atlantic Treaty Organization (NATO), or the European Union (EU), have proliferated considerably more rapidly than states. International nongovernmental organizations, such as Greenpeace or Amnesty International, have grown even more quickly than either IGOs or states and now number about 24,000. The existence of these social institutions across state borders reflects the growing interdependence of the world's peoples and their desire for governance responsive to that interdependence.

The pressures for democracy provide another indication of that desire for governmental responsiveness. Democracy in the modern era is about as old as the industrial revolution and, although subject to more setbacks and less regular growth, has spread at a generally similar pace. Figure 2.23 traces the percentage of countries in Latin America and Europe with what Ted Gurr, Keith Jaggers, and Will Moore (1990) call a "coherent dem-

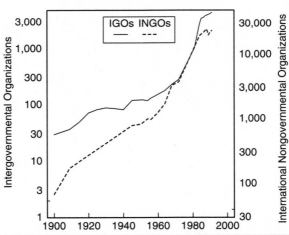

FIGURE 2.22 Growth of international organizations. *Source:* Union of International Organizations (UAI), *Yearbook of International Organizations* (Brussels: UAI, 1991, 1994). *Note:* Criteria for counting international organizations have changed over time, generally becoming more inclusive. Criteria for counting INGOs/NGOs were tightened in 1989 to exclude less active or less international groups.

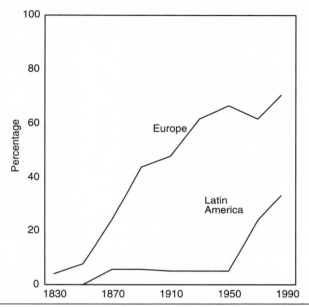

FIGURE 2.23   Coherent democratic polities as portion of regional polities. *Source:* Ted Robert Gurr, Keith Jaggers, and Will H. Moore, "The Transformation of the Western State," *Studies in Comparative International Development* 25, no. 1 (Spring 1990):94.

ocratic polity." Theirs is a somewhat more demanding test of democracy than that of many other observers.

There are, of course, many uncertainties with respect to all of these social and political trends. For instance, a flowering of democracy characterized the period immediately after World War I (with which some compare the contemporary post–Cold War era). By the late 1930s many of the flowers had wilted and died. Once again we must be wary of simple extrapolation.

CONCLUSION

Throughout this chapter we have simultaneously utilized trend extrapolation and inveighed against the uncritical extension of trends into the future. It is impossible to know whether a trend will continue or reach a sudden limit, pass an important turning point, or even end abruptly with a threshold change in the underlying process. Nonetheless, trends are of great use in helping us understand the present and anticipate the future. Many patterns will continue to evolve much as they have in the past. In addition, critical examination of trends moves us quickly to a consideration of the causal dynamics that might underlie change in the patterns. In this chapter I have already suggested many causal linkages that we shall investigate further in subsequent chapters.

In addition to the complexity of choosing an appropriate form for extrapolation of trends, many readers will have noted a second difficulty that also pushes us toward causal analysis. Specifically, many of the patterns we have seen interact with one another. Although we have attempted to look at trends in isolation, there has been recurrent pressure to consider that interaction.

In spite of the limitations of trend analysis, *we must keep in mind the dilemma that we face: There are pressures for us to act (including forgoing action alternatives), even in the face of inability to know the future.* Our examination of trends has given us a better idea of where change is taking us. That knowledge will assist us in moving to a consideration of the kind of future we want and the leverage we have in bringing it about.

THREE

Using IFs to Investigate Change

A careful examination of global trends, like the one we undertook in Chapter 2, contributes considerably to helping us understand where change is taking us. We saw in that chapter, however, that it is not a trivial matter to extrapolate trends into the future. For instance, it is often far from clear whether a trend will follow an exponential growth path, trace an S-curve, or peak and decline. Our examination of trends often forced us to make some additional assumptions about the world. In short, the difference between trend extrapolation and causal analysis may not be as great as we initially suggested. In reality, trend extrapolation inevitably takes place within the context of a broader understanding of the world around us. We bring an understanding of that world, a mental map or model of it, to any investigation of trends.

One difficulty with mental maps or models is that they often remain largely implicit. A second is that they are frequently very simple. Consider again the issue of forecasting the weather. You ask a friend what the weather will be tomorrow and she says "warm and sunny." You know that it is warm and sunny today. How do you judge the reasonableness of her forecast for tomorrow? Is she simply extrapolating the weather from today? Did she look at the weather map in this morning's paper and see that no new weather front is moving this direction? Or did she hear a forecast on the radio that was based on a complex computer model?

If the weather tomorrow is important to you, perhaps because you are planning a long hike, you may ask your friend how she knows it will be warm and sunny. That is, you may begin to explore her mental model and to compare that with your own. You may have more trust in her forecast if it is based on the weather map and even more if it is based on computer-generated forecasts that have in the past proven quite accurate. Presumably our understanding of the future adequacy of global food supplies and the quality of the earth's environment merits asking the same question: "How do you know?"

This chapter introduces a computer model called International Futures (IFs) as a tool for investigating global futures. Computer models formalize mental models mathematically. They are not automatically superior to mental models because of that formalization. In fact, many computer models are less sophisticated than a good mental model and produce unreliable forecasts.

Nonetheless, the careful use of computer models has some significant advantages. The first is that a computer model is highly explicit. One can examine the model very carefully. In contrast, we often have difficulty explaining our own mental models and may find ourselves "clueless" with respect to the mental models of others. Even if we reject a computer model, careful examination of it might well add sophistication to our own mental model. In fact, that is probably the single most important reason for using computer models: Because they represent the mental models of others, sometimes the cumulative understandings of many others, they help us learn.

Second, a computer model sometimes can attain a level of complexity that surpasses our mental models. That complexity might allow the computer program to probe the secondary consequences of change and action in ways that we cannot. For instance, computer models of chess probe the implications of moves far more fully than the typical human player. (It is also important to remember, however, that complexity can also introduce error.) Third, we can often use a computer model to investigate experimentally a variety of different assumptions. For instance, we might examine the possible consequences of several courses of action, as chess programs typically investigate far more possible moves than the average human player can. Or we might investigate the consequences of a single plan under differing assumptions about the workings of some key element in the environment of our action.

Those readers who do not intend to use the computer model that accompanies this book should proceed directly to Chapter 4. We invite those who do continue this chapter to sit down with it next to their computer. Like riding a bicycle, the best way to learn to use a computer model is to do it.

SOME BACKGROUND ON INTERNATIONAL FUTURES

There are many models of specific issues such as world population, the world economy, and the world climate. There are even more models of specific issues that have limited geographic scope (a country or region). The first model to devote attention to both the environment and the economy, and to do it on a global scale, was the one used to produce a book called *The Limits to Growth* (Meadows et al., 1972). That volume received worldwide attention for its pessimistic forecasts of the global future. Many models, some producing optimistic forecasts, followed that one in the 1970s and 1980s.[1]

IFs draws on many of the features of other world models (Hughes, 1985b, 1988). It represents a greater range of elements from what we earlier called the "human development system" than do most other world models. Specifically, it represents human demographics, food production, energy supply, the economy, and some aspects of political structure. It allows us to look at these elements individually and in interaction.

Our use of IFs will proceed in two stages. First, in this chapter we will look in turn and individually at the same global trends that we considered in Chapter 2. This reexamination will allow us to learn how to use IFs and also to learn something about how it operates—that is, about the mental model that underlies it. Second, in subsequent chapters you will have the opportunity to begin investigating the complex interaction of various elements in the model—to do substantial causal analysis of the future.

EXAMINING FORECASTS

Chapter 2 traced trends that are reshaping the world in seven issue areas. This section will assist you in using the IFs model to examine those same trends or forces. The use of IFs to examine the trends is, however, significantly different from the simple extrapolation of those trends in the last chapter. The most basic difference is that IFs is a fully integrated computer model; changes in any part of the model affect the rest of it. Thus, demographic, energy, environmental, and economic trends in IFs are very much interactive, even when we look at each individually. Although the results IFs produces may be very similar to the figures and tables presented in Chapter 2, they will never be identical. And even quite minor changes in any of the assumptions of IFs will affect all forecasts. Although we use IFs in this chapter to examine individual forecasts as if they were extrapolations, IFs is a complex causal model.

▶ **Starting IFs and Examining the Main Menu**. Before you can investigate trends, you need to know how to use IFs. You should install IFs on your computer using the instructions on the diskettes. (In case of installation errors, see the READ.ME file on Disk 1.) Then you should be able to initiate IFs from Windows simply by double-clicking on the IFs icon in the IFs program group. (If you are using IFs on a network and someone else did the installation, you may need additional instructions.) An older, DOS version of IFs is also available, and if you are using it you should refer to the first edition of this book for instructions; the instructions here support the Windows edition of IFs.

As IFs begins to run, you will see an introductory or "splash" screen that identifies the model and the version of IFs you have (see Figure 3.1). IFs loads its data files as it displays the introductory screen. You can use "speed keys" throughout IFs. Note that the "C" is underlined on the Continue button. That means that the speed key is Alt-C; you can hold down the "Alt" key and type "C" to proceed without the use of the mouse. It is, of course, normally easier just to use your mouse to click on the Continue button.

Figure 3.2 shows the Main Menu. Selecting any item on the menu with either a click of the mouse or the use of a speed key will take you deeper into IFs with either additional menu options or another screen. For instance, click on ProfFeatures (Professional Features). You will then see a submenu of four additional options. If you have the student edition of the model, only one of those options, IdentifyRegionMembers, will be available to you (the other options are available in the professional rather than the student edition and are the ONLY elements of IFs not available in the student edition). To explore further,

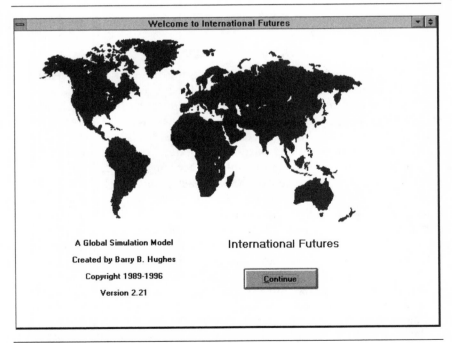

FIGURE 3.1   Introductory screen.

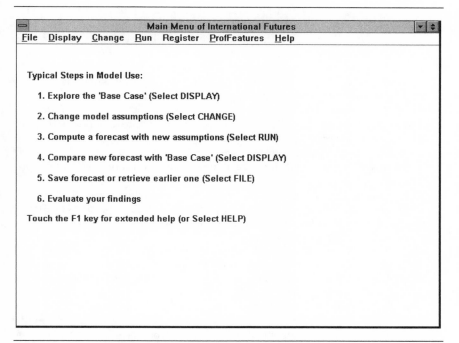

FIGURE 3.2   Main Menu.

click on IdentifyRegionMembers and you will see a screen with a listing of the "regions" into which IFs divides the world—some are individual countries and some are country groupings. Clicking on a region name will display the member countries of a region. IFs represents the world in regions because the representation of each individual country would demand too much computer capability.

Return to the Main Menu by clicking on the Exit key. Now explore the Help option. You can always obtain information about the model with this option or by touching the F1 function key on your keyboard. Help is "context sensitive" so that touching F1 will provide help related to the part of the model from which you touch it. Within Help, click on Overview to obtain some basic information about the model, or click on Model Detail to look at flow diagrams and even equations. There is a great deal of information available in the Help system and you should look for it as needed.

Exit from Help (click on File-Exit or double-click on the little dash in the upper right-hand corner of the Help screen) and return to the Main Menu. Note the text below the menu that describes the typical steps in model use. Model use normally has several steps that together constitute a process that we call "scenario analysis." These steps are:

1. *Explore an initial forecast or scenario of the model called the "base case."* The base case is *not* a prediction of the future. It is a statement of how the future might look *if* the initial conditions, equations, and base case parameter values of the model were all correct (and they never are). You will compare the base case with your own expectations or with forecasts from other sources (like those in Chapter 2). The base case will help you begin thinking and learning about the initial conditions, equations, and parameters of the model.

2. *Change assumptions of the base case.* IFs makes it easy to change initial conditions or parameters (see Table 3.1 for some important definitions). IFs even allows you to make some equation changes by using "switches."

3. *Run the model again to obtain a new forecast or "scenario."* Your changes will often create what you consider to be a more accurate (or more desirable) representation of the world.

4. *Compare the forecast generated by the new assumptions with the base case.* Make sure that you understand why the new scenario has produced different results. Your search for understanding may require still more changes of assumptions and runs of the model.

5. *Save your new scenario with the embedded changes you have made for future use (optional).* You will sometimes want to save the scenario so that you can later either build still more changes into it or compare it with additional scenarios.

6. *Evaluate what you have learned about the model and about the world it represents.* To what degree are the results you have obtained artifacts of a model that you either do not understand or with which you disagree? To what extent have you stretched your own understanding of the world and therefore improved your own mental model of it? Your work with a computer model can productively continue until you feel that your mental model is superior to the computer model (and can continue still further if you are then willing to extend the computer model itself).

These steps are somewhat idealized, but you should periodically refer back to them. They will help you make the most efficient use of IFs. In this chapter we will initially restrict our efforts primarily to the first step, exploration of the base case. We elaborate the other steps near the end of the chapter so that you know how to do them in anticipation of subsequent chapters. A copy of the base case is included with the IFs model and was loaded into computer memory when you initiated interaction with IFs. We therefore can now proceed to examine that base case.

DEMOGRAPHIC CHANGE

Research Questions. How large is the world's population? How fast is it growing? Is the rate of growth increasing or decreasing? How does population growth differ in various parts of the world? Where is it growing fastest? Are there any parts of the world in which it has stopped

TABLE 3.1   Important Terminology

Scenario	A forecast with a (computer or mental) model based upon specified initial conditions and parameters. The scenario helps us consider the possible implications of those specifications upon the evolution of variables of interest.
Parameters	Numbers in the equations of a model that specify the strength and even character of causal relationships among variables.
Variables	Concepts (such as population) that vary over time, dependent on their initial conditions, the behavior of causally related variables, and parameters that link them to such causally related variables.
Endogenous	Internal to the model (computed).
Exogenous	External to the model (user-specified).

growing? Is it decreasing anywhere? Is global population growing because birth rates have increased or because death rates have decreased (or both)? What might be the population of the world and its growth rate in 2050? You will be able to use IFs to answer these and similar questions by the time you finish this section.

▶ **Examining Variables in a Scenario: The Basics.** To examine any variable in IFs (a **variable** is a measure, such as global population, that changes over time), you need to click on Display from the Main Menu. You will then see the Display Menu (Figure 3.3) with several additional options. The primary display forms are tables of numerical values (either shown on the screen or printed), line graphs of variables over time, bar graphs of variables again over time, pie charts of variables at a single point in time, and scatterplots of two variables at a single point in time.

Before we can see a table or graph, however, we have to select the variables we want to see in it. Click on SelectVariables and you will see a submenu with two ways of doing this: Standard Subset and Full Set. The former option lets you easily select the most commonly examined variables, and the latter allows you to identify nearly any variable or parameter in the model for display.

Click on Standard Subset and you will see the screen of Figure 3.4. In the upper left you will see a set of variables that are world totals—for instance, world total population, population growth rate, and gross domestic product (GDP). Click on Population. Note that in the Status Box at the bottom of the screen, "WPOP[0]" appears. This is the variable name in the model for "world population."

Now click on Exit to Display, which will return you to the Display Menu. Select Table and you will see a table with the forecast in the base case of world

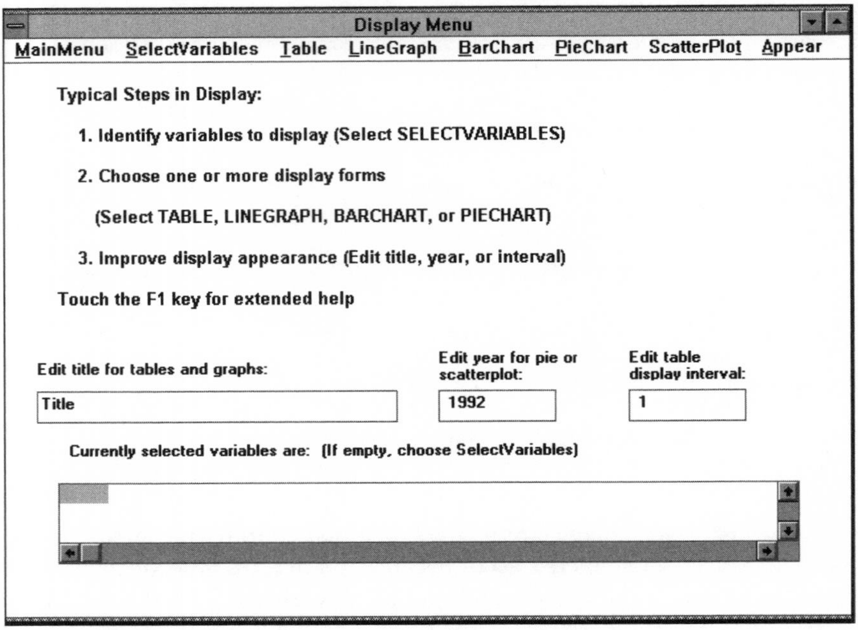

FIGURE 3.3   Display Menu.

population. Note that at the bottom it has options for either printing the table to an attached printer or saving it (as a comma-separated-variable file suitable for import into a spreadsheet). After looking at the table (using the arrow keys at the right to move up and down in it), click on Continue. Now try the Line-Graph option. You will obtain suboptions for different types and styles of line graphs, but simply choose Graph Display to produce a graph. Again, you can print or save the graph (as a windows metafile suitable for insertion into a word processing file). Return to the Display Menu and experiment with changing the figure title or display interval (try every fifth year). You will not be able to create a PieChart with a single variable over time; that option requires multiple variables.

Note that the graph of global population suggests that, although it is continuing to grow, it may begin to approach a level value sometime in the next century. That possibility implies that the growth rate of global population is slowing. To verify that, graph (or display in tabular form) the rate of growth of world population (WPOPR) by returning to Select-Variables and the Standard Subset. If you click on World Population Growth Rate it will add it to the Status Box at the bottom. Should you

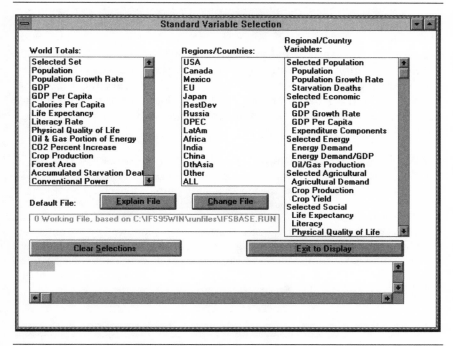

FIGURE 3.4   Standard Variable Selection.

want to look at World Population Growth Rate alone, Clear Selections and then click on it.

Population growth is far from identical in countries around the world. IFs calculates population (and most other variables) for each of its geographic regions.

▶ **Examining Variables by Region.** Again click on SelectVariables from the Display Menu and on Standard Subset. Clear Selections. Note that on the right-hand side of the screen (Figure 3.4) is a double box from which you can choose a region name on the left and a variable on the right (always in that order). Try clicking on All as the region and Population as the variable. You should see POP by region appear in the Status Box. Exit to Display and look at these in tabular or graphical form (a line graph may be too "busy"). Also create a pie chart for regional population in 2000 and again in 2050 (when there are many variables on a pie chart, the labels may overlap).

The world is now in the middle of a global demographic transition from high birth and death rates to low birth and death rates. During that transition, death rates initially declined faster than birth rates, especially in economically less developed countries (LDCs), causing population to grow rapidly. To see this phenomenon more clearly, look at the crude birth rate (CBR), or number of births per 1,000 population, the crude death rate (CDR), and the net population growth rate (POPR) for a single developing region like Latin America. To do that you can go into VariableSelect and the Standard Subset screen. Clear Selections. Click on Latin America (LatAm) and then on Selected Population, and those three variables and several others will appear in the Status Box and are ready for display.

▶ **Examining Variables: Flexibility.** If you want to look only at those three variables (CBR, CDR, and POPR), however, or more generally to access nearly all variables and parameters of the model in any combination, click on SelectVariables and on the Full Set option. That will produce the screen in Figure 3.5. (Clear Selections if the Status Box shows any earlier choices.) In the box on the top you can type "CBR" or any other variable name, followed by the Enter key. Or you can use the arrows on the right to scroll through the exhaustive listing of model variables until you find CBR, and then use your mouse to click on it. You could also click on Population/Demographic in the Subset box at the

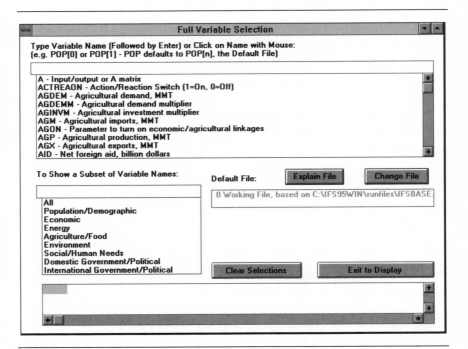

FIGURE 3.5   Full Variable Selection.

lower left, watch the demographic variables alone appear in the box at the top, and more easily move to and click on CBR. Whichever approach you use, after you have selected CBR, a list of regions will appear and you can click on one. Again the Status Box will help you keep track of what you have selected. Experiment, because you can always Clear Selections.

Explore the population model on your own by looking at population (POP), population growth rate (POPR), total fertility rate (TFR), crude birth rates (CBR), crude death rates (CDR), total births (BIRTHS), total deaths (DEATHS), life expectancy at birth (LIFEXP), and/or infant mortality (INFMOR) for a variety of countries and regions.

You may now be asking how the model generates these numbers. The model keeps track of the number of people in each of 19 age categories or cohorts. The first is of infants, and the next 17 represent five-year groupings (people from 1–5 years of age, 6–10, 11–15, and so on). The last cohort combines all those 86 years of age or older. The model also represents a fertility distribution by cohort. That is, it has recent data (by region) on the number of births per 1,000 people for those 16–20 years old, 21–25 years old, and so on. By multiplying the fertility distribution by the age distribution, the model calculates the number of births, and those infants are added to the bottom cohort. Finally the model maintains a mortality distribution that records recent data on the portion of each cohort that dies in an average year (obviously that portion is greater for older cohorts). Multiplying the mortality distribution by the age distribution provides the number of deaths in each cohort, and those deaths diminish the cohort each year. In addition, one-fifth of each cohort passes to the next age group in every year.

Fertility and mortality patterns change in response to other variables within the model. For instance, fertility responds to changes in assumptions about contraceptive use (assumptions you will be able to alter); mortality changes in response to availability of adequate food supply (you cannot directly alter food availability, but you can affect it by modifying other assumptions). Both fertility and mortality change with income level and income distribution. We will return to these determinants later. To learn more about model structure, use the Help system.

FOOD AVAILABILITY

Research Questions. Is food production in the world as a whole growing as rapidly as population? Where might it be growing more rapidly and where less rapidly? Do some parts of the world rely on food imports to maintain adequate calorie levels? In which regions of the world is starvation a danger?

Another critically important force that is reshaping our world is growth in food production and the "race" between it and population growth. You can display world agricultural crop production (WAPRO) in a table or plot it on a graph. It is measured in millions of metric tons. At the dialog level (if you use the Full Set option) you will need to specify whether you want to look at crop or meat production (build a table, or graph with both). You can also look at agricultural production (AGP) by region. Or you can examine agricultural imports (AGM) or agricultural exports (AGX).

Information on food availability may be more meaningful when it is converted to calories available for consumption, whether produced locally or imported. Look at world calories per capita (WCLPC). The units are in thousands of calories per day. On a region-by-region basis you can look at calories per capita (CLPC). The model also calculates millions of potential starvation deaths each year in each region (SDEATH) and the accumulated starvation deaths (since 1990) for the world (WSDACC). Explore for more food and agricultural variables of interest via the Agriculture/Food subset on the Full Set display screen.

How does the model make these forecasts? The model calculates crop production (AGP) by multiplying the million hectares of land devoted to crops (LD) by the tons of food yielded by each hectare (YL). Land under cultivation depends on the capital investment made in improving land (KAG) and the cost of clearing additional land (CLD). Yield levels depend on the use of inputs such as fertilizer. Both investment in land and the use of yield-boosting inputs depend in turn on the price of food. Meat production depends on the livestock herd size and the slaughter rate.

The model determines human food demand (FDEM) as a function of population, income levels, and prices; the more you earn, the more you spend on food (but you allocate a decreasing portion of your total income), and the higher prices are, the less you spend on food. The coefficients (parameters) that represent the responsiveness of food consumption to income and price are called the income and price **elasticities** of food demand. The model calculates the demand upon crop production for livestock feed (FEDDEM) as a function of herd size and grazing land availability. It further calculates an industrial demand for agricultural production (INDEM) (for instance, demand for cotton) as a function of economic size. The sum of these components reflects total agricultural demand.

▶ **Creating Ratio and Percentage Relationships Between Variables.** To look at the food demand for crops in the United States as a portion of the total demand for crops, you can create a ratio or percentage by using the "/" and "%"

symbols after the variable in the numerator. Specify FDEM/ as the variable, selecting the United States on the country/region dimension. Then specify AGDEM, again selecting the United States and identifying crop as the food type. The Status Box will indicate the ratio's calculation, which you can display as usual. You could even specify FDEM/ for ALL countries/regions, followed by AGDEM for all.

The model maintains buffer stocks (inventories) of agricultural products so that a surplus of supply relative to demand in one year will increase those stocks, whereas a surplus of demand relative to production will decrease them. Because food price (FPRI) affects both food demand and food supply, it is a critical variable in the model. It is calculated by the model **endogenously** (internally), rather than being given **exogenously** (externally) to the model by the user. When the buffer stocks rise, they depress food prices; when they fall, they increase prices. Prices then affect both demand and supply in the next year. Thus, changes in buffer stocks and prices act to bring supply and demand into balance over time. In reality, there are always some imbalances and the process chases balance or equilibrium rather than reaching it; such imbalances account for some of the irregularities you will see in model forecasts.

ENERGY TRANSITION

Research Questions. What primary energy form supplies most of the world's energy? How much does it provide? What countries or regions consume the most energy? Which produce the most? Which import and export the most? How big are the world's known reserves of oil and gas? How do those compare to the reserves of coal? How large might unknown (undiscovered) oil and gas resources be?

The world's relative dependence on oil and gas is declining steadily, even as the production and consumption of oil and gas continue to increase. In fact, the world is fairly steadily making a transition from an energy system predominantly dependent on oil and gas to one that will eventually rely much more heavily on some combination of coal, nuclear, and solar (renewable) energy inputs.

To explore this phenomenon in the base case, we can begin by looking at world energy production (WENP). Use the Full Set display option. IFs calculates production of four primary energy forms: oil and gas combined (because they face comparable production futures); coal; renewable sources (including biomatter, photovoltaic, hydroelectric, and other forms); and nuclear (which fusion as well as fission plants could eventually supply). When you select WENP to display, you will be asked to select one or all of these forms. A line graph of WENP in all categories provides a good picture of how the energy supply pattern may change over time. Look also at energy production on a regional basis (ENP).

Oil and gas production (OILGPR) as a portion of total energy production most clearly shows the energy transition. Look at it in either tabular or graphical form. It declines in the long run because the world has limited supplies of oil and gas. The variable RESER (for "reserves") contains estimates by region of known and producible oil and gas in the initial year and thereafter (WRESER carries the world total). Production decrements that variable over time, and new discoveries augment it. The total regional resource base of oil and gas, RESOR, ultimately bounds new discoveries (WRESOR shows the world total). Note how much greater global resources are for coal than for oil and gas.

One of the key characteristics of the world energy system is the concentration of oil and gas production in OPEC countries, with economically more developed countries accounting for most energy demand (ENDEM). You can see this phenomenon by looking first at the pie chart of ENDEM across all regions and then creating a pie chart across all regions of ENP for oil and gas.

A more direct way of examining the gap between production and consumption is to look at energy exports (ENX) or energy imports (ENM). Note that it is possible for a country or a region to be both an energy exporter and importer—even the United States exports some refined products, for instance.

How does the energy submodel of IFs work? It has much in common with the agricultural submodel described earlier. Specifically, it calculates demand, supply, and buffer stocks to balance demand and supply in the short run. Changes in buffer stocks lead to changes in prices, which in turn affect demand and supply in the longer run, so that the model always chases equilibrium (balance).

Energy demand is a function largely of economic size, as measured by GDP, and energy prices (see ENPRI for regional prices and WEP for a world average). Because of the resource constraints on oil and gas, and because of base case assumptions about the capital costs of alternatives (QE), the model forecasts some initial increase in energy prices as the transition proceeds. This method leads to slower growth in energy demand than in GDP (ENRGDP is the ratio of energy demand to GDP and is an interesting indicator of energy efficiency).

Energy is a highly capital-intensive industry. Thus the major determinant of energy production in any energy type is the capital investment that has been made over time in its production. That investment increases or decreases with the price of energy relative to the cost of energy production. For instance, if the price of energy increases less rapidly than the cost of oil and gas production does (because of ongoing resource depletion), capital investment in oil and gas will decline. If the price of energy increases, however, while the capital cost of renewable energy declines (owing to technological progress), capital investment in renewable energy will increase substantially. Thus the supply side of the energy submodel determines not only how much energy each geographic region will produce but also the balance among production levels of various energy forms.

You have probably realized already the importance of the assumptions in the base case about resource bases, current capital costs of various energy types, the future changes of those costs, and the responsiveness of energy demand to price changes. The uncertainty of such assumptions is the reason we earlier said that any single forecast of a model should be examined very skeptically. We will learn later how we can identify and change these and many other assumptions.

ENVIRONMENTAL IMPACT

Research Questions. How much damage are humans doing to the environment? What is the rate of global deforestation? How does the progress of deforestation vary by region? How fast is the growth of atmospheric CO_2?

As populations grow, food production increases, and energy production rises, some environmental damage is inevitable. Increases in agricultural production depend on either additions in land under cultivation or improvements in yield per hectare of cropland. Thus, forest area (including rain forests) tends to decline as a result of conversion to cropland.

Two of the potential environmental problems of greatest concern to scientists and environmentalists today are the greenhouse effect and global deforestation. Fossil fuels contain carbon, and burning them (oxidization) inevitably adds carbon dioxide (CO_2) to the atmosphere. Carbon dioxide allows sunlight to pass through easily, but it retards the radiation of heat back into space (like the glass in a greenhouse). CO_2 is the primary "greenhouse gas," the set of gases that may ultimately cause the earth's climate to become warmer.

You can display or plot the increase in atmospheric carbon dioxide over time. The model tracks that phenomenon in terms of the parts per million that CO_2 constitutes of the atmosphere (CO2PPM) and also in terms of the percentage increase in carbon dioxide (CO2PER) relative to the amount in the atmosphere early in the industrial era (around the year 1800). These measures have interest because some scientists have estimated that a doubling in carbon dioxide might raise average global temperatures (WTEMP) by about 2 degrees Centigrade. The impact of increasing CO_2 is not, however, a threshold phenomenon; that is, temperature rise will not suddenly occur when CO_2 doubles but will instead happen throughout the process.

To examine the impact of human activity on forest area, look at the amount of land (LD) in various categories and regions, measured in millions of hectares. In many countries and regions, there have been increases in cropland and land used for urban areas (and other human developments, such as roads) and decreases in forest area. You can also look at the decline in total world forest area (WFORST).

How does the model calculate these environmental indicators and how do changes in them affect the model's assessment of human well-being? Deforestation is a side effect of agricultural and other human activity. As described earlier, investments in agriculture often bring new land under cultivation. (The model determines the relative economic efficiency of investing in new land and investing in increased inputs, such as fertilizer and machinery.) Although there are important ramifications of forest destruction for humanity, including the extinction of plant and animal species with important pharmacological potential, the costs of the process are essentially incalculable. The model therefore does no more than indicate the extent of deforestation.

Similarly, the generation of carbon dioxide is an inevitable side effect of energy consumption. There are some uncertainties, however, about its impact; one debate, for example, concerns how many billion tons of carbon dioxide the oceans and forests absorb annually. The model therefore represents that absorption as a parameter (CARABR). As important, scientists have begun to speculate about the implications of increased global temperatures on agricultural productivity. The model therefore includes a linkage between rising CO_2 levels and diminished or increased agricultural yields (the parameter is ELASAC).

TECHNOLOGICAL CHANGE

Research Questions. How much does technological advance contribute to economic change? What portion of increase in agricultural production is a result of technological improvement? How rapidly is the technology of global destruction progressing?

Technological change is pervasive in the world around us. It affects medical treatment and thus life expectancy. It alters our agricultural system and thus food availability. It changes the costs of extracting or producing energy and therefore the price and availability of that energy. It is often very difficult to draw out measures of technological advance from the broader processes of change.

One way of looking at such deeply embedded technological advance is to compare over time the resources that go into a production process and the output of that process. For instance, you can obtain a table or graph over time comparing the amount of land used for crop production (LD) with the amount of crop (agricultural) production (AGP). Similarly, you can examine the amount of total production by any sector of the economy (ZS) relative to the amount of labor (LABS) used in that sector (create a ratio).

Chapter 2 suggested, however, that technological advance brings not just economic efficiency gains but also improvements in the destructive power of humanity. Beginning with the American Civil War, sometimes considered the first modern war, humanity has added machine guns, torpedoes, exploding shells, a variety of chemical and biological agents, and both atomic and hydrogen warheads to its armory. It has added submarines, metal ships, aircraft, tanks, and a wide variety of missiles to its list of delivery vehicles. Most of these implements of destruction originated in Europe or North America. All of them have now proliferated around the world. Additional countries continue to adopt them annually, and the world total of most rises steadily.

IFs has no individual measures of this weaponry. Instead you can examine their spread only in the aggregate, by looking at conventional and nuclear power (CPOW and NPOW). For instance, look at the growth of conventional power of various less-developed regions of the world in comparison with the power of Russia (or even the United States).

Forecasts of conventional power are uncertain, but forecasts of nuclear power are little more than wild guesses. We have little idea how fast nuclear weaponry might proliferate in the South. Nor do we know whether contemporary arms control agreements in the North really will substantially reduce inventories of both bombs and rockets in the long run. Such uncertainty in no way diminishes the importance of identifying the underlying trends of weaponry improvement and spread.

How does IFs forecast technological change? IFs does not contain a separate model of technological change. Instead, as the above discussion suggests, such change is represented in various ways throughout the model. In the agricultural sector, improvements in agricultural yield (YL)—metric tons of crops per hectare of land—reflect various other changes. Simple increases in the intensity of agriculture (the amount of capital and labor provided to the land) account for some. IFs also contains, however, a parameter that specifies the annual rate of increase in the efficiency of capital use (RKEF). A similar parameter (RLEF) strongly influences the rate of increase in the efficiency of labor use, but expenditures on education influence that rate as well. In short, the improvements in technology are partly specified from outside the model (exogenously) and partly from within (endogenously).

ECONOMIC RESTRUCTURING

Research Questions. What are the major changes taking place in the world's economy? Which region has the largest economy and how fast is it growing? What region will have the largest economy in 2050 (making all the assumptions embedded in the base case)? What economic sectors are growing most rapidly?

There are at least two important and highly interrelated structural changes reshaping the world economy. First, the economically less developed countries (LDCs) of the world were at one time overwhelmingly producers of raw materials such as minerals and agricultural products. They are now increasingly industrialized economies, supplying larger portions of their manufactures to the economically more developed countries. Second, the service sector (including advanced information and communication activities) increasingly forms the dominant sector of the more developed countries. In short, manufacturing is shifting to the poor countries while the rich countries are concentrating more on services, including high-tech ones.

The basic measure of economic activity in all countries and regions is the gross domestic product (GDP), defined as the total production for final demand of goods and services. You should begin exploring the economic submodel by looking at the variable GDP across geographic units—consider pie charts as well as line graphs. Explore also the rate of GDP growth (GDPR) and the GDP per capita (GDPPC). You can also look at world GDP (WGDP) and world GDP per capita (WGDPPC).

How much of the world's manufacturing is located in the South (the less developed countries are often physically south of the more developed)? How fast is that portion increasing? The percentage share is summarized in the variable SMAN. Its values suggest the speed of manufacturing growth in the South.

To see more clearly how the manufacturing sector is becoming an increasingly large part of the economies in southern regions, however, we must look at those regions individually. The economic submodel calculates production for each country or region in five sectors: agriculture, primary energy, other raw materials, manufactures, and services. For instance, gross production by the manufacturing sector (ZS) in Africa shows that manufacturing will become an increasingly important portion of the economy. Look also at how manufacturing in Africa compares with manufacturing in other regions.

Even more substantial changes are occurring in global services. The service sector is already the largest of the five in the United States, and the dominance of that sector appears likely to increase (see again ZS). Relatively faster growth in service production and consumption is occurring in both other richer, "northern" countries and in the South.

How is the increase in manufacturing in the South and the continued rise of services in the North affecting the aggregate world economy? The percentage of the world's production in each sector (WPROD) will give you the answer. Note especially what is happening to the share of agriculture.

▶ **Examining Relationships Between Variables in Scatterplots.** You may also want to investigate the relationship between two variables. For instance, you may believe that GDP per capita of countries (GDPPC) affects the rate of investment (IRA) as a portion of GDP. To look at this possible relationship, select GDPPC for ALL countries/regions and then select IRA for ALL countries/ regions. Exit to Display and select the Scatterplot option. To test that you have fully mastered display techniques, try creating a scatterplot showing the relationship between GDPPC and the portion that manufacturing constitutes in economies. The model contains no variable showing the manufacturing portion, so create a ratio of value added (VADD) in manufacturing over GDP (GDP) using the "/" symbol (VADD/). That is, select GDPPC for ALL countries/regions as the independent variable, select VADD/ for ALL countries/regions (manufacturing sector), followed by GDP for ALL countries/ regions to create the dependent variable, and then produce a scatterplot.

The economic submodel is in many respects the core of IFs, because nearly all other portions of the model provide input to it or utilize calculations from it. *How does it work?* Like the agricultural and energy submodels, it has demand and supply sides, balanced by changing buffer stocks and prices.

On the supply side, production in each sector depends on the availability of labor (LAB) and capital (KS). The production function that combines those factors is called a **Cobb-Douglas function.** Assumptions about the annual rate of improvements in the quality of labor (RLEF) and the technological sophistication of capital (RKEF) also influence production. Over time the labor force grows with the population (depending also on how much of the population participates in the commercial economy) and the capital stock in each sector grows with investment (in new buildings and machinery). Much of gross production (ZS) goes to satisfy the production requirements of other sectors (for instance, steel production goes into the production of screws and bolts, which in turn goes into the production of cars). These intersectoral flows are subtracted from gross supply to calculate how much of gross production is actually available to meet what we call **final demand** (PFD), consumption by households and government plus investment. We use a technological coefficient matrix (or input-output matrix) to calculate those intersectoral flows (A); each coefficient represents the portion of gross production used by another sector.

The (final) demand side begins with total income (dependent on production levels) and allocates part of that to government (G) through taxes. It then splits the remaining portion between investment (I) and household consumption (C). Government, investment, and consumption all make demands upon the supply side of the economy by sector. The government (GS) primarily buys services. Investment (INVS) largely requires manufactures and construction. Private or household consumption by sector (CS) demands largely food, manufactures, and services (the model uses a linear expenditure system, which shifts the allocation of household spending as income rises).

Exports by sector (XS) and imports by sector (MS) among countries depend on the past pattern of trade (there is a strong inertial element in trade flows) and the relative prices of products in the various geographic regions modified by exchange rates (EXRATE). You can also look at total exports (X) and imports (M). IFs does not have a monetary sector and does not represent inflation. Prices and exchange rates are real, relative to initial conditions.

Local demand (from government, investors, and households) and foreign demand (from exports) reduce inventories or buffer stocks in a sector. Local and foreign supply (from imports) increase buffer stocks. Change in the level of stocks (and the rate of their change) determines the rise or fall of prices (PRI). Rising prices increase investment in sectors, depress consumption, and increase net imports. Thus the entire economic model chases balance between demand and supply, using the buffer stocks to absorb temporary imbalance. This is the same process in the economy as a whole that we saw earlier in the agriculture and energy submodels. In fact, the demand and supply calculations from those two single-sector submodels, because they are based on a more detailed representation of the sectors than that in the economic submodel, override the calculations in the economic submodel (unless the user wishes to turn off those linkages).

Many key assumptions obviously influence the behavior of the regional and world economies in the base case. These include the relative importance of labor and capital in the production process, the rates of increase in labor efficiency and capital sophistication, and the portion of income taken by the government. We will see subsequently how to change these and other assumptions.

SOCIAL-POLITICAL CHANGE

Research Questions. Are citizens around the world becoming more involved in politics and collective social action more generally? If so, why?

It now appears that democracy as we know it in North America, Western Europe, Japan, Australia, and New Zealand is spreading around the world. Multiple changes of government in Latin America, Central and Eastern Europe, and Asia provide support for such a hypothesis. It seems also possible that the level of public involvement in political and social interest groups (including international ones such as Greenpeace and Amnesty International) and in street protests (such as those that toppled governments in Czechoslovakia, East Germany, and Rumania) may be rising. In short, the mobilization of people behind social purposes of various kinds seems to be increasing (some manifestations, like terrorism, are violent).

Why might that be? One part of the explanation is that people are now more able to participate. They are more literate and they have much greater access to the electronic media of communication than ever before. A greater portion also live in cities where they can more easily have face-to-face interaction. A second part of the explanation may be that larger numbers have satisfied the basic needs of existence and therefore can direct their attention to other human objectives.

Some of the indicators in IFs verify that the changes that might facilitate social mobilization are indeed under way. Look, for instance, at the numbers for literacy by region (LIT) and globally (WLIT). Consider also the trends in GDP per capita (GDPPC and WGDPPC) and those in life expectancy (LIFEXP and WLIFE). Consider again regional and global calorie availability (CLPC and WCLPC). Improvements in a physical quality of life indicator (PQLI and WPQLI) summarize much of what happens regionally and globally. That measure often serves as a noneconomic summary of the human condition—it combines literacy rate, infant mortality, and life expectancy with equal weighting.

How does IFs capture and handle the important phenomenon of social mobilization? The model incorporates some important mechanisms that drive the levels of key variables for social mobilization, such as life expectancy and literacy. For instance, government spending flows to both health and education and influences progress on the measures. Although IFs thus represents a number of key aspects of socialization, it does not yet link them causally to democracy. Instead, it represents democracy via an exogenous variable called FREEDOM. The initial values of that variable are set from data of Freedom House and are the sum of the two scales of that organization into a single measure of freedom running from 2.0 (most free) to 14.0 (least free). There should also be a number of "forward linkages" from social mobilization and freedom to other variables in the model. The only one of importance now included is of FREEDOM (democracy) to propensity for warfare—we shall discuss that relationship in Chapter 7. One can also imagine linkages of social mobilization to the nature and distribution of government expenditures. This is just one example of many potentially important linkages that IFs does not contain. No computer model can ever be as rich as our imagination (although it can often be more consistent than our memories and more coherent than our understandings).

You now have a basic understanding of the structure of IFs and have seen how the model allows you to more carefully consider important trends or forces that are reshaping the world. There is, however, a great deal more that one can do with the model; it has several additional levels of complexity. For example, although we have examined only the base case of the model, we have already emphasized several times the importance of various assumptions. We thus need to learn how to change the assumptions of the base case and to construct scenarios (alternative futures based on alternative assumptions) that we can compare with the base case.

CHANGING FORECASTS

Up to now our use of IFs has been relatively passive. We examined the base case and saw one possible way in which the world might evolve. In this section we become more active. Through the procedure of scenario development, we investigate how humans may alter the directions of development relative to the base case. In the last section we learned how to examine the output of the model through tables and graphs. In this section we learn how to manipulate parametric assumptions of the model, in some cases even changing model structure.

Changing parameters requires greater understanding of model structure and parameters than you now have. Subsequent chapters will help you gain that understanding. This section will simply introduce the mechanics of parameter change and model use for examining alternative understandings of the world or the impact of alternative human behavior (refer to Important Note 1).

China, like most countries, presumably has a desire to increase its power over time (or at the very least to avoid decreases in it). In this section we want to explore how China might pursue that aim. To do so, we need to learn about steps 2–5 of model use and scenario analysis, as listed earlier and shown on the screen of the Main Menu: (2) change the parameters of IFs, (3) run the model with new parameters, (4) compare results from the new run (scenario) with those of the base case, and (optionally) (5) save a result set or scenario file based on the new parameters.

▶ **Changing Parameters.** A **parameter** is an exogenously specified number (or series of numbers over time) that influences the relationship between variables

---

Important Note 1

The Help system of IFs lists the major parameters of IFs and describes how to use them. It also contains a discussion of parameter types that will help you better understand parameters. It further contains extensive detail on the model structure, from causal diagrams to equations. It is a very good idea to use Help heavily while developing your own scenarios of the world—otherwise you may find yourself making changes quite different from those you intend.

---

in the model. To change a parameter, it is necessary to know its name. The parameter that controls the allocation of government spending among categories is GK (governmental spending coefficient). The Help system provides more detail on GK and other parameters. Look at GK's value in the base case for China across all types of spending (military, health, and so on). Note that the values for China are fixed, indicating that (in the model) China always allocates a constant percentage of government spending to the military and other categories. One approach China might take in attempting to increase its power in the world is to boost its military spending at the expense of other kinds of spending.

To change the value of Chinese military spending, click on Change from the Main Menu and you will see the same options that you saw when you worked with Display, namely, Standard Subset and Full Set. Analogously with their use in Display, these options allow parameter selection from either a selected subset or all parameters.

Choose the Standard Subset and the screen shown in Figure 3.6 will appear. If you click on the Domestic Government/Political subset (lower left), you will see parameters in that area, including GK. Click on it and then, when prompted, on China as the region and Military as the spending category. When you do that the Change Values screen (Figure 3.7) will appear.

The little graph in the upper right will show you the current value of GK over time for military expenditures in China; note that it is flat or constant. You are able to create any pattern of GK that you desire with the tools on this screen and watch the value of GK change in the graph as you do so (see Important Note 2).

Important Note 2

For variables such as population (POP) you can provide only the initial conditions; the model limits your changes to those initial conditions and computes subsequent values itself. For most parameters, however, you can provide different values for each year.

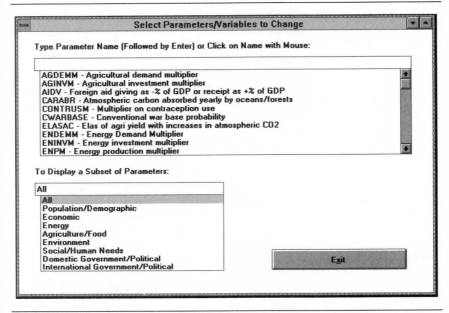

FIGURE 3.6   Standard Variable Change.

You have many options on this screen. One is to select a new single value that will be repeated at a constant level for many years. A second is to indicate first and last values over a time period and to let the model compute intermediate values itself (it **interpolates** linearly—that is, it gradually and steadily changes the values for the years between first and last). A third is to proceed year-by-year and to specify unique values for each year.

Using these options (including some mixing of them), we can create a new arms spending pattern for China. In this case, let us begin by keeping the level unchanged for five years, then increasing it steadily for another five, thereafter holding it at the higher level. Although we could specify this pattern by typing in a value for each year (using the Current Value box near the top left to enter value after value), there are some tricks that make the introduction of this scenario easier:

1. *Repeating values.* To repeat the initial value (shown as the current value for 1992) from the base case for the first five years, type "5" as the number of Repeat/Interpolate Years, then click on the Repeat option among the Action Options. You will see the working year advance by five years and the graph remain flat.

2. *Ramping values up or down.* We can increase the value from its level in this advanced year to a higher level five years later. For instance, type "5" again as the number of Repeat/Interpolate Years, type ".25" in the Final

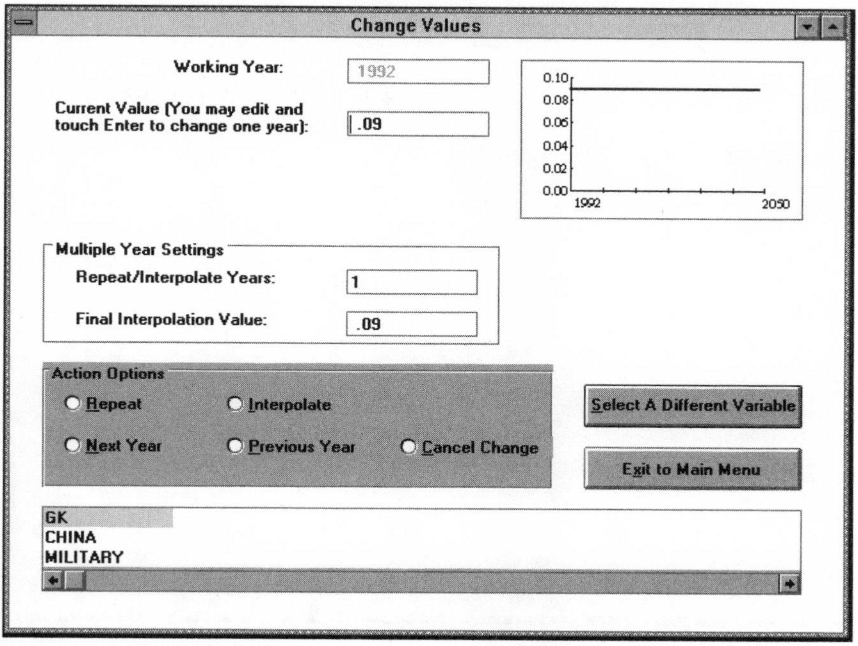

FIGURE 3.7   Change worksheet.

Repeat/Interpolate Value box, and select Interpolate as the Action Option. You will see the working year advance again, and the graph will change to show the increase in GK over time.

3. *Stabilizing the value.* To hold the new value for the remaining years, simply type some number in the Repeat/Interpolate Years box that is sufficient to extend the Working Year beyond 2050 (obviously, for example, "70" would do the trick) and click on the Repeat option. You should see the graph adjust to the new value for China through 2050.

Running the Model. You are now ready to run the model (although you have changed an important parameter, its change will not affect variables until you run the model). Exit to the Main Menu and select the Run option. The Run Screen of Figure 3.8 will appear. Your only choice here is the number of years that the model will run. On slower machines even a 19-year run (the default) will take considerable time, and 19 years is sufficient to see the results of our scenario. So just click on Start Run. As the run progresses you will see the computation of selected variables. When the run is complete you will be able to press Continue to get back to the Main Menu.

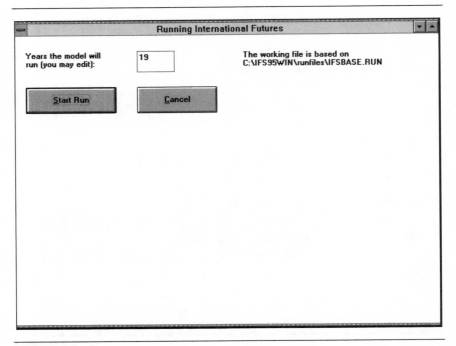

FIGURE 3.8   Run screen.

Comparing Results from One Model Run (such as the base case) to Others. In order to compare results across model runs, it is necessary to understand a bit about files. IFs keeps track of files by name and also with a number assigned to them. The base case is always file "1." That file is always available to you, as is a second file called the "Working File," known as file "0." When you start up IFs, the Working File is immediately set equal to the base case. You may have noticed that whenever you have displayed a variable from IFs, it has always appeared in the Status Box at the bottom of the page (and in table or graph headers) with the number "0" in brackets. You have been looking at the Working File, which during most of your use of IFs has been totally equivalent to the base case.

The Working File keeps track of changes, however, and as soon as you changed the parameter GK, the Working File changed (but not the base case, which never changes). When you ran the model, the Working File changed further as variables were computed using the new value of GK. For instance, the actual government spending in various destination categories (GDS) changed for China, with military expenditures rising and other spending falling relatively.

To see the changed level of GDS, go to Display from the Main Menu, choose SelectVariables and the Full Set suboption, and look again at the Full Variable

Selection screen as shown earlier in Figure 3.5. Note that on the center right there is a box labeled "Default File." The Default File is the file from which a variable is chosen unless you specify otherwise. It should be the Working File, file "0." In the Type Variable Name box, type "GDS" and select China and Military expenditures. The Status Box will show GDS for file "0," your scenario result. To compare it with the value of GDS in the base case, always file "1," you can do one of two things:

1. Type "GDS[1]" in the Type Variable Name box, again selecting China and Military.
2. Click on the Change File button and note that the Default File changes from "0" to "1," the base case. Now type "GDS" in the Type Variable Name box for Chinese military expenditures.

In either case you should see GDS[1] in the Status Box next to GDS[0]. Exit to Display and compare the two in a table or graph. You can obviously display other comparisons from the two scenarios, such as GDP[0] and GDP[1].

Saving Your Scenario for Future Use. You will often wish to save the parameter changes that create a scenario (especially when they accumulate in complexity) and the resulting variable changes from a model run in order to look at them further or to make additional changes at another time. To do so, go to the Main Menu and select the File option. Among the suboptions, select Save. The dialog box shown in Figure 3.9 will appear. You can potentially save model result files (all of which approximate 1.4 megabytes in size) at various locations on your hard disk or on a floppy disk. The default location is the Runfiles subdirectory of the IFs directory on hard disk C. Use the Drives box or the Directories box to change that location as necessary. Then type the file

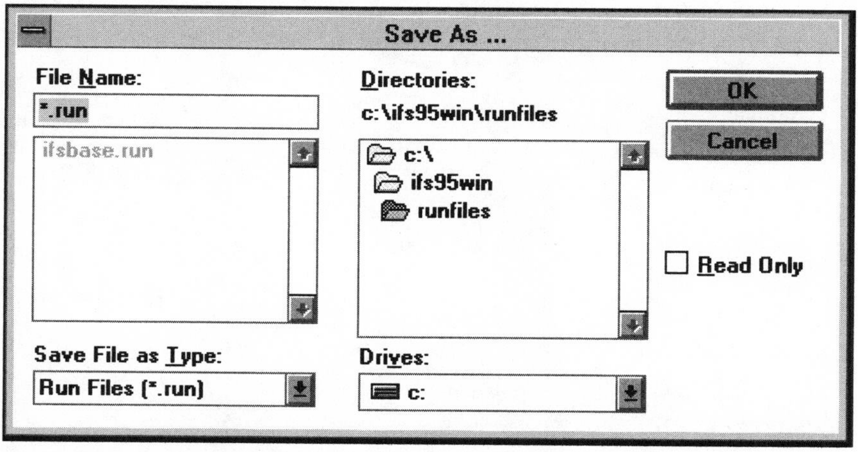

FIGURE 3.9   Save As dialog.

name in the File Name box (always using the ".run" extension to the file name) and click on OK. Call the scenario for China "HIMIL.RUN" and save it. Until you save a file, any changes you have made exist only in the Working File; when you exit from IFs, the Working File is lost (to be *re-created* as the base case when you reenter IFs).

Selecting Scenarios for Display. When you return to the use of IFs at a later time, IFs will not automatically know that run files exist on your hard disk or floppy disk (it cannot look everywhere you might put them). To tell it file locations and your interest in displaying them, you must choose File from the Main Menu and the Select suboption (see Figure 3.10). You should be able to find the scenario "HIMIL.RUN" on your Runfiles subdirectory (if you saved it as discussed immediately above). Type it as the File Name and click on OK (or just double-click on "himil.run" itself). Try that now. The first file that you select in this process automatically becomes file number "2," the second will be file number "3," and so on (remember that the base case is always number "1"). After you select a file, and only after you select it, can you choose variables from it for display. Go to Display and to the Standard Variable Selection or Full Variable Selection screens (Figures 3.4 and 3.5); use the Change File button and note that it can now advance the Default File to HIMIL.RUN. The Explain File button will give you a brief refresher of this explanation about files.

Making Additional Changes to an Existing Scenario. When you choose the Change option from the Main Menu and then choose either the Selected Subset or Full Set suboption, you will move to screens for the selection of parameters and initial conditions. It is important that you understand that these screens and the change process only allow you to change values in the Working File. Thus if you wish to change a scenario file (such as HIMIL.RUN) at a later date, you must first File-Open it, which will make it the Working File. Then change parameters, run the model again, and resave the file, either using

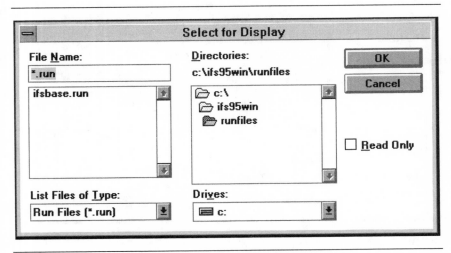

FIGURE 3.10   Select File dialog.

the same name (such as HIMIL.RUN) or a new name in order to record the changes for the longer term. Whenever you exit the model, the Working File itself, and all changes you have made to it, are lost.

Explore further the "high-Chinese-military-expenditure" scenario you have created. For instance, compare the conventional and nuclear power (CPOW and NPOW) and a measure of aggregate power (POWER) of China with values in the base case. Although you have increased the military power of China, you probably suspect that this was not without cost. Graphically compare education spending and the physical quality of life (PQLI) or some of its components, such as literacy (LIT), with values from the base case.

There is a substantial debate concerning the implications of military spending for economic growth. Specifically, does military spending put people to work and increase the GDP, or does it divert resources from other uses (including education and health spending) that make a greater contribution to economic performance? Look at the GDP or GDP per capita (GDPPC) for China relative to the base case and determine the IFs model's answer to that question. You should be aware that IFs does not give the definitive answer— the results of IFs depend totally on the structure and parameters of the model.

That dependency raises another issue. How does the model translate increased military spending into the measure of overall relative power (POWER)? It does so by weighting four elements of power (population, GDP, conventional military power, and nuclear power). The weights it uses are in the parameters PF1, PF2, PF3, and PF4, respectively. Those weights are arbitrary and you can imagine different decisionmakers applying different weights (since World War II the Japanese seem to have weighted GDP more highly than conventional or nuclear military power, for example). You may wish to look at and perhaps alter the power weights within IFs before you feel content with the scenario you have created.

When you are satisfied with the high-Chinese-military-expenditure scenario, it would be useful for the analysis in Chapter 7 to save your working file into one called "HIMIL.RUN" (you probably have already done this). Consider using a bookmark or paper clip to identify for later use these pages on changing parameters, comparing results across scenarios, saving files, and selecting files. You will want to review them later.

▶ **Changing Model Relationships via Table Functions.** You will use parameter changes to create most scenarios. In some cases, however, IFs specifies relationships between variables by table functions rather than parameters. For instance, total fertility rates, contraception use, and meat consumption are functions of GDP per capita in IFs. You can change these functions by selecting the Table Function suboption of Change. Experiment on your own with change in one or more of these functions as the basis for a scenario.

CONCLUSION

You now have all the basic tools that you need to use IFs fully. Although you may not yet be totally comfortable in working with a computer simulation, especially for scenario analysis, what you primarily need now is experience. In addition, Chapters 2 and 3 have explored the first of the three questions that we identified initially: Where do current changes appear to be taking us?

Chapter 4 begins a discussion of causal logic that takes us beyond simple extrapolation. It is the formalization of complex causal connections that makes computer models especially useful. In Chapter 4, I shall introduce causal logic; Chapters 5 through 7 will continue our exploration of the future through causal thought and the use of IFs. In all of those chapters we will be asking two questions: How do we want the future to look? What leverage do we have?

FOUR

Understanding the World Development System

In Chapter 1, we identified an important dilemma: *People must act in the face of an uncertain future.* We proceeded by asking three questions:

1. Where do current changes appear to be taking us?
2. What kind of future would we prefer?
3. How much leverage do we have to bring about the future we prefer?

Chapters 2 and 3 explored the first question. Our principal approach to forecasting, especially in Chapter 2, was trend extrapolation. This chapter shifts our attention to preferred futures and human leverage. In order to address these issues, it is necessary to add investigation of causality to our tool kit of forecasting techniques.

CAUSAL UNDERSTANDINGS

As we looked at trends and attempted extrapolations in the last two chapters, we quickly found that simple linear and exponential extrapolations were very often inadequate. Some growth processes are clearly limited. For instance, literacy cannot surpass 100 percent of the population and oil production cannot grow indefinitely in the face of a fixed resource base. We therefore began to introduce alternative forms of extrapolation, such as S-shaped and bell-shaped curves, that *implicitly* recognized those limits.

Causal analysis helps us *explicitly* recognize such limits and more generally assists us in understanding how complex processes might evolve in the future. At the root of causal analysis is the distinction between independent and dependent variables, or between cause and effect, respectively. Up until this point we have discussed population growth as if it were a phenomenon independent of any other. We all know, however, that a large number of factors affect population growth. For instance, the availability of contraception changes birth rates. So, too, does the availability of opportunities for employment of prospective mothers. Similarly, the quality of medical care affects death rates, as does the prevalence of diseases such as AIDS and cancer. Thus, changes in the availability of contraceptives, employment of women, medical technology, and incidence of disease are all causes (independent variables) of population growth (the dependent variable).

We generally divide causal relationships into two categories. **Positive relationships** exist when an increase in the independent variable (such as AIDS) leads to an increase in the dependent variable (such as the death rate). In such instances, of course, decreases in the independent variable lead also to decreases in the dependent variable. In contrast, **negative relationships** exist when an increase in the independent variable (such as contraception availability) causes a decrease in the dependent variable (such as the birth rate). In those cases, decreases in the independent variable will also lead to increases in the dependent variable. Parameters control the strength of both positive and negative relationships.

It is, however, sometimes difficult to distinguish independent and dependent variables so clearly. For instance, a high rate of population growth in an Asian country might lead (cause) the government to institute a family planning program and increase the availability of contraceptives, which we have already suggested might cause the population growth rate to decline. In such a situation, we have a system of variables that *feed back* on each other in complex cause-and-effect relationships.

If population growth gives rise to family planning programs that control that same population growth, the process is reminiscent of a home thermostat that controls temperature by turning heat on and off as necessary (when temperature increases, the thermostat assures that heating ceases, which in turn leads temperature to decline). Figure 4.1 portrays the two causal linkages in both the family-planning and home-heating examples. Note that one linkage in each case is positive and one is negative and that changes in a variable like population eventually feed back in a loop of linkages to that same variable. We call such a combination of linkages a **negative feedback loop.** As these two examples suggest, such loops tend to produce relative stability in the processes they represent. A feedback loop becomes a negative loop whenever it includes an odd

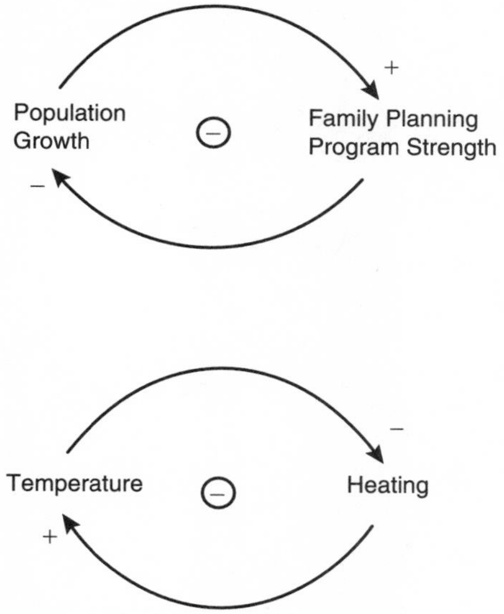

FIGURE 4.1   Negative feedback loops.

number of individual negative linkages (for instance, one, three, or five negative linkages out of six or seven total linkages).

In contrast, consider what might happen if the death rate from AIDS in an African country overwhelmed the medical establishment in that country, which in turn made it impossible to cope medically with AIDS and led the incidence of AIDS to rise further. This situation would be similar to that of a thermostat with its "wires crossed"—sensing too high a temperature, this rogue thermostat turns up the heat. Figure 4.2 portrays the two causal linkages in each of these examples. We call the dynamics in these examples **positive feedback loops**. Note in the heating example that both linkages are positive. A feedback loop will be positive or self-reinforcing whenever the number of negative linkages is zero or even. In the heating example, there are zero negative linkages, whereas in the AIDS example, there are two. Thus, the AIDS example is also a positive feedback loop. Processes in positive feedback loops tend to either collapse precipitously (like population in the AIDS-ridden country) or grow without bound (like the temperature in the afflicted home).

Many growth processes are combinations of positive and negative feedback loops. Consider, for instance, the growth of world oil production. On one hand, increases in production facilitate further increases in

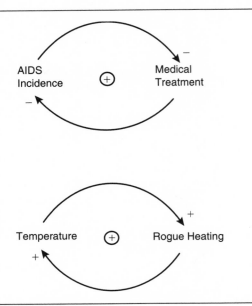

FIGURE 4.2   Positive feedback loops.

production (for instance, by leading to improved technology or by fueling deeper drilling). On the other hand, increases in production begin to deplete resources, which leads to restraints on production. If the first and positive loop is dominant, as it was globally for most of this century, oil production grows exponentially. When the second and negative loop becomes dominant, as it has been in the United States and may soon become globally, oil production stabilizes and eventually declines. It is specific parameters in the equation representation of the loop linkages that will determine dominance. Figure 4.3 represents this interacting pair of feedback loops.

Causal models greatly help us understand change. All of us already have at least rudimentary causal models concerning the world development system in our minds. As a way of helping you think about your own causal models, and to help you compare yours with those of others, the rest of this chapter sketches five common models (and some variations) that many individuals draw upon. Each of the five tends to focus heavily on a single aspect of the evolving global system:

1. States (countries) struggling with the eternal need to provide their own security in the face of potentially hostile power from other states.

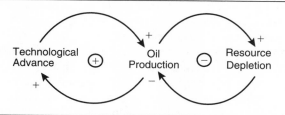

FIGURE 4.3   Interaction of feedback loops.

2. A global community of individuals seeking stability and peace and bound together by increasingly integrated and powerful markets providing an abundance of goods.
3. Rich and poor classes interacting in structures that tend to maintain their relative position in those structures.
4. An ecosystem containing many species, including humanity, whose growth strains the ecosystem's balance.
5. Knowledge and technology conferring benefits on humanity in a process by which human progress begets still more progress.

Each of these models can organize a very rich understanding of the world. In fact, the models can be so rich that some individuals rely almost exclusively on one or a select set of them. These models thus become their **worldviews.** As we sketch in turn each of these causal models or world-views, consider how they compare with your own.

STATES AND THEIR INTERACTION: REALISM

The state is a universal modern variant of what we can call a "security group"—that is, an organization devoted in significant part to assuring the physical security of its members. Other examples include tribes, em-pires, clans, criminal associations, and street gangs. Every state (or street gang) has a territory with reasonably well-established borders, a defined population, a functioning government (or its equivalent), and recognition by other states (or gangs) as a legal equal (or rival). We commonly desig-nate states as countries (although Taiwan is a country that some states do not recognize as a sovereign equal and therefore do not treat as a state).

States have functions other than the provision of security for their citi-zens. The security function is so central to their existence, however, that we frequently define their pursuit of it as "high politics" and designate struggles over economic, environmental, or other benefits they might provide as "low politics."

The world has no organizational units that can dictate to states or maintain order in conflicts among them. In fact, the global environment for states is fundamentally anarchic. Thus states act to provide their own security, although they may enter into alliances of convenience with other states. Again, one can see the analogies with a society that has powerful clans or street gangs but lacks effective central police authority (Somalia, for instance). Alliances of convenience also form in such societies but seldom persist. It is often said that "states have permanent interests, but no permanent friends or enemies."

According to the worldview we call **realism**, the world is a "self-help" system. States that want to protect or enhance their own security must rely on their own efforts and skills to do so. Frequently this endeavor requires the development of substantial military capabilities. Power is a central concept or variable in the realist worldview. It is such an important means to the desired end (enhanced security) that it practically becomes an end of its own. Central to the purposes of states must be the protection and enhancement of power.

The pursuit of power may set in motion positive feedback loops. Those states that have power may be able to use that power to obtain still more. In the colonial era, for instance, Spain used its naval power to conquer most of Latin America and to extract gold and silver from its new territories. It could then use that plunder to build more ships and motivate more soldiers. Figure 4.4 represents that positive loop.

Similarly, an economically powerful country like Britain during the eighteenth century could use its high productivity to conquer foreign markets and exchange its products for raw materials that it could bring home and use to further enhance its productivity. Moreover, it could use those economic strengths to hire nationals in its colonies to create overseas military capabilities with limited drain on its domestic resources. The overseas military forces could then, in turn, assist traders in opening up further markets for the British. For instance, the British shipped opium produced in India to China. When the Chinese banned the import in 1839, the British responded with military action. A series of opium wars and treaties following British victories opened an increasingly large number of ports in China to British trade. History abounds with examples of power begetting power that are perhaps less odious, but little less clear-cut.

As these examples suggest, power includes but is not limited to military capabilities. It also benefits from economic and demographic strength. The most powerful countries of the world today are, in general, the economically and demographically largest: the United States, Russia, China, India, Japan, and Germany.

Although a country's power may enhance its own security, it will threaten others. Those others will normally react by establishing counter-

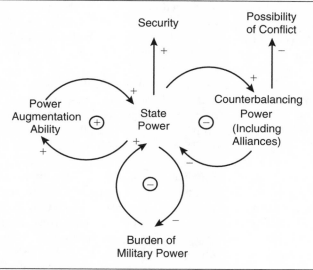

FIGURE 4.4   A simplified model of realism.

balancing capabilities, thereby bringing under control the power of any state that threatens to become dominant and potentially aggressive. In so doing they will not only increase their own security but lessen the probability of conflict. Conflict among relative equals will inevitably be expensive and the outcome will be uncertain. Therefore a balance of power makes conflict an irrational enterprise and less likely (see again Figure 4.4). Realists argue, however, that some military conflict is inevitable in relations among countries because there will always be conflicts of interest among them and there is no central arbiter.

It is, of course, not always possible to offset the power of others by building up one's own—Turkey could hardly have been expected to cope alone with the buildup of the Soviet Union during the Cold War. Thus, alliances become necessary because they augment the negative, counterbalancing feedback loop on power. Most of Europe joined an alliance against Napoleon's France when that country's power was growing without clear limits. Similarly, Turkey joined with much of Europe in NATO to counteract the growing power of the Soviet Union after World War II. One might argue that most of Europe has now also joined an economic alliance called the European Union (EU) to balance the overwhelming economic power of the United States and Japan.

Realists also often argue that the growth of potentially overwhelming state power (through the positive loop of power breeding power) is further controlled by the economic burden it begins to place upon the country. Historically, empires have not always ceased to grow simply because they met opposing power. They sometimes have overreached their ability to sustain a military buildup and thereby weakened the economic base of that military. Paul Kennedy (1987: xvii) argued that the Hapsburg monarchs "overextended themselves in the course of repeated conflicts and became militarily top-heavy for their weakening economic base."[1] The United Kingdom did the same in the nineteenth and early twentieth centuries and, according to Kennedy, both the Soviet Union and the United States reached critical points more recently. Figure 4.4 represents this additional negative feedback loop as well.

The prescriptions of the realist view are quite obvious from its causal portrait of the world. Each state, in the absence of any protective central authority, must fend for itself in the anarchic global system. It can do so in two ways. First, it can build up its own power and wisely use its existing power to attain still more. Second, it can join in temporary alliance with other countries to oppose any state that threatens to achieve a dominant position.

There are, as with any recipe of this type, complications in the implementation. Consider modern Germany, faced with the very proximate power of Russia. To what degree should Germany rely upon building its own counterpower? There are dangers there, including overburdening the economy and eliciting attempts by other states to balance the power of Germany in turn. And to what degree should Germany trust other countries to be faithful in their NATO alliance commitments to Germany, should Russia once again become a significant military threat? There are also dangers there.

In the modern world economy, the United States faces a significant economic challenge from both Asia, especially Japan, and the EU. Should it react primarily by strengthening its domestic economy, or should it enter into economic alliance, perhaps with Canada and Mexico? Realists see international politics as much more an art than a science. Great diplomats and leaders have historically been able to strike the critical balances among strategies, but lesser souls have failed.

THE GROWTH OF GLOBAL COMMUNITY: LIBERALISM

There is another prescription, however, that competes with the realist set. It rejects the premise of inherently antagonistic relations among countries or between economies such as the United States and Japan. It argues instead that extensive and ongoing cooperation is possible on a broad scale internationally. It views the world not solely through the lens of state system anarchy, state interest, and power, but in considerable part through the lens of growing global community.

The perspective of **liberalism** generally begins with an attack on realism. First, it criticizes the assumptions that states will behave as rational, unitary actors. Misperception of power balances and the intentions of other actors are so common that those balances do not sufficiently dampen conflict. Internal forces within a state (from intense nationalism to religious or ideological dogmatism) may drive even experienced and otherwise cautious leaders into unwise foreign adventures. Thus, say liberals, the realist is too sanguine with respect to the ability of power-seeking and power-balancing to produce security and relative peace. Remember that Iraq attacked Iran in 1980 and invaded Kuwait in 1990. Neither war secured the gains that Iraq anticipated, but both cost very large numbers of lives (casualties in the Iran-Iraq war approached 400,000). Efforts at power-balancing in the Middle East by Iran, Saudi Arabia, the United States, and even Iraq itself did not prevent catastrophe.

The critique goes further. The attempt to balance power with power, say the liberals, often sets up a destructive positive feedback loop. What one state views as a defensive buildup in reaction to the overly great power of another, the second will likely view as a potentially offensive threat. Thus it will, in turn, undertake a buildup. Both realists and liberals know this logic as that of the **security dilemma**. Liberals argue that the logic sets up arms races that increase the probability of war. They point to the arms race before World War I as one example. Perhaps increasing levels of arms will by themselves raise the probability of their use. Perhaps one state will finally achieve an advantage or recognize an imminent disadvantage and therefore initiate conflict.[2] Figure 4.5 represents such a destructive pattern of interaction, and Figure 4.6 shows one possible real-world result of that dilemma, the arms race between the United States and the Soviet Union during the Cold War.

If it is too dangerous to rely on rational judgment of states in power balances, and the competitive logic of the security dilemma constantly works to initiate and fuel dangerous arms races, what can liberals offer in place of the realist vision? Fundamentally, they put forward a competing vision of growing global community, accompanied by increasing levels of cooperative interaction (see Figure 4.7). The mutual strengthening of community and cooperative interaction creates a positive feedback loop that makes war increasingly expensive (by disrupting valuable interchange), unproductive, and difficult to initiate, thereby encouraging peace.

Liberals point to the increased integration of world economies via trade and financial flows. They draw our attention to steadily increasing levels of interpersonal contact across borders through tourism, business travel, and governmental linkage. They argue that rising demand for international approaches to transboundary environmental problems underlie additional cooperative initiatives. They claim that the sharp rise in

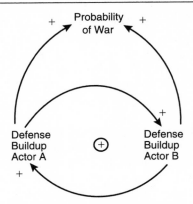

FIGURE 4.5   The security dilemma.

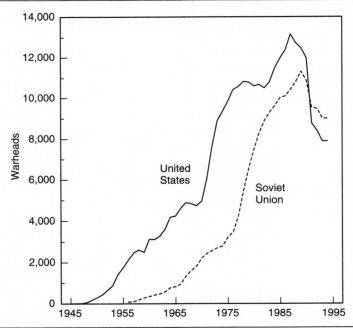

FIGURE 4.6   Strategic nuclear warhead balance. *Source:* Worldwatch Institute, Worldwatch Database Diskette, 1995. *Original Source:* Robert S. Norris and William M. Arkin, "Estimated U.S. and Soviet/Russian Nuclear Stockpiles, 1945–94," *Bulletin of the Atomic Scientists,* November/December 1994.

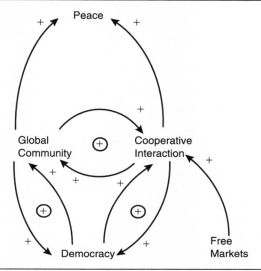

FIGURE 4.7   A simplified model of liberalism.

numbers of intergovernmental and international nongovernmental organizations that we saw in Chapter 2 verifies the climb in global community and cooperative interaction.

Realists are quick to point out that increased interaction does not always lead to cooperation. The United States had a lower level of interaction with Europe during the nineteenth century than during the twentieth and managed in the former century to avoid most involvement in European disputes; Britain had closer interaction with much of Asia prior to 1950 than subsequently, and its relationships have been better in the postcolonial period.

Liberals acknowledge this issue and emphasize that it is the combination of growth in global community and increased interaction that is beginning to dampen international conflict. Moreover, to the extent that the global community is becoming increasingly unified around the principles of Western liberalism (individual freedoms, market economies, and political democracy), that community promises to be even more peaceful. Although democracies have frequently fought with nondemocracies, it is perhaps impossible to cite examples of true democracies going to war with other democracies. Some have suggested that the War of 1812 and the American Civil War are such examples.[3] Yet the War of 1812 between the United States and Great Britain preceded the British Reform Bills of 1832, 1867, and 1884 that granted voting rights to the middle and working classes. The Confederacy that fought the Union not only protected slave-holding but never existed prior to the Civil War. In the case of essentially all exceptions, the commitment of one or both countries to democracy appears shallow.

MARKETS AND THEIR BENEFITS: COMMERCIAL LIBERALISM

A close relative or variant of the political liberalism we have been discussing is **commercial liberalism**. Although Europeans will recognize classical liberals as those who support free-market-oriented Liberal parties in Britain, France, and elsewhere, citizens of the United States will confusingly identify commercial liberals as economic conservatives. The U.S. political system has quite thoroughly adopted commercial liberalism and its emphasis on free markets—thus modern economic conservatives want to preserve (conserve) that orientation. In much of the rest of the world, however, restrictions on free markets are more common, so commercial liberals in Liberal parties often seek to change the system by freeing the market, while Democratic Socialist parties often become the "conservatives" (in Russia after the breakdown of the USSR, the communists ironically became the conservatives and the free-market or commercial liberals became "radicals"). In this book I adopt a more universal terminology because I wish to clearly and directly associate commercial liberalism with liberal or free markets, both domestically and internationally. It is very useful to have concepts that are less place- and time-bound than contemporary political labels in the United States or elsewhere.

At the core of commercial liberalism stands the proposition that freely functioning markets produce benefits for all participants in them. Economic exchanges must reward both buyers and sellers, whether they trade goods, labor, or capital; otherwise the transactions would not occur. Free domestic and international markets lead to an expansion of economic product because participants can specialize in the production of whatever they make with relatively greatest efficiency—they will have a **comparative advantage**.

On regional and even global bases, free exchange will therefore lead to increasing specialization of production in a division of labor. In much of the eighteenth and nineteenth centuries, the United States and the countries of Central Europe (such as Poland) provided grain and other agricultural and mineral products to England, France, and Germany. Those more industrialized countries (especially England) provided the capital and equipment to build the railroads that brought such products from the American heartland to the coastal ports. The expansion of output facilitates reinvestment by producers into the capital (buildings and machinery) with which they can produce still more goods or services for the open markets. More output and trade lead to even more capital investment, setting up a strong growth cycle.

Figure 4.8 portrays in simplified form these positive feedback loops at the heart of commercial liberal thought. Economic output both benefits from and contributes to capital formation and increased market exchange. Because of these positive feedback loops (or virtuous cycles), both political and commercial variants of the liberal perspective incorporate an inherent sense of progress. In fact, as we saw earlier, many international political liberals look to the progressive expansion of world markets as one of the driving forces behind the growth of global community.

The emphasis by liberals on positive feedback loops continues still further. Figure 4.8 indicates also that the processes of capital formation and participation in free markets will lead to ongoing economic restructuring. Economic structures and divisions of labor, once established, do not remain fixed. Changing technology and the steady march of capital accumulation continue to alter the most efficient divisions of labor. In general liberals feel that economies will progress through stages, although the progression will be far from uniform across countries or time.

Whereas economies may initially specialize in agricultural products and minerals (the primary economy), they will eventually begin to pro-

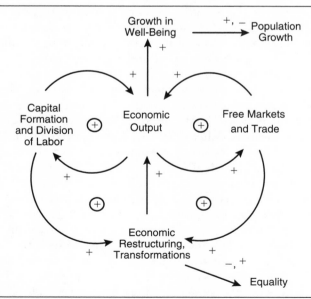

FIGURE 4.8   A simplified model of commercial liberalism.

duce manufactured goods (the secondary economy). In fact, the relative poverty of many food producers in largely agricultural economies attracts industrial capital because it means low wages and low costs of production. Hence, we can understand the rush of British capital to the United States late in the nineteenth century, the movement of U.S. capital to Latin America in much of the twentieth century, and the surge of Japanese investment throughout Asia in the late twentieth century. Eventually, however, increased investment and production lead to such high labor demand that wages rise. Moreover, the satisfaction of many material demands by industrial production begins to shift the attention of consumers to other issues, including education, health care, and leisure time. Thus, economies increasingly become more mature and service-oriented (the tertiary economy). Canada, the United States, most of the countries in Europe, Australia, New Zealand, and Japan are at this advanced stage of development. Other countries around the world, liberals generally argue, will follow similar paths of economic development.

These constantly ongoing economic restructurings, which the steady advance in capital formation and technological progress drive, and which open domestic and international markets facilitate, contribute to steady advance in economic output. They thereby set up additional positive feedback loops in the simplified liberal model (see again Figure 4.8) and further improvement in average well-being.

Most classical liberals recognize, however, that even while average well-being improves, the condition of some may stagnate or even deteriorate. Early in the industrialization process of any country, only a few really benefit. For the large mass of farmers, conditions of life may not change at all. For those in the sweat shops of new industry, conditions may actually deteriorate.

Both the specialization within international divisions of labor and the transformations in those divisions obviously have costs for some in society. English farmers in the 1800s found it difficult to compete with food imported from countries richer in land and inexpensive labor. Those who wanted to begin manufacturing businesses in Central Europe or the United States found it difficult to compete with producers in countries possessing well-established industrial sectors that boasted advanced capital and skilled laborers. When the U.S. economy industrialized rapidly in the late nineteenth and early twentieth centuries and dramatically improved efficiency in agriculture, the less productive agricultural producers suffered. As the United States transforms itself into a predominantly service-oriented economy, many manufacturing workers are suffering.

Although classical liberals recognize the burdens borne by those working within sectors in relative decline, they believe the pain to be temporary and to be offset by increased opportunities elsewhere. Thus, after a transition period the manufacturing jobs of mid-twentieth-century America provided greatly improved living standards for the farmers who initially struggled to survive in a declining sector and then abandoned their farms for the cities. Presumably the "Okies" who lost their land and migrated to California, sometimes surviving only as seasonal farm laborers, doubted that the new industry of California would ever offer much to them or their children, but it eventually did so.

Similarly, it is argued, service-sector jobs will eventually improve the conditions of those forced from manufacturing in the United States during the contemporary era, and new manufacturing jobs in Mexico and Taiwan will similarly improve the conditions over time of those leaving the farms in those countries.

Thus the effects of economic growth and restructuring on equality are complex in the liberal model. Any restructuring, but perhaps particularly the early stages of industrialization, condemns some to relatively and even absolutely worse conditions, thus lessening equality. In the later stages of the restructuring, however, large numbers of workers enter the newly dynamic economic activities and equality improves. The Kuznets curve (Figure 4.9) shows the pattern of equality that this process should

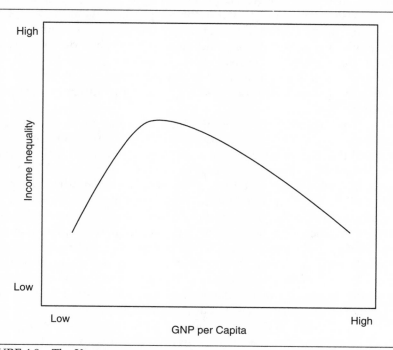

FIGURE 4.9   The Kuznets curve.

generate across countries at different levels of GNP per capita (as a proxy for different stages of economic development). In reality, however, the empirical evidence for the relationship is very mixed and the debate remains quite intense. Moreover, the Kuznets curve grew out of analysis of restructuring associated with industrialization. It does not explicitly represent that associated with the transformation to service-oriented economies.

Commercial liberals do not, however, restrict their attention only to overall economic performance. The logic of individuals rationally pursuing improvement in their economic conditions through exchanges in the market has more general implications. For instance, individuals may also make rational decisions with respect to family size in order to improve their economic conditions. In poor societies it may be rational to have large families. The costs of raising children may be low when they do not expect expensive brand-name clothing and college educations. The benefits of raising them may be high when they go to work on the land or on the street at a very young age and later care for their aged parents. In rich societies, the cost-and-benefit calculus changes dramatically.

Liberals thus provide a causal basis for the model of population growth that demographers characterize as the demographic transition (we discuss it in more detail later in this chapter). As economic well-being begins to improve, individuals quickly (and rationally) improve their diet, sanitation, and health care and thereby lower their death rates. This factor raises population growth rates. Over time, however, birth rates begin to decline, through the logic just described, whereby the cost-and-benefit analysis leads rich societies to have fewer children, and the population growth rate falls.

The same assumptions of individually rational economic behavior help liberals to elaborate many more specific causal understandings of the world that Figure 4.8 does not show, but that models like IFs capture. For instance, liberal economists emphasize how higher prices lead to decisions by consumers to reduce consumption of a product. Empirical studies allow economists to estimate the percentage reduction in consumption of a specific good, such as natural gas, for every percent increase in its price. They express the ratio of the percentage reduction in consumption to the percentage change in price as a parameter called the "price elasticity of demand." Similarly, they can express the percentage increase in demand for cars as a ratio to the percentage increase in income of consumers as an "income elasticity of demand." The IFs model takes advantage of such elasticities in many of its calculations.

The prescriptions of the liberal model follow quite clearly from its elaboration. Most important, we should not interfere in any significant manner with the workings of free markets or capital accumulation, because these are the mainsprings of an efficient economic system. In fact, we should work to increase the extent of both. Many modern liberals, sometimes called "compensatory liberals," do argue, however, that society should ease the pain of transition for those who suffer it most.

REALIST UNDERSTANDINGS OF ECONOMICS: MERCANTILISM

A school of economic realists called **mercantilists** has argued for centuries that economic and political power reinforce each other and that the state must act to protect and enhance both. With respect to economic power, mercantilists desire a strong economy capable of producing all that the state needs, including the instruments of war and the goods necessary to survive economic isolation during war (thereby increasing military power). In addition, mercantilists desire the accumulation of wealth in the hands of the state, either in the form of gold and silver reserves or in the form of claims upon the resources of other states (in holdings of their currency). And mercantilists favor putting their own citizens to work within their own country rather than seeing potential jobs lost to other countries. Figure 4.10 represents the simple mercantilist view.

Many of these desires of mercantilists obviously put their states in direct conflict with other states. Not all states can simultaneously export more than they import, thereby providing jobs for their own citizens and increasing their treasury's holdings of gold and foreign currencies. Figure 4.10, like much state-centric mercantilist thought, ignores these obvious systemic problems with the argument. Because mercantilism suffers from such obvious contradictions at a systemic level, few elaborate it explicitly as a creed; nonetheless, it remains the implicit basis for many urgings to restrict market access by other countries and simultaneously increase market penetration of those countries.

Mercantilist proposals directly contradict those by liberals for letting markets work, even at the expense of periods in which imports exceed exports. Liberals argue that such periods are inevitable and self-correcting—when the exports of a country become large relative to imports, attempts by other countries to obtain the currency of the exporting country in order to pay for those exports will drive up the value of the exporter's currency. When the value of a country's currency rises, it automatically raises the prices of its exports, decreasing demand for them, and also encourages the mercantilistic country's citizens to import relatively inexpensive foreign goods (see Figure 4.11). Thus mercantilist policies may work for a while, but they inevitably prove fruitless. The steady rise of the Japanese yen in recent decades will, liberals say, ultimately balance its trade (all else being equal).

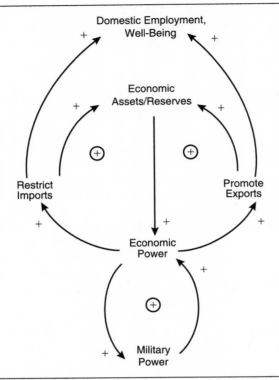

FIGURE 4.10   The mercantilist variation of realism.

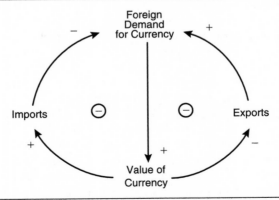

FIGURE 4.11   The liberal view of self-correcting trade and financial markets.

THE PERSISTENCE OF INEQUALITY: STRUCTURALISM

The structuralist perspective moves equality from the peripheral position it holds in liberalism (and in realism) to the center of consideration. Structuralists see inequality to be a direct result of the concentration of economic power in relatively few hands. Structuralists do not make a strong distinction between politics and economics. On the contrary, they argue that concentrations of political and economic power strongly reinforce each other in a positive feedback loop. Figure 4.12 portrays that loop and its implications for equality (namely an increase in inequality).

Much like realists, structuralists claim that power begets power. Those who have economic power are able significantly to affect the terms of exchanges. Whereas liberals focus on the fact that no two parties will freely enter into an agreement unless both benefit, structuralists draw our attention to the fact that they may benefit very unequally. In a society with much unemployment, for instance, an employer may be able to hire the

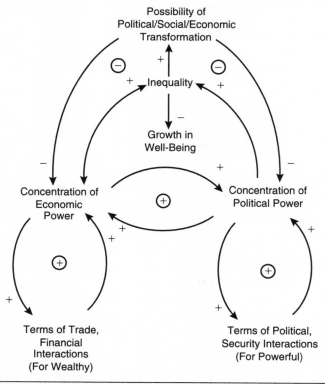

FIGURE 4.12   A simplified model of structuralism.

labor of a worker for little more than survival wages but sell the fruits of that labor for a very considerable price. Similarly, a rich country with the capability of producing most of its own needs will find itself in an enviable bargaining position relative to a country with little to sell other than bananas or coffee and no ability to produce cars or computers.

In such unequal relationships, the economically more powerful country may be able to influence strongly the **terms of trade,** that is, the prices of the goods it sells relative to the prices of the goods it buys. Similarly, the richer individual or society may be able to shape the terms (interest rate and repayment period) at which it lends money to the poorer, as long as the desire to lend money is less pressing than the need to borrow. The desperation of many Latin American and African debtors in the 1980s, a decade many label the "Lost Decade" for those countries, suggests the power that comes with lending money.

On the political side, we have already discussed (with respect to realism) how political-military power may be self-reinforcing. We can extend that notion to a discussion of political-economic power. When rich countries set up the formal institutions that give guidance for international trade and capital flows (such as the World Trade Organization, the World Bank, and the International Monetary Fund), and often reserve for themselves an overwhelming majority of the votes within those institutions, it is likely that those institutions will seldom challenge the interests of their founders.

Thus Figure 4.12 shows two loops that reinforce the concentration of political and economic power via the terms of political and economic interactions that the rich and powerful set in dealings with the poor and weak. Together with the loop linking political and economic power, the system suggests a very powerful self-reinforcing dynamic that works against any relative advance of those at the bottom of it.

Structuralists disagree among themselves, however, with respect to the degree to which this cluster of positive feedback loops works to increasingly intensify the divisions among global classes or simply to maintain them. Some structuralists argue that the developed world emerged only in the process of "underdeveloping" the rest of the world and that the process of impoverishment continues with little diminished intensity. Others see some advance in the absolute position of the global poor and weak, even while the relative gap between them and the rich and powerful remains undiminished. In light of the empirical evidence we saw in Chapter 2 with respect to the absolute advances made around the world in life expectancy, literacy, and even income, it is difficult to accept the former and stronger structuralist position.

One source of the dispute is some uncertainty with respect to the negative loops at the top of Figure 4.12. Traditional Marxist perspectives foresaw increased inequality leading to increased pressure for political, social, and economic transformations that would redress the balances by eliminating the concentrations of economic and political power (and transferring that power to the masses). Marx and others believed that the inequality would intensify to the point of a social explosion and that the transformations would be revolutionary. That is, they saw the negative feedback loops as having a threshold character—they either functioned or did not.

It is possible that the processes of transformation may be more continuous, at least in some societies. Thus, some ongoing transformations may occur that redress at least partly and intermittently the concentrations of wealth and power, thus restricting the growth of inequality. One could argue that the New Deal policies of the Roosevelt era, and, more generally, the welfare programs established by all developed Western states, illustrate the possibility of such partial transformations. One could also argue, however, that these examples simply illustrate the ability of rich states to buy off their own relative poor, but that the global system provides no such option to the Nicaraguas or Haitis of the world.

Structuralists do not ignore economic growth. In fact, they commonly argue that reducing inequality will facilitate that growth. Illiterate, underfed workers are not highly productive ones. Studies have investigated the relationship between economic growth and the emphasis a less developed country puts on basic human needs such as food, housing, and medical care. For many years, for instance, structuralists pointed to Sri Lanka as a success story because it achieved growth by satisfying basic needs. Like the studies looking at the liberals' Kuznets curve, however, those linking attention to basic needs with growth have not been definitive.

Although the model of structuralist thought presented in Figure 4.12 oversimplifies the complexity of that perspective, it does suggest some of the key leverage points for improvement that structuralists identify. For instance, some reforming structuralists look for ways to weaken the positive feedback loop linking concentration of economic power to the terms of trade and financial interaction. Examples include global agreements that would purposefully alter the terms of trade or forgive indebtedness. Similarly, other suggestions target the second lower feedback loop of that figure, including substantial revisions in the voting and operating structure of international financial institutions (IFIs) like the World Bank. Proposals in the 1970s for a New International Economic Order (NIEO) included many such elements.

Structuralists also look to strengthening the negative feedback loops at the top of Figure 4.12. More moderate structuralists differ little from compensatory liberals in their calls for transfers from rich to poor as a way of reducing economic concentration. More radical structuralists see such measures, as well as most proposals in the NIEO, as mere palliatives. The only real solution, they argue, is thorough system transformation through revolution, breaking once and for all the control by the rich and powerful over economic and political power.

ECOLOGICAL SUSTAINABILITY: ECO-WHOLISM

The central concern of **eco-wholism** is sustainability.[4] All species place demands upon the ecosystem(s) in which they function. Periodically, the numbers of a species grow because their food supply surges or a predator population declines. For nonhuman species such growth is, however, always temporary and limited. Ultimately, the population will bump up against new limits or old ones will reemerge.

Ecosystems are seldom, if ever, in a steady state. Populations of some organisms grow and those of others decline. Cycles of growth often lead a species temporarily to exceed the long-term **carrying capacity** of an environment. For instance, deer protected from their canine and human predators will expand in numbers until they overgraze their environment (they "overshoot" a carrying capacity). After a delay, the despoiled environment will no longer support the overgrazing—in fact, because of destruction to the vegetation it will no longer support even the population that it could once comfortably feed. Therefore the population of deer will collapse as they become vulnerable to starvation in winter and to micropredators (disease). Gradually the vegetation will rebound and the deer population will begin another cycle.

Figure 4.13 portrays a negative feedback loop that links human population to the environment in roughly the same way. The primary difference is that the demands of humans on their environment are more variable than those of deer on theirs. As humans increase the scale of their economic activities per capita, they multiply their individual demands on the environment—each person demands more water, energy, and other goods. Whereas the demands that most animals place on their environment are limited to food inputs, humans require a variety of energy and mineral inputs as well. In addition, human outputs back to the environment include extensive waste from industrial activities. Both input demands and outputs detrimentally affect the environmental quality necessary to satisfy future human needs.

Negative feedback loops like that depicted in Figure 4.13 often produce cyclical behavior around a target value (in this case the environmental carrying capacity). We earlier discussed a household thermostat as part of a negative loop linking the temperature of a home and its heating system. Although good thermostats maintain temperature within a fairly narrow range, temperature will alternately exceed and fall short of a specific target value.

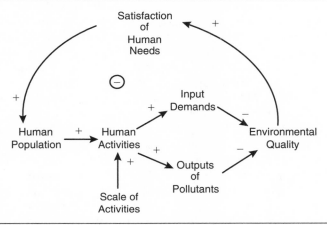

FIGURE 4.13   A simplified model of eco-wholism.

Historically, human populations have exhibited such cyclical variation in their interaction with the environment. There remains much debate over the causes of historical collapse in a variety of early Middle Eastern, Asian, and American civilizations. Scholars attribute such collapse to invasion from the outside (potentially due to the invaders having exceeded their carrying capacity or to the weakening of the invaded as they exceeded their own); to exhaustion of soils or their damage from salts in irrigation water (and therefore to famine); to social breakdown (sometimes a consequence of food shortages); and to a variety of other factors. The relationship between humans and their environment has often played a key role.

Obviously we cannot now know with certainty how far humanity has progressed, if at all, into a condition of overshoot (use of the environment beyond sustainable limits). Nor can anyone predict accurately when collapse might occur and how severe it could become. Finally, no one can be certain how rapidly humanity might recover from a collapse. Eco-wholists emphasize, however, that the costs of recovery can often substantially exceed the costs of anticipatory and preventative action. For instance, it may be impossible to restore a tropical rain forest once destroyed; humans can drive a species to extinction, but we have no means of recovering a lost species. Similarly, heavy soil erosion may leave little choice but abandonment of agriculture over the area involved. In terms of the models of extrapolation we saw in Chapter 2, environmental change can involve threshold changes that we can make in only one direction. Eco-wholists therefore point out that the costs of preventative and ameliorating action are generally small in comparison with the potential costs of inaction.

The concept of carrying capacity is obviously very important to eco-wholists. They believe in the existence of reasonably definite limits to the sustainable level of economic activity in the long term, while generally admitting that such limits remain uncertain until activity overshoots them. A famous computer modeling project (Meadows et al., 1972) produced forecasts suggesting that human population and economic growth faces a wide variety of interacting limits early in the twenty-first century. The project circulated the results in a best-selling book called *The Limits to Growth*. Lester R. Brown (1981) also sought to specify the limits and argued that the fisheries, cropland, grazing land, and forest area of the world would ultimately sustain only about 6 billion humans. The world population will reach that level near the turn of the century. He argued that substantial parts of the world have already exceeded local limits.

There are by definition limits to what we call the nonrenewable resources of the world, including the mineral wealth and especially the fossil fuels. We saw in Chapter 2 that most of the world's energy now comes from such fossil fuels. Almost no one questions that the speed at which new fossil fuel sources are discovered is dramatically slower than our rate of fossil fuel use. Thus, with respect to those energy forms humanity has already significantly overshot the level of sustainability (although existing stocks may last for many decades).

Yet many eco-wholists devote less attention to the limits that affect inputs than to those on outputs, especially global pollution of air and water. Chapter 2 already documented the increase in environmental pollutants such as CFCs and carbon dioxide. Although collective global action is now rapidly reducing the production and use of CFCs, there is less prospect for substantial near-term reduction in the production of carbon dioxide, in part because fossil fuels have proven to be more plentiful than many pessimists believed twenty years ago.

Many analysts identify the nature of ownership as a factor complicating the relationship of humans and their environment. When individuals control their own environment and can restrict access by others, they have an incentive to maintain it. Unless under great economic stress, ranchers do not build their herds so large as to destroy the vegetation on their own land. When individuals have common access to an environment, however, they have an incentive to derive as much utility from it as possible for themselves, even at the expense of others. Ranchers sharing access to government land have an incentive to add a few additional cattle, even if it reduces the viability of vegetation in the long term and the average weight-gain of each animal. Ranchers calculate that they will benefit from their own additional cattle and have little concern with the weight-loss of cattle owned by other ranchers. This collective destruction of an environmental area open to many is called the **tragedy of the commons.**

Consider another example. Should a single company be given a very long-term lease to the timber rights in a forest area, the company would have an incentive to see that the area continues to produce trees over that long term. Were the government to permit multiple companies periodic access to the same area, each would want to extract the timber as quickly as possible before its rivals did so. Very long-term leases begin to approximate private ownership and elicit similar concern with longer-term environmental quality.

Many global environments remain open to common use by humans who have no clear ownership. It is impossible to subdivide the atmosphere, and it would be extremely difficult to allocate the deep ocean regions to individuals or countries. Even within countries, most waterways and many forests remain common property.

Although the establishment and enforcement of property rights over grazing land, energy resources, and forests may reduce the rate of their use dramatically, it cannot guarantee that the rate will drop to one sustainable in the long run. Eco-wholists see the continued growth of human populations and the scale of individual human activities as severe threats to the environment whether the resources are collectively or privately owned. Given the centrality of population size to the simplified model in Figure 4.13, it should surprise no one that eco-wholists place especially great prescriptive weight on slowing or stopping global population growth. Chapter 2 traced the rapidity of growth in both human numbers and economic activity per capita.

Eco-wholists worry, however, that the growth in human population has a great deal of momentum and therefore will not cease in the near future. A good predictor of the growth in the population of a country for the next 30 years is the size of the population now under 15 years old and therefore about to enter the most fertile years. Although the population under 15 in more developed countries averages 20 percent of the total, in less developed countries that age group constitutes 35 percent of the total (Population Reference Bureau, 1995).[5]

It is often argued that population growth in the less developed countries will follow the same declining trend as that in the more developed countries. In the latter, birth rates and death rates were both high at the beginning of the nineteenth century. Death rates have declined quite steadily over the past 200 years, falling at times enough below birth rates to cause population to grow at rates of 0.5 to 1 percent annually. Yet birth rates also declined, and in recent decades they have dipped so close to the much-reduced death rates that overall population growth in many rich countries has ceased.

The movement from high birth and death rates to low birth and death rates, via an intermediate period in which births exceed deaths, is known as the **demographic transition**. It is generally argued that a variety of improvements in the quality of life of Europeans gradually caused them to reduce their birth rates to the level of their death rates. As incomes of societies go up, the costs of raising children climb while their contribution to the average family declines. As opportunities for women in the work force have increased over the past two or three decades, the costs of forgoing those incomes and staying home with children have climbed quite sharply. We earlier described this logic from the viewpoint of a liberal.

The decline of death rates in poorer countries began largely at the end of World War II and was so sharp that the gap between birth and death rates came quickly to exceed that in rich countries at any time during their own demographic transitions (see Figure 4.14). This decrease in death rates led to population growth rates of as much as 4 percent annually—for comparison, the rate that now characterizes Africa on average is 2.8 percent (Togo leads with a population growth rate of 3.6 percent annually).

What worries eco-wholists is that this rapid growth in Third World populations, which have less outlet for migration than the European countries had during colonial times, may so overwhelm the environment that the economic and social transformations that eventually slowed the birth rate in the developed countries will never occur. If environmental deterioration prevents improvements in income, the poorer countries could find themselves not in a demographic transition but a **demographic trap** (Brown, 1988)—a situation in which inadequate food supplies and economic opportunities prevent these societies from experiencing rising incomes and slowing birth rates. Continued high birth rates would in turn maintain the pressure on the environment. Figure 4.15 portrays the demographic trap in terms of a positive feedback loop. (Remember in examining any feedback loop first to assess the sign of each individual linkage by asking what happens to the variable in front of the arrow when that behind it increases; after determining the sign of each linkage, characterize an entire loop as positive if the number of negative links is zero or even.)

Even if the developing world and therefore the world more generally manages to escape the demographic trap, eco-wholists worry, the environmental impact of each individual human being is constantly increasing. Figure 4.13 represented this scale-of-activity factor as external, or exogenous, to the feedback loop. We know, however, that it is closely tied to economic activity that exacerbates the impact of humans on the environment. Year after year, the average human being places greater demands on the environment. Average calorie and protein consumption continue to climb and more of the protein comes from meat, thereby requiring still greater increases in agricultural output. Energy use rises, especially in developing countries, with fossil fuels contributing the bulk of the increase.

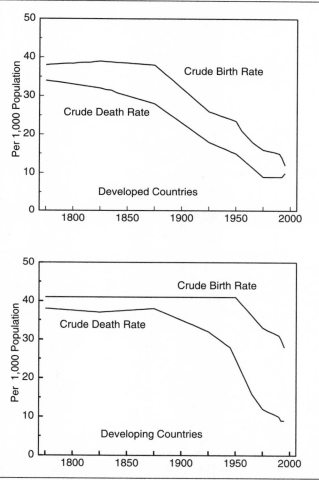

FIGURE 4.14 Demographic transition. *Source:* Nancy Birdsall, *Population and Poverty in the Developing World,* World Bank Staff Working Paper No. 404 (Washington, D.C.: World Bank, 1980), 4; Population Reference Bureau, *World Population Data Sheet* (Washington, D.C.: Population Reference Bureau, 1986, 1988, 1992, 1995).

The eco-wholist sees in this pattern the near certainty of overshoot and collapse in the relationship of humans to the environment.

Ironically, other observers often look to precisely the same trends in food and energy consumption as strong evidence of progress. They see in them increasing human mastery of the environment. We turn to that perspective.

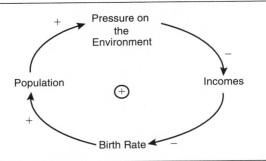

FIGURE 4.15   The demographic trap.

TECHNOLOGICAL PROGRESS: MODERNISM

The core of **modernism** is technological progress. Figure 4.16 represents that model in very simple form. The more important feedback loop in that model is the one that links human technological knowledge to itself. The stronger our existing base of understanding, the faster and easier scientists and engineers add still more to that base. This process creates exponential and even superexponential growth in knowledge. Modernists frequently point to the facts that more scientists and engineers live today than in all of prior human history and that technical publications continue to proliferate at ever more rapid rates.[6]

Whereas eco-wholists place humans squarely within their environment, modernists tend to put humanity in a privileged and superior position relative to it. The body of cumulative human knowledge, efficiently transmitted across generations and augmented in each, allows humans to increasingly control and shape their environment—for instance, to grow more food on a given area of land or to extract more oil from deeper pools. That increasing control, in turn, allows us to devote ever more resources to building the knowledge base for even greater control. The prospect that humans could actually put a relatively self-sustaining colony on the moon or Mars captures the enthusiasm that modernists often exude.

Note that the dominant loops in Figure 4.16 are positive and represent virtuous cycles of ever greater knowledge and therefore of steady improvements in human welfare. This model contrasts sharply with the dominance of a negative feedback loop in the simple eco-wholist model (Figure 4.13).

Modernists frequently acknowledge the concerns that eco-wholists have with respect to the steady growth of demands upon the environment. They tend to see that growth not as overshoot of sustainable limits,

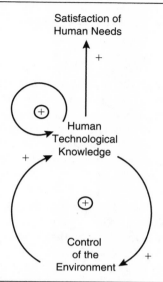

Satisfaction of
Human Needs

+

Human
Technological
Knowledge

+

Control
of the
Environment

+

FIGURE 4.16   A simplified model of modernism.

however, but as the steady pushing back of limits that face other species or that faced humans in earlier eras. Certainly we now require more food than ever before, as both populations and average per capita consumption grow. Yet the productivity of agriculture in places like Japan, where rice yields are multiples of those in most of Asia, suggests the tremendous potential for yet greater production. The benefits of the Green Revolution that began in Mexico in the 1950s continue to spread around the world; modernists attribute much of the difficulty that Africa has in meeting its food requirements not to environmental limits but to the lesser impact that the Green Revolution has had there. They argue that genetic engineering of plants and animals has only begun to push agricultural yields up to an even higher plateau.

Similarly, some generally eco-wholistic studies in the 1970s (like *The Limits to Growth*) suggested that the world was in imminent danger of exhausting its supplies of fossil fuels. They argued that the oil price shocks of that decade were harbingers of an era of very high prices and increasing scarcity. In fact, global energy production and consumption have continued to increase; natural gas production grew by 65 percent between 1976 and 1991 (British Petroleum Company, 1992: 21).

Modernists point out that when economists study economic growth, they often initially look for its roots in increasing *quantities* of capital (machines and buildings devoted to production) or of labor devoted to production. What they generally find, however, is that improvements in the *quality* of capital and labor, that is, in technological capability, provide 50 percent or more of gains in production.

Frequently such gains in productivity actually reduce the need for raw material inputs, including energy, and also reduce the outputs of waste to the environment. Consider the rapidly increasing power and capabilities of the personal desktop and laptop computers with which most of us now process information. Just a few years ago, a computer with the same capabilities would have filled a good-sized room and required heavy duty air conditioning to prevent overheating.

Aggregate data suggest the scope of improvements already obtained in such material use efficiency. Between 1974 and 1988 the world's economy grew by approximately 52 percent (CIA, 1990b: 36). Over the same period of time the world's use of energy grew by about 35 percent (Council on Environmental Quality, 1991: 302). These relative growth patterns have broken a longer-term pattern in which there was a nearly one-to-one relationship between growth in economies and energy consumption.

Agriculture provides an even more striking example. Between 1950 and 1989 total output in the United States grew by 87 percent. The Department of Agriculture estimates that total inputs to the sector actually decreased by 17 percent. Although chemical inputs increased very sharply during the period, labor requirements dropped rapidly and mechanical inputs stagnated (Council on Environmental Quality, 1991: 339). As a result of productivity increases such as these around the world, the price of U.S. wheat in constant 1980 dollars fell from $296 per ton in 1950 to $91 in 1990.[7]

Modernists anticipate that the long-term trend for many individual human requirements (including food, energy, and minerals) will be downward, reflecting the ever-increasing efficiency with which human technology satisfies needs. This contrasts sharply with eco-wholist expectations that such trends will be upward, thereby exerting increasing pressure on the environment.

Julian Simon, an active modernist author, convinced Paul Ehrlich, an outspoken eco-wholist, to place a wager on the price trend of commodities during the 1980s. Simon bet that prices would move down and won the wager.[8] In reality, improvements in efficiency of input use have increasingly become an area of some common ground between eco-wholists and modernists. The former prescribe such improvements and insist that they are urgent; the latter anticipate that obtaining them will be relatively easy.

Because the output of pollutants back to the environment tends to be highly correlated with the demand for resources from it, modernists expect little difficulty in gradually reducing pollution. They typically point to improvements in air and water quality in much of the United States over the past two decades as evidence for what can and will be done globally. Between 1980 and 1992 the average number of days during which air registered unhealthy levels in 23 major cities dropped from 27 to 14 (*The Universal Almanac 1995*, 1994: 608). Over the same period the Environmental Protection Agency measured declines in national emissions of sulphur oxides, carbon monoxide, and ozone.

Few modernists even attempt to foresee the specific technologies that might arise to augment food production, provide new energy sources, improve the efficiency of commodity use, and reduce pollution. Many would agree with the old saw, "Necessity is the mother of invention." Overall their model is much simpler than that of the eco-wholists, and many would remain much happier simply extrapolating progress into the future rather than delving into complicated and uncertain causal analyses.

CONCLUSION

It is important to make clear that the IFs model does not represent the worldviews sketched above in the form discussed here. Although understanding of and sensitivity to all of the worldviews helped in the structuring of IFs (Hughes 1985b), model development drew upon theory and research in areas as disparate as population growth, trade, and military spending. Worldviews influence theory in disciplines such as demography, economics, and political science, but that theory does not strictly elaborate those worldviews. In some instances no clear tie exists between causal linkages in the model and any worldview.

The causal model of IFs is actually considerably more extensive than these sketches of worldviews. You can explore that causal model by calling up the model's Help system and asking for model detail. That will allow you to investigate a large number of causal diagrams for various portions of IFs. You can, in fact, go one step further and look with the Help system at the equations of the model.

There have been several reasons for this chapter's presentation of worldviews.[9] First, this discussion may have helped you clarify your own thinking about the world development system and may have added some complexity to your understandings. Second, the worldviews nicely illustrate causal dynamics, something that we must understand in thinking about the future. Third, because the worldviews all provide important insights into dynamics of the world development system, they have been very influential, if not determinate, in the design of IFs.

A fourth reason, and perhaps even the most important one for our elaboration of the worldviews, is that consideration of their causal logic forced us into discussion of values and conflicts among values. What values do you bring to your thinking about the future and how do you rank them? For instance, do you value harmony with the environment? Do you also value human progress? Might progress ever disrupt the environment? Similarly, do you value economic well-being? How about equality of opportunity for individuals at birth? Is there any tension between the value you probably place on both well-being and equality of opportunity? For instance, might an emphasis on efficient economic growth lead to increased income rewards for highly productive individuals and therefore the birth of more children into homes characterized by relative poverty? Do you value maintenance of national security against external threat? Do you also value the development of cooperative and peaceful interaction among countries? If you value both, might there be some tension between those two values? For instance, might not actions intended to enhance national security, such as developing a new weapons system, actually threaten global peace?

If your eyes begin to glaze over in reaction to such a barrage of questions, you are not alone. Nonetheless, stop to think for a moment about those questions. Not one of them is unimportant. In fact, they are all central to choices about the future of humanity. You do not need to answer them to your satisfaction now, and the fact is that you may never be able fully to resolve the trade-offs and hard choices they demand of you. It is, however, required of citizens in democracies that they regularly grapple with these questions.

FIVE

□ □ □

The Pursuit of Progress and Sustainability

In the past two decades, environmental questions have surged upward on national, regional, and even global agendas. Citizens and leaders recognize that the current and projected scale of human activities could pose a threat to the long-term availability of food and fossil fuels and the long-term viability of the oceans and atmosphere as envelopes for life on earth. The 1992 United Nations Conference on the Environment and Development in Rio de Janeiro issued a call for what is, in effect, a new global environmental order. Such an order might require forgoing the use of some modern technology (6 billion people or more cannot reasonably use automobiles in the way Americans now do). Technological advances such as nuclear energy have often presented new environmental challenges; there is an old advertising slogan that would now draw as many jeers as cheers: "Better living through chemistry."

At the same time, we have witnessed unprecedented technological progress in a variety of fields, including miniaturization of electronics, exploration of space, and understanding of the workings of living organisms. The new technologies promise untold benefits for humanity. Already, in fact, they have been used to clean up air pollution, improve water quality, cure disease, and increase the production of food, both total and per capita. The technologies have clearly and substantially improved the quality and length of life for peoples around the globe.

CONTEMPORARY ISSUES

Chapter 4 sketched two competitive images of the relationship of humans with their broader environment. In the modernist image, humans increasingly dominate, even control, that environment and can look forward to continuing progress with respect to food and energy availability, material well-being, and life expectancy. In the eco-wholist perspective, humans are a part of their broader environment and may well be placing unsustainable demands on it; humanity faces increasing challenges in feeding a growing population and maintaining a quality of life that the rich of the world take for granted and the poor wish to emulate. In this chapter we move from these general images to specific issues. Namely, we will focus on the growth of population, the availability of food and energy, and the quality of the environment. Our principal purpose is to investigate the leverage that humans have in these issue areas.

Population

Chapter 2 presented forecasts with respect to global population growth for more and less economically developed portions of the world and for geographic regions. Those forecasts were based in substantial part on extrapolation of current trends. Because the total size of global population is fundamental to forecasts of food sufficiency or environmental quality, it is essential that we devote some attention to the accuracy of such forecasts and to the leverage that humans have with respect to them.

Figure 5.1 compares three forecasts of the global population. Note that by 2050 the high and low forecasts vary by approximately 4 billion people, roughly two-thirds of the current global population. Although such alternative forecasts, or **scenarios,** purposefully range from one extreme to another, and most analysts expect reality to fall somewhere in between, the great variation suggests considerable uncertainty. That uncertainty in turn suggests some latitude for human intervention.

How do analysts make such forecasts? And on what does the variability in them depend? The simplest forecasts, including some of the highest global population forecasts, are no more than pure extrapolations of current growth patterns. They may use a "simple growth model," an equation that computes population at time point (t) as population at a prior point (t − 1) times the sum of 1 plus a growth rate (r).

$$POP_t = POP_{t-1}(1 + r)$$

Computer models can generalize this formula to predict population at any time point in the future, based on an initial point (t = 0).

$$POP_t = POP_{t=0}(1 + r)^t$$

Yet, not a single demographer believes that population growth rates will fail to change over a long period of time. They therefore rely on a

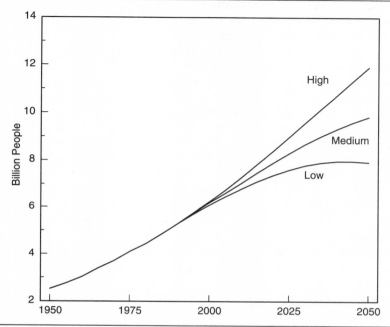

FIGURE 5.1   Scenarios of global population. *Source:* Ronald Bailey, ed., *The True State of the Planet* (New York: The Free Press, 1995), 399. *Original Source:* United Nations, *World Population Prospects: The 1994 Revision-Annex Tables* (New York: United Nations Population Division, Department for Economic and Social Information and Policy Analysis, 1994), Tables A-1, A-2.

more sophisticated approach to forecasting population called cohort-component analysis. Cohort-component analysis represents the population of a geographic region by age category, or "cohort," and sex. Demographers refer to these data as age-sex distributions. It is common to maintain the categories for age groupings spanning five years, such as people 6–10 or 21–25 years of age. Demographers also collect and maintain data on the number of births that occur annually for every 1,000 women in each age category and the number of deaths that occur each year per 1,000 people in each age category. These data constitute fertility and mortality distributions, respectively. Like age-sex distributions, they vary by country. It is quite simple to combine age-sex, fertility, and mortality distributions into a dynamic model of population growth.

This approach to forecasting population directs our attention to fertility and mortality rates. Figure 5.2 shows fertility rates over time for more and less developed countries in the form of the total number of births that a woman can expect to have during a lifetime, a measure called the total fertility rate (TFR). Why do the figures vary across countries and across time? One of the most widely recognized explanations for variation is income per capita (usually approximated by Gross National Product [GNP] per capita). Rich countries tend to have low fertility and mortality rates, whereas poorer countries tend to have higher rates (look again at Figure 4.14 showing the demographic transition). The explanation for the impact of income on mortality is fairly obvious. Individuals in societies with higher income are more likely to have access to good nutrition, clean water, safer working conditions, better health care, and other supports of a longer life. The explanation for the depressing effect of higher income on fertility is only slightly more complicated. Whereas children in poor families actually provide economic benefits through both early earnings and support of parents in old age, in rich families the costs of child care and education more commonly exceed any income that children add to the family.

Although differences in income across countries can explain much of the variation in fertility and mortality rates, many other factors are also involved. These include income distribution. In general, the greater the income equality within a society, the lower the mortality and fertility rates. Because increases in individual income from very low levels lower fertility and mortality more than do increases in income from high levels, societies that raise the incomes of nearly everyone simultaneously can logically attain greater reductions in fertility and mortality.

Another very important factor in reducing fertility is the status of women in a society. When women have more access to education and job opportunities, the average number of children they bear in a lifetime decreases sharply. Governmental or private programs that make available information about family planning and that provide access to contraceptives also have an unmistakable impact in reduction of fertility.

This review suggests that humans actually have considerable leverage on the growth of population. They can affect it substantially through policies that change economic growth rates or the distribution of income. They can also affect it through programs that improve the condition of women or that support family planning activities.

Efforts to apply that leverage became notable in the 1960s as global population growth reached its peak rates slightly in excess of 2 percent annually. At the national level, family planning programs had begun appearing in the 1950s. By 1995 they existed in 65 countries. Contraceptive use in Latin America grew from less than 20 percent of married couples in 1960 to nearly 80 percent in 1990. Many more developed countries have been active in supporting such programs through the mechanism of economic development agencies. For instance, the United States took a lead-

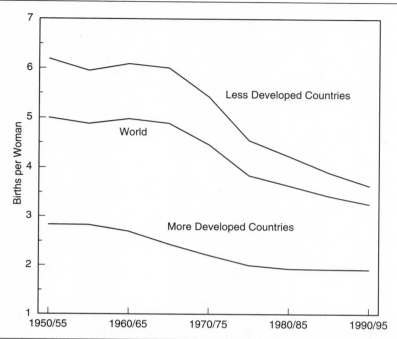

FIGURE 5.2   Total fertility rate. *Source:* Ronald Bailey, ed., *The True State of the Planet* (New York: The Free Press, 1995), 401. *Original Source:* United Nations, *World Population Prospects: The 1994 Revision-Annex Tables* (New York: United Nations Population Division, Department for Economic and Social Information and Policy Analysis, 1994), 112 and 126.

ership role through the Agency for International Development in the 1960s.

International activities have intensified over the past 30 years. The UN has sponsored three World Population Conferences: Bucharest in 1974, Mexico City in 1984, and Cairo in 1994. Although important actors in Bucharest (especially China) and Mexico City (notably the United States) resisted global commitment to reduction of fertility, and despite the right-to-life controversy that drew most media attention, there was considerable consensus on the issue in Cairo. Moreover, participants at Cairo drew special attention to the importance of improving the status of women. The UN provides ongoing support for family planning through its Fund for Population Activities.

African and Islamic countries have lagged in their commitment to national and international activities and their implementation of family planning programs. In many cases, cultural, especially religious, beliefs have supported higher rather than lower fertility. The strong opposition in some countries to abortion, a common means of family planning in other countries, has circumscribed international support for family planning. Yet the substantial reduction in global birth rates in just three decades preceding 1995, from approximately 5 per woman in a lifetime to about 3 per woman, indicates the leverage that societies have with respect to fertility. And a global increase in life expectancy, from 55 to 65 in the same three decades, shows similar leverage with respect to mortality.

Food

Famines in the Soviet Union in 1934, in Bengal in 1943, and in China during 1958–1961 each claimed several million lives (Eberstadt, 1995: 39). Although the famines were caused partly by gross political mismanagement, the absence of much cushion in regional food supplies contributed significantly. Chapter 2 showed that food production per capita has increased globally and in all regions except Africa over the past several decades, making it likely that the total number of starvation or famine deaths around the world over the next 25 years will be lower than the estimated 20–25 million that occurred in the last quarter of the nineteenth century, an era of much lower global population (Avery, 1995: 54). Yet the number of malnourished people in the world remains in the hundreds of millions, and famines, especially in Africa, still claim tens and even hundreds of thousands of victims. Again we want to ask what kind of leverage we have with respect to forecasts of food production and availability.

In the most basic terms, food production depends on the amount of land under cultivation and the productivity of that land. For most of human history, increases in the amount of land were more important than land productivity, a fact that obviously predisposed leaders and peoples to invasion and conquest of their neighbors as well as to more extensive cultivation of their own domains. Figure 5.3 shows the amount of land devoted to grain production globally (grain is still our most basic and most important food) and the total production of grain. Although there is some potential for expansion of cultivated land (such as the area removed from farming in the United States and on the pampas of Argentina), it is obvious from that figure that essentially all of our increase in production now comes from improved yields on a largely stable cultivated area.

Those yields in turn now depend on a combination of increased investment in agricultural equipment; heavier use of fertilizers, pesticides, and herbicides; and improvements in the genetic stock of the grains that we grow. Beginning most notably with the success that Norman Borlaug had with Mexican wheat in the 1950s, new strains have increased the world's

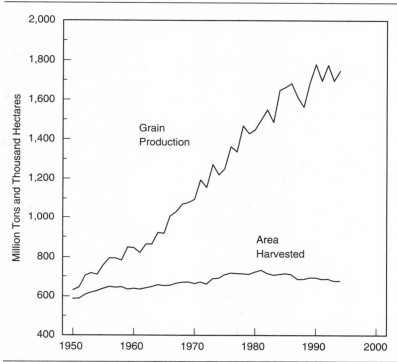

FIGURE 5.3   Global grain production and area harvested. *Source:* Worldwatch Institute, Worldwatch Database Diskette, 1995.

grain yield from 1.1 tons per hectare in 1950 to 2.6 tons in 1992 (Brown, Lenssen, and Kane, 1995: 43). Increased use of fertilizer supported productivity advance in the 1960s and 1970s, and heavier use of pesticides and herbicides, in combination with "conservation tillage" (generally involving less plowing), increasingly supports continued advance in the 1990s.

Debates surround both the continued possibility of productivity improvements and the best ways to pursue them. The private market obviously provides a critical foundation for productivity, as farmers and the companies that sell supplies to them strive for increased yields and profits. The global community has, however, played an important role also by building a global network of agricultural research institutions on the initial successes of Borlaug and the Ford Foundation in Mexico. The Consultative Group on International Agricultural Research (CGIAR) brings together states, international governmental organizations, and nongovernmental organizations in a partnership that in 1995 supported 16 research centers on all continents.

Those centers and vast private efforts have contributed to improvements not only in grain production but also in global meat production since 1950, quadrupling it in total amount and doubling it in per capita terms (Brown, Lenssen, and Kane, 1995: 31). Meat consumption is now rising very sharply in Asia. Still, Asian consumption averages only 14 grams of animal protein per capita per day, in comparison with 55 grams in Japan and 71 grams in the United States (Avery, 1995: 51).

Governments and voluntary organizations also sometimes turn to food aid for countries in special need. For instance, substantial transborder efforts helped limit deaths in the African famines of 1972–1974, 1984–1985 (Jansson, Harris, and Penrose, 1987), and 1992–1993. Although long-term decline in food production per capita and periodic droughts are major causes of famine on the African continent, so too are the kinds of political failures that characterized the very large famines earlier in the century. For instance, a Socialist government in Ethiopia after 1974 and a civil war in that country disrupted food production, as have a long ethnic war in the Sudan and a nearly complete breakdown of civil order in Somalia during 1992. This problem has made it difficult for outside agencies to obtain information about pending food shortages or access to populations during them. Such agencies also worry about creating long-term dependence on foreign food supplies, particularly if donations undercut the prices needed by local farmers to increase production. Thus food aid has become a less heavily used tool in the arsenal of weapons with which we strive for adequate global food supplies, while increased investment and improved technology have become more heavily used.

Although the world's fish catch is only about 5 percent by weight of the world's grain production, it is only about one-third less by weight than global meat production. Fishing therefore provides a critical global source of protein. The ocean fish catch has advanced little for more than a decade, and many observers believe that fleets have reached the peak of production. Because more than half of the world's fisheries are either fully exploited or overexploited (Jeffreys, 1995: 296), human leverage is increasingly applied to managing fisheries rather than expanding production. The Third United Nations Conference on Law of the Sea established 200-mile exclusive economic zones for coastal states, thereby providing both the incentives and the means for those countries to manage many coastal fisheries.[1] Yet competition of fleets from the same country within those zones, global competition within the open ocean, and state subsidies to their fleets result in both consistent financial losses on the global fish catch and continued management problems.

One bright spot in the world fish catch is a rapid expansion of aquaculture or fish farming (sometimes called mariculture), especially in Asia. The total production of aquaculture reached 14 million tons in 1993 (Brown, Lenssen, and Kane, 1995: 32), about a doubling in a decade. Figure 5.4 shows the production of both ocean fishing and aquaculture, as well as of meat.

This brief discussion of the dramatic changes in food production patterns and quantities in recent decades suggests the tremendous possibilities for human leverage with respect to food supply. Farmers operating in free markets are central actors. States often intervene in those markets, sometimes distorting prices and therefore incentives. There has been a persistent tendency in the post–World War II period for governments in economically developed countries to support prices above market levels in order to protect the incomes of farmers. Governments in economically less developed countries have often held prices below market levels in an effort to protect the diets of consumers. The former policies have created

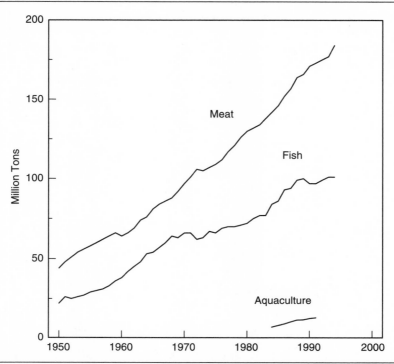

FIGURE 5.4   Global meat and fish production. *Source:* Worldwatch Institute, Worldwatch Database Diskette, 1995.

surpluses and the latter have contributed to shortages. At the same time, international research efforts and food aid have sought to assure both long-term supply increases and short-term food adequacy. They, too, have had very important effects on the global food system.

Energy

With sufficient energy one can grow grain on the top of Mount Everest or extract all minerals needed by an advanced industrial economy from seawater. Thus, energy is the "master resource." Energy issues, like those of population and food, present us with both important choices and considerable leverage.

The instability of global energy markets received widespread attention at about the time of the first contemporary African famine, when world oil prices quadrupled in 1973–1974. Although global market prices eroded a bit thereafter (in constant or real dollars, that is, after subtracting inflation), they doubled again in the second oil shock of 1979–1980. They subsequently collapsed in the mid-1980s. They would have again risen sharply during the UN-Iraq war of 1991 had not Saudi Arabia opened its oil taps. Figure 5.5 shows the quite dramatic oil price instability of the past 25 years.

Explanations for this supply and price instability abound, including: (1) the attempt by OPEC members to exercise power over their primary resource and to extract maximum revenues; (2) the ethnic and religious ri-

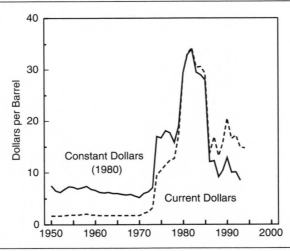

FIGURE 5.5   World oil prices. *Sources:* World Bank, *Commodity Trade and Price Trends, 1987–88* (Baltimore: Johns Hopkins University, 1988), 80; British Petroleum, *BP Statistical Review of World Energy* (London: British Petroleum, 1995), 12.

valries of the Middle East that have interrupted oil exports with warfare; (3) the failure of Western oil-importing countries to develop and utilize other energy technologies; and (4) the geologically limited resources of world oil and gas and the inevitability of some supply constraints regardless of political and economic decisions in the region.

Whatever the explanation, both the sharp increases in oil costs and the price instability have given countries, especially large oil importers like Japan, reason to search for ways in which to exercise greater control over their own energy futures. They have generally tried to achieve some leverage on oil prices and price stability in at least four ways: (1) increasing their own production of oil or other sources of energy to achieve energy independence; (2) reducing energy demand through conservation; (3) establishing domestic reserves and sharing arrangements with other countries in order to provide some insurance against further disruptions; and (4) diversifying external supply sources. Let us consider each of these policy levers in turn.

Immediately after the 1973–1974 oil shock, the United States launched "Project Independence," an effort to increase its own energy production so as to eliminate oil imports by 1980. Although the effort proved futile, it bears consideration. Such an attempt can focus on the production of oil, the production of alternative fossil fuels, or the production of alternative energy forms such as nuclear and solar. When countries have ready access to large reserves of fossil fuels, that strategy can succeed. It did for Norway and for Great Britain, which turned to the supplies of the North Sea, and for the Netherlands, which exploited its large natural gas reserves. The United States found, however, that even with the addition of new oil resources from Alaska, it did not have the oil and natural gas reserves to achieve independence. For Japan, with minimal fossil fuel resources, it was not even an option.

On a global basis, natural gas production increased by considerably more than 50 percent between 1973 and 1994; meanwhile, world oil production has been fairly stable (British Petroleum Company, 1995: 6, 21). There is potential for further expansion in production of both oil and gas. Figure 5.6 shows that the ratio of reserves to production (which is used to calculate the number of years that known global reserves would last at current production rates) has increased for both fuels, especially gas. Even without further discoveries, a prospect against which we can bet safely, world oil supplies would last more than 40 years and world gas supplies would extend for 60 years at current production rates. The cost of those supplies does, however, remain a key issue as we drill deeper and locate wells in more inhospitable locations.

Economists refer to the percentage increase in energy supply as a result of a 1 percent increase in price as the price elasticity of supply. If a 1 percent

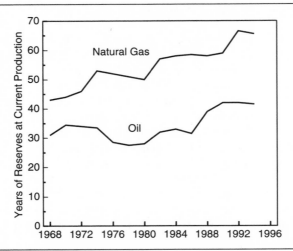

FIGURE 5.6   Lifetime of fossil fuel reserves. *Source:* British Petroleum, *BP Statistical Review of World Energy* (London: British Petroleum, 1995), 6 and 21.

increase in price gives rise to an increase in supply (after some time delay) of greater than 1 percent, they say that supply is elastic; if the response is less than 1 percent, they say that it is inelastic. They attempt, however, to be more precise and to actually specify the elasticity as a number (a 1.5 percent or elastic response, for example). Obviously, the supply elasticity for fossil fuels depends heavily on the fossil fuel base.

The supply elasticity of nuclear energy depends relatively little on the resource base (the cost of uranium itself is minimal in the overall cost of nuclear energy). It depends instead on the capital costs associated with the production of electricity from nuclear energy and with the environmental acceptability of nuclear energy to particular countries. Uncertainties surround the real costs of nuclear waste disposal, risks of accidents, and even the decommissioning of older nuclear plants. Thus, various countries assess the environmental acceptability very differently. Although the growth in nuclear energy production has slowed around the world in recent years because of concerns with both cost and safety, it more than tripled between 1980 and 1993 (British Petroleum Company, 1991, 1994).

Solar energy, whether from hydroelectric plants, wind farms, or photovoltaic cells, also has capital cost and can cause environmental damage. Passive solar construction and photovoltaic cells, however, have few environmental costs, and even the capital costs have dropped as the technology has improved (see Figure 5.7). Therefore, the price elasticity of

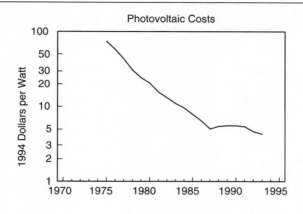

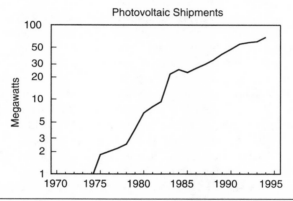

FIGURE 5.7   Solar energy costs and sales. *Source:* Worldwatch Institute Database (Washington, D.C.: Worldwatch Institute, 1995).

solar energy has been generally increasing with that technological change. Industrial and governmental sponsorship of research on such technologies can provide leverage.

The surprise to many observers of energy systems in the 1970s and 1980s, however, was that with limited exceptions the price elasticities of supply proved lower than expected and the price elasticities of demand proved higher. That is, we discovered that the ability of consumers to reduce energy consumption in the face of higher prices is considerable. For many years, energy demand had grown in near lockstep with economic size (represented by GDP) in developed countries. That relationship has been broken in the past two decades. For Western developed countries, energy consumption per unit of GDP dropped 31 percent between 1970 and 1990 (Bailey, 1995: 437). Energy conservation can involve either eliminating some consumption (such as driving less) or substituting more efficient technology (buying a more efficient car). In both cases, the environmental consequences can be quite positive. Thus, environmentally minded observers have argued that governments should focus their attempts to gain leverage in energy on conservation. They recommend, for instance, higher taxes on energy, like those that European governments put on gasoline, and government sponsorship of research on recycling.

After the 1973–1974 oil shock, oil-importing countries established the International Energy Agency (IEA) to coordinate energy policies. They charged the IEA with restraining demand, encouraging alternative energy sources, and preparing plans for cooperative action should future supply shortages develop. The IEA has encouraged member countries to build strategic petroleum reserves to provide cushion in the face of future oil supply disruptions. Many, including the United States, have done so. The IEA has also put in place plans for sharing of the burden should additional disruptions of supply from the Middle East occur.

The IEA and member governments recognize, however, that the ultimate measures of success in energy policy are: (1) reduction of dependence on energy from unstable supply sources, and (2) downward pressure on energy prices. We have already seen that real energy prices have fallen dramatically from the peaks of the early 1980s and are, in fact, not substantially higher than those of the 1950s and 1960s. Dependence on the OPEC countries of the Middle East, however, continues. Despite supply disruptions that caused the oil shocks of the 1970s and 1980s, in the decade ending in 1994, OPEC's share of world oil production rose from 31 to 41 percent, and the Middle Eastern share rose from 20 to 30 percent (British Petroleum Company, 1995: 5). Although OPEC lost some of its own leverage over the global energy system in the 1970s and early 1980s, it has subsequently regained much of that leverage.

The Environment

It is difficult to make general statements about trends in the quality of the natural environment. Some trends appear clearly negative. For instance, there is no question that levels of carbon dioxide in the atmosphere are increasing. Landfills (that is, covered garbage dumps) continue to proliferate, as does nuclear waste. The air quality of major cities in developing countries is deteriorating noticeably as automobile congestion grows.

At the same time, however, some trends are clearly positive. The air quality of the major cities in most developed countries is markedly better than it was two decades ago. The water quality of many streams and lakes in those countries has improved. Although it may be many years before we see an impact on ozone levels in the upper atmosphere, the emissions of the CFCs that have been depleting ozone are dropping precipitously (the ironically named congressional Representatives DeLay and Doolittle tried in 1995 to reduce U.S. commitment to the phaseout of CFC production).

With respect to other aspects of the environment, it is difficult to be certain about improvement or deterioration. Data from 1600 to the mid-1900s show a steady increase in the number of species extinctions globally. It is possible, however, that extinctions peaked at the middle of the century and that there now is some decline in annual disappearances (Edwards, 1995: 218). Moreover, the amount of land put aside in protected areas has grown from practically nothing at the beginning of the twentieth century to 800 million hectares, or 5.9 percent of total land area, by 1993. Such areas are essential to protecting biodiversity.

Patterns in deforestation similarly are somewhat mixed. Moreover, they illustrate the tendency for the good news to appear in more developed countries and the bad news to emerge with development from low levels. Plantings and reversions of agricultural land to temperate forest in developed countries have been massive. In the United States, forest area has grown in this century even as the country became the world's largest producer of timber and greatly expanded timber production. Forests have also expanded in Canada and Russia. European forest area grew sharply in the 1980s (Sedjo, 1995: 201) and is now expanding in China, another temperate-zone country.

In contrast, the rate of deforestation in the tropics continued to rise during the 1980s, averaging 0.8 percent annually over the decade. Given the pressure on the agricultural systems of developing countries for higher production, as well as the need of many such countries for revenues from hardwood exports, that trend should not surprise us.

On the surface, development itself appears to explain a substantial portion of the environmental picture. Agricultural land, industries, and cities expand rapidly in the early stages of development, and countries with low levels of income find many environmental systems overwhelmed. As development proceeds and wealth accumulates, however, some of that expansion slows and countries not only begin to limit damage to the environment but also to repair it.

We should beware, however, of a picture of an economic determinism that includes no explicit role for the leverage of human environmental decision and action. Because environmental damage is outside the economic calculation of most producers and consumers, they commonly pay little attention to limiting it, even in the most developed countries. Although some aspects of the environment, such as many forests, could be better preserved if they were privatized, because owners would be more likely to look beyond immediate economic survival and have reason to treat their property well over the long run, air and water systems generally remain public. Thus it has been the growth of voluntary and sometimes selfless individual action, the support of nongovernmental organizations within and across countries, and the pressure of legal and institutional machinery both within and across countries that have led to progress where it occurs.

At the interstate level, the United Nations Conference on the Human Environment, held in 1972 in Stockholm, was a milestone. It preceded the creation of the United Nations Environment Program in 1973 and an explosion of activity protecting domestic and international environments. Global conventions and treaties are proliferating along with nongovernmental organizations. Improvements in environmental quality, or at least reductions in the pace of deterioration, do not just happen as countries become wealthier. Human effort must flow into action consciously targeted at ameliorating the damage of other human activity.

Perhaps two classes of global environmental issues remain most pressing. The first, as we have already indicated, is a broad range of problems in developing countries: tropical deforestation, species loss, and air and water quality deterioration. The second is a set of truly global issues in which developed and developing countries interact. Even when more developed countries are prepared to attack problems of the atmospheric and oceanic commons (and they still are frequently not so prepared), developing countries often face what they determine to be more pressing needs. The pollution (from carbon dioxide to sulphur dioxide and from toxic chemicals to nuclear wastes) that large developing countries like China, India, and Brazil spew into the global commons will almost certainly increase in the next few decades.

Issues, Leverage, and Action Decisions

In brief, there appear to be many points of leverage, both for private individuals and for governments, with respect to issues around progress and sustainability. Fertility and mortality patterns do change in response to variables such as income level, income distribution, and government programs. Food production rises or falls as a result of policies on land use, technological innovation, and pricing. Energy security responds to dependence on imports, physical resource constraints, efforts to conserve, and the costs of alternatives to fossil fuels. Environmental quality varies with development levels, but more immediately with direct attention to its protection. It is, in reality, difficult to influence many of the variables that shape the condition of our world on these issues. Yet many others are clearly within our ability to manipulate. We do have leverage.

Knowing that, the key question becomes one of action. Do you believe it desirable to seek lower global population growth rates, and if so, how should it be done? Should we work to improve diets in Africa and reduce starvation levels, and if so, how? Is it important to reduce tropical deforestation? Among the most important questions is, What unanticipated secondary and tertiary consequences might our specific actions have?

The dilemma that we all face has not changed. We must still act in the face of an uncertain future. And we must still consider how best to balance potentially (although not always) competing values such as progress and sustainability. You always have the choice, of course, of leaving the decisions to others, of failing to cast your own ballot or to speak your own mind. Should you believe it possible, however, to help create through your action a world superior to the one that your inaction would equally shape, the next section may assist in your evaluation of options for action. Remember to distrust the results of computer simulations like IFs, but at the same time to use them in helping you think through the issues.

EXPLORATION OF INTERNATIONAL FUTURES

The IFs model allows you to investigate how you might help shape a future consistent with your own understandings and values. You will do that through scenario analysis. Specifically, you will first select a set of indicators upon which you wish to focus. Then you will begin manipulating parameters within the model that represent points of possible human leverage in order to push those indicators in the directions you desire. This will be a process of trial and error and one that will help you think through causal linkages, constraints, and trade-offs.

You will often actually select two sets of indicators upon which to focus as you develop scenarios. The first set will be specific to the issue area in which you are exploring leverage (population, food, energy, and so on). These will show you the immediate impact of the parameters you manipulate and will help you make certain that the scenario you are developing is being introduced into the model as you desire. We shall discuss these issue-specific indicators below. The second set of indicators will consider the bigger picture. For instance, in looking at global futures with an eye to progress and sustainability, you might wish to look at world and region-specific GDP per capita (WGDPPC and GPPPC), physical quality of life (WPQLI and PQLI), calorie availability per capita (WCLPC and CLPC), literary rates (WLIT and LIT), the global level of atmospheric carbon dioxide (CO2PPM and CO2PER), and the world forest area (WFORST).

Chapter 3, particularly in its final section, provided basic information on the use of IFs for scenario analysis. Return to that chapter if you need to refresh your memory on the mechanics. The Help system of IFs includes an extended discussion of parameters available within the model and their use. Take a moment to look at that by accessing Help within IFs and exploring.

Population

To repeat, the first step in scenario analysis is always to identify some indicators of importance to you. In looking at the issue area of population, some issue-specific indicators of interest would obviously include global and region-specific populations (WPOP and POP) and their growth rates (WPOPR and POPR). You may also want to look at regional crude birth and death rates (CBR and CDR) or at life expectancy (LIFEXP). Remember, however, that you will also want to look at general global and regional indicators of progress and sustainability.

The second step in scenario analysis is to ask yourself what changes might conceivably shift the values of the indicators you have chosen in directions you desire. With respect to population size, we have already talked about fertility and mortality rates as key variables. You can introduce changes in fertility and mortality directly by altering values of multipliers on them (TFRM and MORTM). There are equivalent multipliers on many variables within IFs.

▶ Select the Change option from the Main Menu of IFs, select the standard set of parameters to change, and identify TFRM as a parameter to change. Then interpolate values of TFRM for all countries and regions from 1.0 to 0.8 between 1992 and 2010 and leave it at that level for remaining years. That reduces fertility rates gradually to 80 percent of the rate that the model would otherwise calculate. Run the model and examine the size of population and its growth rate in comparison with the base case. How much effect does that assumption have by 2010? You may have to run the model until 2050 to see any really significant change.

It is important that you think through the basis for the changes you make in multipliers or other parameters. Do you believe that technological breakthroughs may prolong life substantially? If so, you might wish to consider changing values of MORTM gradually (via the interpolation option in parameter change) from 1.0 in 1992 (no change) to 1.3 in 2050. Do you, however, believe that the spread of diseases such as AIDS or the development of treatment-resistant infections will shorten average life expectancies? If so, you might want to change the values of MORTM from 1.0 to 0.8 over time. (Refer to Important Note 3.)

Important Note 3

When you introduce a scenario into the working file via parameter change, your change stays in the working file until you explicitly reverse it or exit from the model. If you wish to introduce another scenario, it is important that you be able to distinguish its impact from that of the earlier parameter change. To do so, either (1) save the working file under a new name (File-Save) and then make your second change, so that you can compare the results before and after the second change, or (2) reopen the base case (File-Open) so that you can introduce your second change and compare results with the base case. It is good practice to build scenarios with one change at a time to the base case and to combine multiple changes in a single scenario only after understanding the individual impact of each change.

We sometimes use multipliers to force into the model changes that we understand might come about in many different ways. For instance, our reduction of TFRM from 1.0 to 0.8 could represent a postulated breakthrough in birth control technology, an intensification of family planning programs, increases in income, more egalitarian income distributions, or improvements in the health and education of prospective mothers. IFs will not always include all of the specific policy levers that you will want to consider. In the population area, however, it does include a substantial number. For instance, CONTRUSM allows you to work directly with assumptions about family planning programs (read about this and other parameters in the Help system). You can increase or decrease the income share of the poorest 20 percent within a country or region (INCSHRM). Or you can increase governmental spending on health or education (GK). Still again, you might accelerate or decelerate economic growth via the multiplier on GDP (GDPM).

▶ For instance, try increasing the income share (INCSHR) of the poorest 20 percent for India gradually by one-half between 1990 and 2005 via the multiplier INCSHRM. Because income distributions do not change very rapidly in most societies (barring major revolution), such a dramatic increase is in reality very unlikely. Look at the impact such a change could have on the crude birth rate (CBR) and the number of births (BIRTHS) in India. Would such an improvement in income distribution have any net impact on population growth, GDP per capita, or quality of life? Keep in mind that improvements in income distribution would also bring better nutrition and health care to the poor and thus have an effect on the crude death rate (CDR) and the total number of deaths (DEATHS) as well. Because demographic variables change slowly, you must run the model for at least 25 years to really see the effect of this scenario. (See Important Note 4.)

Important Note 4

If you change a parameter, run the model, change another parameter, and
enter Run again, you will find the model positioned to start running again in
the final year of your last run (this option allows you to alter a scenario as
you develop it through time). You will normally want to reset to the initial
year before starting your next run.

Food and Agriculture

Indicators of potential interest in this issue area include agricultural
production (AGP), yield per hectare of land (YL), agricultural demand
(AGDEM), and agricultural imports and exports (AGM and AGX). Many
variables in this portion of the model have separate values for crops and
meat. Often, however, it is useful to focus on indicators that summarize
the condition of human nutrition. Consider calories per capita per day
(CLPC), the number of annual starvation deaths (SDEATH), or an overall
physical quality of life index (PQLI).

There are many parameters of potential interest in food and agriculture. There are direct multipliers on agricultural demand (AGDEMM),
agricultural investment (AGINVM), and yield per hectare (YLM).

▶ The yield multiplier (YLM) can introduce assumptions of accelerated technological advance in agriculture. Its normal value is 1, but an increase to 1.1 between 1990 and 2005 would gradually increase agricultural production by 10
percent relative to the base case (with the same inputs). If you believe that
rapid technological breakthroughs in crop genetics through biotechnology are
probable, this scenario could be appropriate. Similarly, a decrease to 0.9 would
relatively decrease agricultural production by 10 percent (and might reflect an
assumption of severe environmental deterioration). Pick a region and experiment with YLM. You may wish, for example, to look at Africa and to see the
impact of yield assumptions on starvation deaths.

Yields per hectare grow around the world in the base case at rates that
many analysts might argue are unsustainable, because the technology will not
emerge, because irrigation water will be inadequate, or for other reasons. Try
setting the maximum yields (YLMAX) for all regions to 10 tons/hectare and
investigate the impact. Look at cumulative global starvation deaths, world
food prices, global calories per capita, and other variables.

You might also want to look at the global implications of technological
advance and change YLM for all regions simultaneously. What impact
does such a technologically optimistic scenario have on world agricultural production (WAPRO) and price (WAP)? How about accumulated
world starvation deaths (WSDACC) or quality of life (WPQLI)? *In this and*

many other scenarios the model will to some degree "fight" the change—increases in agricultural productivity through technology will put some downward pressure on food prices and that will in turn shift some resources out of agricultural production. You may need to exaggerate a scenario to achieve the desired behavior.

Agricultural breakthroughs could also occur in aquaculture. The mariculture parameter (MARIC) allows you to increase or decrease exogenous assumptions about the domestic cultivation of fish by region (in million metric tons of fish annually). The ocean fish catch parameter (OFSCTH) similarly allows change in assumptions about global oceanic fish supply. You might consider a scenario in which the global fish catch, which has been relatively stable for some time, increases by one-third by 2005, perhaps because of improved harvesting or management methods. The regional share in the fish catch (RFSSH) determines the geographic distribution of that catch.

Many observers of agriculture, especially in the Third World, have been distressed at the amount of food that reaches maturity in the fields but never reaches the table because it is lost to rodents, in the harvesting process, or through inadequate shipping and storage. You can see an estimate of the portion that regions lose in these ways (LOSS) and change assumptions about that loss via a multiplier (LOSSM) or via the table function that relates LOSS to GDP per capita.

Energy

Indicators of possible importance in energy include energy production (ENP), energy demand (ENDEM), the ratio of energy demand to GDP (ENRGDP), and energy prices (ENPRI). You may be very interested in the global pattern of energy production (WENP) or prices (WEP).

As we discussed earlier, there are many places where we may be able to exert leverage on local or global energy systems. One area is the production of oil and gas, coal, or nuclear or renewable energy (the categories within IFs). You can experiment with such leverage directly via a multiplier on production (ENPM). In fact, within resource constraints you can even force a particular growth rate for an energy form via a parameter controlling energy production growth rate (EPRODR). The normal value for that parameter is zero, allowing the model to compute energy production by region and energy type. Nonzero values, such as 0.035, say, force a production growth rate upon the model (in this example, a rate of 3.5 percent each year). Again, see the Help system for more explanation of specific parameters.

▶ The energy production multiplier (ENPM) is a technological multiplier on energy production by energy type. Try assuming technological progress that increases the production potential of oil and gas or renewable energy in all regions by 20 percent in 2010 (increase the value of ENPM gradually from 1.0 to 1.2). What impact does that assumption have on global energy price and economic output? You might look also at the impact it has (if any) on the relative North-South gap (NSGAPR). Why might global energy production efficiency and the North-South gap be connected?

Although these parameters will force the model to produce more or less of a given energy type, the model also includes parameters controlling specific aspects of the energy system that might give rise to different production levels. For instance, one key factor that will affect energy production futures is the availability of fossil fuel resources. Go back to the base case and look at the values over time for global oil and gas reserves (WRESER). These reserves peak and begin to fall even before 2025, and their fall constrains oil and gas production. Even if you assume via ENPM technological improvements in extracting the resource, the constraint of total reserves remains. Because oil and gas tend to be less expensive than other energy forms (such as coal or nuclear or renewable energy), that constraint puts upward pressure on world energy prices (WEP).

Some observers argue that pessimists have routinely underestimated the amount of oil and gas in the earth (for instance, by predicting that the United States would run out at the turn of the century, before the discovery of the big Texas fields). Perhaps the assumptions about ultimate oil and resources (WRESOR) in the model are too conservative.

▶ You can introduce more optimistic assumptions about world energy resources by changing the value of the resource factor (RESORM, which works as a multiplier on resources). Try doubling it for oil and gas resources of all regions. Simultaneously double the discovery rate (RDM) of that oil and gas for all regions. What impact does that have on world reserves and prices? Does it affect world GDP per capita (WGDPPC) or quality of life (WPQLI)?

Some might also question the assumptions in the base case concerning the cost of future production of energy. Technological progress could increase the production of energy possible with the same investment levels.

▶ If you are interested, you can explore the implications of decreasing (or increasing) the costs of energy production on a region and energy-type specific level. The multiplier on energy capital costs (QEM) allows you to do that. This is a good way of investigating possible changes in the cost of renewable energy technologies. (As with other multipliers you should leave the value in 1992 at 1.0 and interpolate to a new value over time.)

Still another parameter on the production side of energy is a multiplier on investment in energy (ENINVM). If you believed that governmental tax or subsidy policies might lead to an increase or decrease in energy investment, this parameter could help you introduce such changes. The parameter increases or decreases total energy investment, letting the model continue to allocate that investment among energy types based on relative cost considerations. Be reminded again, however, that the model often "fights" changes that you introduce through such policies. For instance, an increase in energy investment forced by the multiplier ENINVM could lead to higher production, lower prices, and therefore lower profits to energy production. That could cause the model's endogenous investment mechanism to begin decreasing the investment to which you apply the multiplier.

We pointed out earlier that there may actually be more potential for leverage on the demand side of the energy system than on the supply side, especially for resource poor regions like Japan. On the demand side, there are two key parameters. The first is, again, a direct multiplier on energy demand (ENDEMM). The second is the price elasticity of energy demand (ELASDE). Note that this elasticity in the base case has a negative sign (as prices rise, energy demand falls). In spite of many attempts to estimate this parameter based on data about prices and demand, its value still remains quite uncertain.

Both oil importers and oil exporters also have the option of setting direct limits on the amount of oil and gas that they import or export. A parameter representing energy trade limits (ENTL) allows you to introduce such policy choices. Normally the value is zero, indicating no interference with market determination of trade. A value greater than 0.001 will limit exports to the value you set, in billions of barrels of oil per year. A value less than –0.001 will similarly limit imports. Because IFs is structured for long-term rather than short-term forecasting, it is probable that the economies in IFs adjust somewhat too easily and too quickly to such limits. Nonetheless, these limits can have substantial impact (try, for instance, the setting of ENTL so as to disrupt the exports of OPEC between 2000 and 2005).

Finally, of course, energy exporters, and to a lesser degree energy importers, have in the past attempted to control directly the price of energy. If you set the parameter ENPRIX to any non-zero value for a region, it will turn off the endogenous computation of energy prices (ENPRI) for that region and substitute the value of ENPRIX.

Environmental Quality

One direct measure of environmental quality in IFs is the percentage of increase in atmospheric carbon dioxide (CO2PER) relative to estimates of preindustrial levels. Another is the amount of the world's land area in forest (WFORST). You can look at regional or country-specific forest areas by examining all uses of land (LD). Still another factor of potential interest is the remaining global fossil fuel reserves for oil, gas, and coal (WRESER).

It is possible to directly manipulate environmental quality through the multiplier on forest area (FORESTM). Increases or decreases in forest area will, of course, affect land available for other uses such as crop production.

In general, however, parameters that affect environmental quality are the same ones that affect the size of the population, the availability of food, or the supply of energy. Thus, essentially all of the parameters discussed in connection with those issues could also affect environmental quality. Your efforts to assure adequate food and energy supplies may have had some unintended environmental consequences. A good first step in looking at the environment is to compare the scenarios you have been developing with the base case.

For instance, your efforts to improve diets in Africa and Latin America may have intensified deforestation in those regions. Explore the interaction of food supply and deforestation. What if Latin America were to greatly slow its conversion of rain forest to other uses (including agriculture)?

▶ The target growth in land parameter (TGRLD) attempts to control the percentage increase in cropland (most of which comes from forest)—again, the model "fights" specific values. Reduce that parameter to 0.0 for Africa (only the value in the first year is meaningful). Run the model and look at the improvement this makes in the amount of land remaining under forest in Africa (LD) and even in global forest area. Note that there is no world economic cost to this change (look at world GDP). But what cost does Africa pay? Consider GDP, food prices, quality of life, starvation deaths, and the necessity of importing more agricultural products (AGM).

Explore similar scenarios for forest preservation in Latin America and South Asia, two other regions in which forest cover is decreasing rapidly. When several southern regions collectively protect their forests, does it affect the North-South gap? Do any northern regions actually benefit by exporting more and higher-priced food to the regions that protect their forests?

Some of the southern regions have argued that if the richer portion of the world wants to protect southern rain forests, it will need to share in the costs of doing so. One possibility would be additional foreign aid (controlled by AIDV, a parameter we will discuss in Chapter 6); another would be debt relief (swapping forest preservation for debt). These are sometimes called "side payments." Develop what you consider to be some options and examine whether they can provide adequate compensation for the economic losses of the South—you may need to read Chapter 6 to learn about options.

Another side payment might be improved agricultural technology to compensate for lesser amounts of land under cultivation. Were the rich countries to support more research and development (R&D) on agriculture, considerable improvements in agricultural yields could result in the South. You could introduce such improvements via the yield factor multiplier (YLM) that we used earlier.

In reality, many of the assumptions of those who focus on environmental quality are mirror images of the more technologically optimistic assumptions we introduced in some of the scenarios above. Food production has managed to stay ahead of population growth in the past four decades only as a result of rapid technological progress known as the Green Revolution. Instead of an acceleration of such progress, which the base case already assumes will continue at a generally comparable rate into the future, the growth rate could slow—environmental damage, ranging from soil loss and desertification through worsened air quality and the spread of pesticide-resistant insects, could contribute to slower growth in yields. The yield multiplier factor (YLM) can simulate such assumptions if you reduce its value below 1.0. And instead of increased ocean fish catch, overfishing could already be depleting stocks of fish and catches could decline.

The problem of growth in global atmospheric carbon dioxide is even more difficult to address than that of forest area. We suggested a possible combination of conservation (saving the forests from the ax) and technological advance (improved agricultural yields) for the problem of global forest area. We can test a similar combination for the problem of carbon dioxide. The primary source of increased CO_2 is the burning of fossil fuels (although deforestation also contributes and other gases add to the greenhouse effect). We will concentrate on the energy connection. Environmentalists suggest that the best way to address both energy and environmental problems could lie in the more efficient use of fossil fuels.

▶ We saw earlier that the energy demand multiplier (ENDEMM) allows you to explore the leverage of energy conservation (without having to specify exactly how it might come about; it might well involve that nasty word "taxes"). Reducing ENDEMM for all regions from 1.0 to 0.8 in 2010 introduces a global reduction of energy demand by 20 percent relative to the base case. Look at world energy production and price (WENP and WEP), the atmospheric carbon dioxide (CO2PER), and world GDP. Are the effects as great as you might have expected? If not, why not?

Remember how the model sometimes "fights" you. In this case, energy conservation may lead to energy price reductions (look at world energy prices, WEP). If so, the normal incentive to conserve energy—higher prices—is reduced in the scenario, and that can offset much of the conservation scenario you added. Consider what might happen if you conserved energy very carefully, reducing the price of energy for your less environmentally conscious neighbor. Again we see the problem of channeling the benefits of protecting the environment to those who pay the cost.

Moving beyond conservation to technological advance, we encounter another suggestion of environmentalists: that the world rely more heavily on renewable energy. This suggestion is often coupled with the argument that government should support more research and development (R&D) on renewable energy so as to lower its cost.

▶ We saw earlier that you can simulate a decreasing cost for renewable energy by lowering its capital cost multiplier (QEM), say from 1.0 to perhaps 0.8 by 2010. Since this multiplier controls all costs for production (operating and capital), a 20 percent reduction over such a period is very optimistic. (The cost of solar cells will, however, almost certainly fall much more than that.) Does this scenario by itself, or in combination with the conservation scenario, significantly lower the production of global fossil fuels? (Look at WEP for fossil fuels compared to the base case.) Does it control the growth of atmospheric CO_2? You may need to run the model many years to see more meaningful improvement.

We should remember, however, that environmentalists are often somewhat pessimistic and tend not to look for technological fixes to solve problems. The assumptions we have been making to this point could be too optimistic. With respect to energy, it may be that we have overestimated fossil fuel supplies—as we exploit them, the remaining supplies may become too expensive to extract. Lower values of the resource multiplier (RESORM) can introduce more conservative assumptions. And some of the costs of nuclear energy, such as disposal of wastes and decommissioning of old plants, have yet to be borne by many nuclear producers; thus the capital cost of nuclear energy (QEM) may rise in the future. Both of these possibilities have implications worth exploring for coal use and carbon dioxide increases—again, you may need to look toward 2050 to see significant effects.

The model also offers a way of investigating environmental damage to the agricultural system from the growth in atmospheric carbon dioxide that your scenarios probably failed to stop. You can raise the absolute value of an elasticity of agricultural production with growth in atmospheric carbon dioxide (ELASAC) on a region-by-region basis to posit greater damage (leaving the negative sign intact); lowering it simulates less damage and a value of 0.0 would turn off the linkage. Positive values represent improvements in agriculture as a result of warming. This elasticity could constitute a proxy for all forms of environmental damage to agriculture (ozone and acid rain are often caused by some of the same industrial and energy practices that generate carbon dioxide).

Even with conservation and technological advance, it is difficult, if not impossible, to control either deforestation or the increase in atmospheric carbon dioxide. Many eco-wholists argue that the rapid ongoing growth of human population, in combination with the efforts we make to feed, clothe, and shelter ourselves (maybe even to buy our cars), inevitably increases the pressure on the environment. Thus, they argue, one of the most fundamental changes we must make is to slow and then halt the growth of human population—to bring it into some kind of balance with the environment. You may want to investigate alternative population scenarios again now that you are focusing on environmental quality. Can you reasonably reduce population growth fast enough to have an environmental impact?

Some eco-wholists also suggest that modern developed economies are extremely wasteful of energy and other raw materials, simultaneously depleting resource bases and contributing to environmental degradation. They propose allowing slower economic growth rates (you can use GDPM) and concentrating remaining economic growth on true improvements in the quality of life. In fact, it is conceivable that the early post–World War II period was extraordinary with respect to general technological advance and that the period since the early 1970s, characterized by slower growth in productivity and economic output worldwide, better indicates the future. You may wish to experiment with more conservative assumptions.

You probably have noticed that the position with respect to technology of those who focus on environmental quality is somewhat ambivalent. Some expect or at least hope that technology will offset the hard choices they prescribe to save the environment. Others see technology as a failed hope and expect little from it in the future.

Research Questions. How might the world of the future look for an eco-wholist (as elaborated in Chapter 4)? Experiment with a variety of what you consider reasonable assumptions about environmental constraints. How much difference do they make with respect to variables such as GDP per capita, life expectancy, calories per capita, starvation, and economic growth? Develop a scenario for what you consider to be an environmentally constrained, but still reasonable, future. Look at the scenario with and without the policy measures proposed by the eco-wholists. Do such policies help the world adapt to the constraints or do they cause additional pain? Remember that it is best to develop scenarios by changing one parameter at a time and examining and understanding its impact before adding more changes.

CONCLUSION

This chapter has been the first of three in a presentation and consideration of specific issues. We have considered the causal dynamics surrounding selected issues, and we have therefore been able to investigate the leverage we may have with respect to them. Overall, we have explored the development of scenarios as a means for investigating the pursuit of progress and sustainability and the possible conflicts or trade-offs in that pursuit.

The representations in IFs of causal dynamics surrounding population, food, energy, and environmental quality come from studies by issue-specific experts (remember that the Help system within IFs elaborates the causal linkages beyond our discussion here). Those representations do not correspond strictly to the stylized discussions of eco-wholism and modernism in the last chapter. Nonetheless, the insights of those two worldviews have been useful in considering the possible tension between the achievement of sustainability and the pursuit of progress.

In the same manner, the next chapter will investigate a range of global economic issues. The tension between the attempts by economic liberals to maximize well-being and the desires of structuralists to achieve some level of equality will give a general shape to our discussion. Remember that our ultimate goal is to facilitate making choices in the face of uncertainty.

SIX

□ □ □

The Pursuit of Economic
Well-Being and Equality

Economic issues always sit high on the agendas of domestic and inter-national decisionmakers when they consider the future. Economic growth has come to be a fixture of the global economy over the past 200 years, and leaders devote much effort to selection of policies that will sustain or even increase growth rates. At first glance, they appear to have been very successful. Between 1960 and 1990 the global product increased by a factor of 2.9, while global population increased only by a factor of 1.4.

Yet there are at least two flies in the ointment. First, in the past two decades global economic performance has faltered. During the 1960s, the world economy grew at an average of 4.9 percent annually. In the 1970s that fell to 3.4 percent, and in the 1980s it dropped further to 2.7 percent (CIA, 1991b: 26).[1]

Second, inequality, both between and within countries, has increased. The per capita gap in GDP between the richest 20 percent of the world's population and the poorest 20 percent has increased from 30:1 in 1960 to 61:1 in 1991 (UNDP, 1994: 35).[2] Figure 6.1 suggests how overwhelming the inequality and poverty of the world appears: In 1990 a large majority of the world's population lived in countries with a GDP per capita of less than $1,000 (World Bank, 1991: 204–205). At the same time, countries with a GDP per capita of more than $15,000 controlled most of the world's economic output.

Although inequality within *developing countries* has increased for many years, much data suggest that income distribution within *developed countries* has also been worsening again since the 1970s, after decades of improvement. Even more, wealth distribution appears also to be deteriorating.

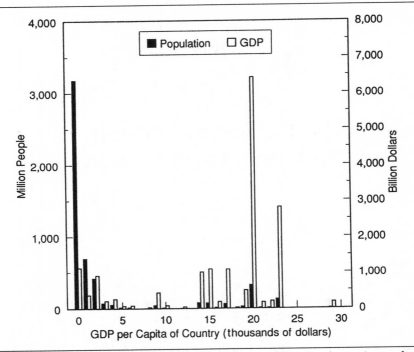

FIGURE 6.1 Distribution of global population and gross domestic product. *Source:* World Bank, *World Development Report 1991* (New York: Oxford University Press, 1991), 204–205 and 208–209.

Figure 6.2 shows that following a long period of movement toward greater equality, the distribution of wealth in the United States began to worsen, especially in the 1980s. Improvements also ceased in other more-developed countries, and the wealth gap between rich and poor may be widening throughout much of the developed world.

Chapter 4 outlined the debates over these issues that rage among commercial liberals, mercantilists, and structuralists. The purpose of this chapter is to focus on some specific issues of global political economy in order to assess how much leverage we have with respect to them.

CONTEMPORARY ISSUES

Although competing worldviews draw our attention directly to the possible tension between growth and distribution as ends, national and global debates tend to focus on narrower, more instrumental issues. Specifically, debates over trade and investment take center stage. In re-

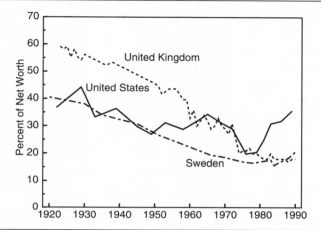

FIGURE 6.2   Share of marketable net worth held by top 1 percent of wealth hold-ers. *Source:* Edward N. Wolff, *Top Heavy: A Study of the Increasing Inequality of Wealth in America* (New York: Twentieth Century Fund Press, 1995), 23. Reprinted with permission from the Twentieth Century Fund, New York. Raw data courtesy of Edward Wolff.

cent years the public mood has somewhat soured on a third instrumental focus of policy, income transfers. Nonetheless, this tool remains a key pol-icy issue around the world. We turn to these issues, focusing on the lever-age that humans have in pursuit of their values.

Trade

In 1995 the international community heralded the arrival of a new in-stitution, the World Trade Organization (WTO). At the regional level, the European Union (EU) has officially replaced the European Community (EC), marking a substantial advance in the integration of economic mar-kets. Similarly, the United States, Canada, and Mexico entered into the North American Free Trade Agreement (NAFTA). NAFTA members held talks with Chile in 1995 concerning further expansion. The continued ad-vance of such organizations testifies to the strength of belief that markets open to trade and capital flows will bring economic benefit.

The standard liberal theory that has dominated both academia and global policy for most of this century posits that when two parties enter into trade, both benefit from it. The mutual benefit has several roots. One is the comparative advantage that trading partners have as a result of varying factor endowments. That is, when one country has a relative surplus of labor, it makes sense for that country to specialize in labor-intensive goods and services, just as a country with a relative surplus of oil and natural gas can efficiently specialize in its production. A second reason that trade can be beneficial is that there may be economies of scale that accrue to the production of larger volumes of the same good. A country producing aircraft may find that the costs of developing a new aircraft type are so great that the unit cost will drop to reasonable levels only with a very high volume of production; that country's trading partner may find that the same logic applies to large ships. Thus, they should specialize and trade. A third reason is that trade competition itself may lead to increased rates of technical innovation as competitors seek to maintain market share. Liberals support markets open to imports and producers who act aggressively to export. The causal logic of this position and the policy prescriptions that follow from it are clear: Freer trade promotes economic growth; therefore, remove barriers to free trade.

So-called strategic trade theorists seldom question the success of trade in enhancing the *combined welfare* of trading partners. Instead, although they may not leap to the labels, they are more likely in the tradition of realists or neomercantilists to ask questions about the *relative benefits* of trade. One country may realize great benefits and economies of scale by specializing in consumer electronics; it is less clear, however, that another country will gain equally by specializing in oil production because of a large factor endowment. The first country puts large numbers of both skilled and unskilled workers into the workplace to produce electronic goods and develops a labor force that might easily move not only into new electronic products but also into transportation equipment controlled by them, robotics, and so on. The second country may find that its oil production requires much capital but puts relatively few people to work and does not develop transferable skills and spin-off industries. Strategic trade theorists in the United States suggest that U.S. exports to Japan of timber and farm products, in exchange for consumer electronics, might have this unequal character. The strategic trade theorist also points out that industries at the cutting edge of technology generally have a higher profit rate, in part because of limited competition, than those that have been widely developed around the world for many years.

We saw in Chapter 4 that the structuralist worldview generally elaborates this same line of argument, while emphasizing the relationship of less developed countries with more developed ones. Moreover, structuralists suggest that over time the trading relationship can progressively deteriorate for less developed countries. Specifically, the terms of trade may shift in such a way that the weaker countries need to export more and more of a good simply to import the same amount of other goods from stronger countries.

Southern countries question their long-term position in the global division of labor. Although with industrialization they have rapidly become much more than the global hewers of wood and drawers of water (that is, providers of primary goods), they still tend to specialize in goods with limited technical sophistication. As many producers of such goods struggle for declining markets in part abandoned by the more developed countries, it is common that deterioration in **terms of trade** (the prices of what they export relative to the prices of their imports) plague the new exporters. Structuralists argue that those at the bottom of the global economy's totem pole constantly face markets that weaken just as they come to dominate them. Even the International Monetary Fund (IMF) has calculated that the terms of trade shifted against developing countries at an annual rate of 2.2 percent between 1982 and 1991 (IMF, 1990b: 152).[3]

The causal logic and prescriptions of mercantilist and structuralist positions are also clear: Trade unequally benefits trading partners; therefore, manipulate trade to gain as much benefit as possible. Given the support that this position has found in both developed and developing countries, it is not surprising that decisionmakers around the world, especially in countries and periods in which imports exceed exports, face pressure from their citizens to "do something" in order to protect jobs and boost the local economy—to exercise the leverage they have. From the early 1970s into the 1990s, the United States found itself in this position, especially relative to Japan, a country that ran trade surpluses often easily linked (for instance, through automobile exports) to the trade deficits of the United States. Those surpluses did not seem to diminish over time as liberal theory had predicted.

In response to such public demands, the United States has pressured a number of countries, especially Japan, to restrict their U.S. sales of goods such as textiles, steel, and automobiles. It argues that the Japanese government relies on mercantilist protection of the home market from outside penetration while supporting export growth, a pattern incompatible with a liberal trading order. One of the tools the U.S. government has used is selective retaliation against sectors of the Japanese economy (such as semiconductors) in a tit-for-tat policy. It is easy to see how a strong economic power like Japan, pursuing mercantilist (realist) economic policies, could engender action-and-reaction dynamics very reminiscent of arms races, resulting in the retaliatory closing by countries of markets to each other.

It is not only Japan that poses a challenge to the liberal trading order of the post–World War II period. A number of countries have similarly, if more recently, adopted export-promotion policies that seek to strengthen their domestic economies by sharply increasing exports. Some of these countries, including Taiwan, South Korea, Singapore, and Hong Kong, belong to the set of newly industrialized countries (NICs). Although a few of these countries, most notably Hong Kong, also open their domestic markets to goods and thus act in a manner compatible with a liberal trading order, others have continued the mercantilist practice of protecting domestic markets while aggressively pursuing foreign ones.

The official advice of the North to the South in a variety of forums remains liberalization—entrance into the world economy with as few restrictions on trade and as few domestic market interventions as possible. Yet less developed countries (LDCs) often find that when they do substantially increase exports of a class of goods, such as clothing, shoes, or consumer electronics, developed countries begin to put up barriers. Needless to say, in light of such behavior, the official liberal advice can appear rather hypocritical to them.

The competing causal analyses give rise to a number of specific questions concerning choice in the face of uncertainty and the leverage that we have with respect to economic well-being and levels of equality. How actively should countries pursue free markets? To what degree might selected protectionist measures weaken or help local economies? How do states committed to free trade deal with a state that takes advantage of open markets elsewhere but protects its own?

Investment

There is considerably less debate about the importance of increasing investment in order to enhance economic performance than there is about trade issues. The standard approach to forecasting GDP is to represent it as a function of several factors of production: Physical capital (K) and labor (L) are the most common, although some analysts supplement them with land, technology, or other inputs to production. To be more specific, one widely used representation is

$$GDP = aK^\alpha L^\beta \text{ (where "a" is a "scaling" factor and alpha and beta are parameters that determine the relative contributions of capital and labor)}$$

The GDP of all countries finds its way via the spending, saving, and taxation decisions of individuals, corporations, and governments to four principal end uses: household consumption on a wide range of goods and services; governmental expenditures for defense, education, health, and other purposes; reinvestment in capital stock; and net exports. The reinvestment in capital stocks normally is sufficient to cause those stocks to grow and therefore to increase GDP in future years.

This widely shared understanding of the dynamic underlying economic growth causes countries automatically to attempt policy formulation that will increase individual, corporate, and governmental savings and therefore reinvestment in capital. Although it sounds as though it would be a relatively simple matter to achieve these goals by this means, it is not. In spite of substantial governmental efforts, the portion of GDP that the high-income Western countries as a whole reinvested in capital between 1970 and 1990 varied only from 18.9 percent to 22.7 percent (World Bank, 1991b: 52–53). Debates rage over the degree to which intervention by government via policies on taxation, spending, or interest rates can increase savings and investment. Therefore, they also rage over whether government should so intervene. A corollary debate concerns how much investment governments should undertake directly (such as in the infrastructure, or public capital of roads, highways, information systems, and so on).

One of the biggest debates centers on the possible trade-off between investment in physical capital and investment in labor force quality, sometimes called **human capital.** For instance, government could spend on highways, subsidize private capital via lower taxes or research and development, *or* "invest" via education and health care in human capital, because better-educated and healthier work forces produce more (the value of "L" in the above equation increases).

In short, consensus surrounds the general exhortation to increase investment, but debate surrounds the definition of exactly what investment is and the causal dynamics by which policy decisions affect it. Moreover, given limited governmental resources, it should not be surprising that laborers would be more enthusiastic about government investment in human capital than are the owners of capital. In spite of such debates, it is safe to say that governments everywhere seek to increase investment and therefore economic growth.

The Interface of Trade and Investment Issues: International Transfers

Investment also takes place across international borders, raising important questions in the process. Countries, especially less developed ones, often seek to attract capital from abroad in the hopes of increasing their GDPs. Funds flow across interstate borders in several forms: foreign aid, public and private loans to governments or companies, purchase of corporate shares (portfolio investment), and direct investment in companies (equity investment). Interstate fund flows may or may not enhance investment levels in the target countries. For instance, recipients of foreign aid might use the money to build physical infrastructure such as roads and electricity-producing dams, or they might spend it on military equipment that contributes little or nothing to economic growth. (Figure 6.3 traces flows of aid from the Organization of Economic Cooperation

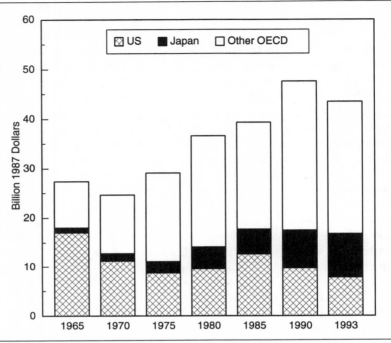

FIGURE 6.3 Net flows of development assistance by donor. *Source:* World Bank, *World Development Report 1992* (New York: Oxford University Press, 1992), 254–255; World Bank, *World Development Report 1995* (New York: Oxford University Press, 1995), 198–199.

and Development, which includes almost all of the economically developed, market economies, since 1965.) Although direct investment from abroad into, say, a new textile factory may seem more nearly certain to enhance overall investment in the recipient country, it may also lead some domestic entrepreneurs to divert their own investment funds abroad or even to redirect them into consumption.

In short, attracting money from abroad has somewhat uncertain implications for the enhancement of investment. Those implications become even more uncertain when, like loans or short-term investment, the funds may again leave the country that attracted them. Third World countries attracted many loans in the 1970s, some of which they used wisely to enhance domestic savings and investment, and some of which simply increased consumption. Whatever uses the loans were put to, LDCs have had a very difficult time repaying their foreign indebtedness from that period. In 1982 the total external debt of LDCs was $836.1 billion; by 1991 that figure had grown in nominal terms to $1,313.5 billion (IMF, 1990b:

184). The debt equaled about 120 percent of exports at both ends of the decade (it peaked at 172 percent of exports in 1986). During the 1980s and early 1990s the international community sought to relieve the LDCs of some of that burden through many schemes: forgiving parts of the debt, reducing interest rates or lengthening repayment terms, and even swapping debt for environmental preserves or ownership of formerly state-controlled industries. For much of the South, particularly countries in Latin America and Africa, foreign indebtedness remains, however, a key international economic issue of the 1990s. After the massive outflow of private funds from Mexico in 1995, the concern of LDCs broadened to include equity investment as well as loans.

It is also unclear whether funds from abroad can improve economic well-being in developed countries. It is important to understand that the inflow and outflow of funding from abroad is closely related to the trade balance of a country. A country like Japan, with a large surplus of exports over imports, achieves that surplus by saving more than it invests domestically. We represent that relationship with an identity that must hold in the economic accounts of all countries:

$$\text{Savings} - \text{Investment}_{domestic} = \text{Exports} - \text{Imports} = \text{Investment}_{foreign}$$

The driving forces in this relationship are complex: Does Japan export so much relative to imports because it has a surplus of savings relative to domestic investment demand? Or do its large net savings reflect the export-oriented character of its corporations and government policies? In any case, Japan uses its surplus of savings over domestic investment to send funds abroad for foreign investment opportunities, buying or building commercial property, factories, stocks, and bonds around the world. Although countries like the United States and Britain often welcome the inflow of investment into industries and its promise of jobs and growth, they also worry, just as LDCs do, that a subsequent return of funds to Japan will create difficulties. Hence, many developed countries have long urged Japan to attack the two imbalances of the above equation by (1) consuming more domestically and saving less and (2) increasing imports relative to exports.

Economic policymakers clearly believe that, both domestically and internationally, we have considerable leverage via trade and investment policy over economic well-being and the distributions of income and wealth. At the same time, however, there are very substantial debates over the causal dynamics of the underlying systems and therefore over the appropriate application of leverage. In the next section we use the IFs model to further explore the issues. You should understand, however, that the answers the model provides are very much built into the model.

Thus its purpose is to assist you in thinking about the issues, arguments, and competing understandings, not to provide "the answers."

EXPLORATION OF INTERNATIONAL FUTURES

In this section we use the IFs model to explore global political-economic futures. Chapter 3 explained the mechanics of using the model. Return to it or use the Help system of IFs if you need a review.

Chapter 5 pointed out that the first step in scenario analysis is to pick some indicators of importance. Only then can you manipulate parameters that you believe real-world policies may affect and analyze potential leverage. Because the focus in this chapter is on the growth of well-being and the level of equality, you will want to look at worldwide and country or region-specific GDP (WGDP and GDP) and at the growth rates in those values (WGDPR and GDPR). Take some time to do an analysis of those values over time in the base case. There are, however, many critics of the emphasis on purely economic indicators of well-being. You may want to also look again at the physical quality of life index (WPQLI and PQLI) or other specific measures of well-being that you determine to be important, such as life expectancy, literacy, and so on.

As you turn to issues of distribution and equality, you will also want to make the absolute and relative values of North-South gaps (NSGAPA and NSGAPR) important indicators in your analysis. Explore those variables in the base case and look in more detail at economic development in some of the poorer global regions. IFs also includes an indicator of domestic income distribution (INCDIS). Specifically, that measure shows what portion of all household income in a country or region flows to the poorest 20 percent of the population. Unfortunately, that measure is an "exogenous" variable in IFs. That is, you can change it externally to the model and thereby see its impact on other variables such as fertility and mortality rates. You will not, however, see changes in it endogenously or internally to the model, because no equations of the model calculate it. You will need to focus your policy analysis concerning income distribution primarily on the global distribution.

When we reviewed thinking about leverage with respect to growth and distribution, we focused on three specific issues: trade, investment, and transfer policies. We will organize our use of IFs in the same way.

Trade

Markets and Restriction of Them: Trade and State Intervention   We want primarily to investigate the implications of openness of markets. We will spend less time on terms of trade. To explore the growth of trade in the base case, look at world trade as a percentage of the world economy (WTRADE). The advocates of free and expanded trade argue that continued growth in trade as a percentage of the economy carries with it many benefits. Tariffs and various nontariff barriers to trade threaten these benefits. Tariffs are taxes on imports and thereby raise the price and reduce the volume of imports. Various nontariff barriers to trade, such as quotas or quality restrictions on imports (health standards on food imports, for example), have the same general effect.

▶ Does IFs show the benefits of greater trade and fewer trade barriers that liberals claim? To explore this question, manipulate the protection multiplier (PROTECM) country by country. When the value is 1.0, there is no change in tariff and nontariff barriers to trade. A value of 2.0 effectively doubles the world prices a region faces on all of its imports. As the value approaches 0.9, the price of imports is cut by 10 percent (the model will not allow you to reduce prices by more than that).

You might begin by asking about the consequences should the United States move away from free trade as many suggest is likely (and some say desirable) in the next decade. For instance, introduce a scenario that effectively doubles the price of goods coming into the United States by ramping PROTECM for the country from 1.0 to 2.0 between the initial year and 2005. What are your expectations? Consider also the possible economic consequences for Japan.

If the global economic impact of U.S. protection is less than you expected, one reason might be that trade protection, like military spending, is often subject to an action-reaction dynamic. IFs does not build in any automatic reaction by other regions to U.S. protectionist measures. You must do that through your scenario(s).

▶ Introduce proportionate reaction to the increased U.S. protection by all other regions in the system (representing an overall breakdown in the liberal trading order). You can do this by ramping up PROTECM for all regions. Look again at the results for the economies of the world. You might also experiment with a severe global trade war—tariffs of perhaps 300 percent. What does it do to global economic growth?

Almost everyone agrees that trade enhances aggregate welfare—the results of these scenarios suggest that the structure of IFs carries that causal logic. Commercial liberals recognize that the LDCs face a particularly demanding world, but they argue that the appropriate response is to use the market fully, not to withdraw from it. They point to the economic success of Taiwan, Korea, and other export-promoting countries as evidence. Go back to the base case (use Files from the Main Menu to Open it) and develop a scenario that incorporates an export promotion policy for the region called "rest of the developed world" (the region that contains many of the NICs like Taiwan and Korea).

▶ There is an export shift (XSHIFT) parameter in IFs that allows you to "force" exports of countries onto the global market. Values of 0 leave exports unchanged from the base case, but positive values increase exports. The effects of XSHIFT are cumulative. That is, a value of 0.05 adds about 5 percent to exports for that year and all subsequent years until other factors in the model dampen the increase. Thus it is best to set the value of XSHIFT fairly low (such as 0.05) for all years. Apply your scenario, for example, to the exports (X) of the rest of the developed world. Then look at economic and quality-of-life indicators. Does this change have any affect on other regions?

How does trade improve economic performance in IFs? Were there both a high level of sectoral disaggregation and a detailed representation of factor costs in IFs, the benefits of trade from comparative advantage and specialization would be implicit. IFs does not have that level of detail. Instead it relies on a mechanism that relates manufactured imports to the efficiency of production. As the ratio of manufactured imports to the GDP increases, the productivity of production in all sectors increases (this relationship is controlled by an elasticity of productivity with manufacturing imports, PRODME). In essence, the linkage serves as a surrogate for two trade benefits: efficiency gains through comparative advantage and productivity gains through the import of manufactures, especially of capital goods that bring advanced technology.

Terms of Trade   Chapter 4 pointed out that even free-trade skeptics seldom question that trade increases aggregate economic benefit for all parties. Instead, they argue that some parties benefit more, perhaps even much more, than others. The key to such claims lies often with terms of trade—the price a country receives for its exports relative to the price of its imports.

In the real world it is difficult to change terms of trade. A country cannot simply begin to charge more for that which it exports and expect thereby to earn more. Charging more would dampen demand and elicit competing supply; the country might ultimately earn less. It may be possible, however, to shift production and exports from goods of less value to those of more value, a strategy that Japan has pursued.

▶ You can explore the North-South terms of trade in the base case, as computed by the model, by looking at the computed variable TERMTR. Does it show a clear trend upward (more relative value for southern exports) or downward (less value for southern exports)? There is considerable debate among those who have studied the terms of trade as to how much the trend historically has shifted to the disadvantage of the South.

We can see how important terms of trade are for the South, however, by simulating the financial impact of an improvement in them. The terms-of-trade parameter (TERMX) is a multiplier on the value of southern exports (and proportionately reduces the value of northern exports). If you change it gradually from 1.0 to perhaps 1.2 in 2005, you can see the impact that a 20 percent improvement in the terms of trade would have for the South (even if it appears inconceivable that real-world policies might accomplish such a shift).

Run the model with such a change and look at the new terms of trade (TERMTR). You might want to look with special care at a particular southern region, such as Africa. What happens to the value of exports (X) and the cost of imports (M)? What happens to the GDP per capita (GDPPC) and the physical quality of life (PQLI) relative to the base case? Does the improvement in export earnings allow Africa to import any more food (AGM)? If so, does that have any affect on potential starvation deaths (SDEATH) in Africa? Overall, how does a change in the terms of trade seem to compare with foreign aid (to be discussed below) in its potential for improving the existence of Africans? Why?

The results of this scenario will likely be very much as you anticipated if it is projected just 30 years. By 2050, however, the scenario produces some "counterintuitive" or perverse results—regions that you expect to benefit from terms of trade intervention on their behalf do less well than in the base case. Explore the results carefully to see why, perhaps by looking at external debt levels (XDEBT) and exchange rates (EXRATE). The discussion later in this chapter on foreign aid will also help you understand such results.

Research Questions. How much benefit do countries gain if they open themselves up to imports? Can one country gain that benefit unilaterally, or must many countries or regions open markets simultaneously? If all countries and regions open markets, do they share equally in benefits? Are the costs of protection comparable to the gains of free trade?

Investment

Fostering Capital Investment Most discussion on investment focuses on increasing physical capital and we will begin ours there. We will then turn, however, to human capital. Commercial liberals devote much of their attention to limiting interventions in interstate trade, and they also decry much involvement by governments in their domestic economies. They argue, for instance, that price controls and subsidies to selected industries either discourage or render less efficient much of the savings and investment that the economy requires for rapid growth. A world to the liking of the commercial liberals would be one in which government actions freed up substantially more savings and created opportunities for investment. Both mercantilists and structuralists see some opportunities for direct governmental investment.

▶ You can simulate increased investment (however it might be encouraged) with the investment multiplier (INVM). When INVM is 1.0, the model computes investment according to internal rules. When the value is 1.5, investment would be 50 percent higher than normal; similarly, a value of 0.5 would reduce investment by 50 percent. Investment changes (I) come at the expense of, or are made to the benefit of, consumption (C).[4] INVM is a regionalized parameter, so if you want to see an entire world in which investment increases you will need to change it for all regions. There have been, however, many calls for increased investment in the United States and you may want to look at the impact in that country alone.

Research Questions. Is a country's leverage over economic performance greater with trade or with investment policies? How much additional economic growth can countries achieve if they either promote exports or increase investment? Because investment increases come at the expense of consumption, can less economically developed countries use this strategy as effectively, or does it have short-term implications for the poorer countries (loss of consumption power, declines in quality of life) that are unacceptable? (For example, can Africa increase investment without worsening immediate food problems?)

Investment in Human Capital   One of the internal strategies for development that many structuralists propose is to focus attention on the poor by providing for the basic human needs of citizens—such as food, education, and health care. You can develop scenarios that devote special attention to the satisfaction of those needs by manipulating government spending on education and health (using GK).

▶ Try shifting governmental spending into health and education (and thereby automatically away from the military) and see the implications. Do not forget also to consider the cost this change may or may not have in terms of power. You might focus on India.

International Transfers

North-South Transfers and the North-South Gap   To this point we have looked at internal resource allocations. We shift now to interstate flows. Although you could undertake some of these same analyses among developed countries, we will focus on North-South relations. Look again at the ratio of GDPs per capita in North and South—that is, at the relative

North-South gap (NSGAPR)—and also at the absolute difference in GDPs per capita in the two global regions (NSGAPA). The persistence of these gaps has led to many proposals for substantial aid programs from northern to southern countries.

▶ A negative aid value parameter (AIDV) specifies the percent of GDP that donor countries give as aid. (That value is unlikely to exceed –1.0 [or 1 percent] in even a very substantial North-South aid program; values like –0.3 are now common.) In this scenario you will presumably want to change the outflow of aid for several aid-giving regions, such as the United States, the EU, and Japan, perhaps ramping AIDV up to −1.0 from its initial value over a 5- or 10-year period. (CAUTION: If you were to alter the values of AIDV in the initial year, the model would compensate to preserve initial conditions—instead, gradually increase aid levels, leaving initial values unchanged.)

The aid given by donor countries goes into a pool that the model then splits among recipients. Positive values of the same parameter (AIDV) mark a region as an aid recipient and specify *desired* aid as a percentage of GDP for a given recipient. The model imposes the actual total aid available from donors onto the recipients proportionately according to the amount of aid desired. AID is the amount of interstate aid calculated by IFs; it is negative for donors and positive for recipients.

Once again, before you run the model with increased North-South aid transfers, consider how much impact you expect the scenario to have on the quality of life or GDP per capita in both donor and recipient regions. How much might the increased aid narrow the absolute and relative North-South gaps? How much impact will the aid have on different recipient regions? Overall, how much leverage does the model suggest we have with this policy "handle" and how does that compare with your expectations?

We saw earlier that change in terms of trade can produce counterintuitive results in the long run. If you look at the impact of increased aid receipts on Africa in the very long run, you may see similar results for similar reasons. Especially if the model results differ from your expectations, you will want to know more about the basis for the model calculation: *How does foreign aid affect the economies of donors and recipients in IFs?*

First, aid affects governmental revenues and expenditures. For recipients it is an addition to government revenues; for donors it competes with other governmental expenditures. In both cases it therefore has secondary implications for other categories of government spending and thereby for the economy. Second, aid affects investment. Those who study aid debate how much an increment in foreign aid adds to the investment (capital formation) within the economy of the recipient. Third, aid is either a credit or debit to the external capital account balance (CAPACT). As such it will affect external debt (XDEBT), the exchange rate (EXRATE), the availability of imports (which in turn affects economic performance), and even investment as a portion of the GDP (IRA). It is this last linkage that can counterintuitively cause either improvements in terms of trade or aid inflows to increase the exchange rate, thereby dampening exports and growth.

Research Questions. Experiment with different foreign aid scenarios. Overall, do these policies prove more or less important than you expected? How do you explain the results? To help understand the results you might want to look at the relative magnitude of arms spending, foreign aid, investment, and trade. And you may want to look 25 years or more into the future for some analyses. How substantially and how rapidly could you reasonably expect a large-scale aid program to narrow the North-South cleavage?

International Borrowing and Debt   There is very often a substantial loan component to what we loosely call "foreign aid." Thus foreign aid contributes with private flows of capital to the foreign debt that accumulates with interest and restricts LDC ability to import. In fact, a considerable portion of that debt, especially for the poorest LDCs, such as many African countries, is public debt owed by one government to another.

▶ IFs computes annual international public borrowing of southern countries as a portion of the aid they receive (AIDLP). It accumulates the total external debt of regions (XDEBT) as a function of both annual trade deficits and such public borrowing. IFs computes the annual repayment of debt (LOANR) depending on the portion that must be repaid each year (REPAYR). When foreign debts are high enough, the amount that must be repaid annually can actually exceed the amount of new foreign aid, actually creating a net aid outflow from poorer to richer countries (compare LOANR with AID). Explore the values of these parameters and variables in the base case of IFs. You might focus on Africa.

Compare the condition of Africa, including the prospects of starvation deaths (SDEATH), under one or more scenarios that reduce or eliminate the loan portion of aid (giving it all as grants by setting AIDLP to 0) or that effectively forgive the outstanding loan (by reducing the repayment rate to 0.0). How much leverage do these policy variables have to improve the condition of Africans? What if *all* the "aid" came as loans?

Research Questions. What might be best-case and worst-case scenarios for the South? They might involve either high or low aid (depending on what you found about the long-term implications of aid). They might involve changes in the terms of trade, export promotion or lack of it, and governmental spending patterns. You now have many possible policy levers with which to experiment. How much leverage do you believe we realistically have to improve the economic problems of the South and which policies take advantage of that leverage?

CONCLUSION

This chapter moved us from considerations of progress and sustainability to those of economic growth and equality. Economic liberals tell us about comparative advantage, division of labor, and the virtue of free trade. They promise some ultimate progress in equality but prescribe attention to economic efficiency. Mercantilists (realists) remind us that states remain central actors and will pursue power and wealth, even at the expense of free trade. Structuralists describe the world in a fashion that perhaps owes more to realists than to liberals. While emphasizing the problems and potential of the South rather than of great powers, structuralists also perceive, for instance, control by the powerful of the terms of trade. Different values and understandings direct our attention to different issues and policy levers. Once again you must draw your own conclusions about the relative or combined merit of the worldviews and the leverage we have with respect to our future.

SEVEN

□ □ □

The Pursuit of Security and Peace

No value is more important to humans than their physical security. History traces the efforts of individuals and groups to protect their persons, their territory, and their wealth against the predations of others. In the twentieth century, the development of ever more powerful weaponry, including of course nuclear weapons, has both continued the search for security and complicated it. The end of the Cold War has in no way fundamentally altered human attention to security needs.

At the same time, however, the development of weapons of mass destruction, capable perhaps even of the extinction of the human race, has also intensified the search for peace. We have developed regional and global institutions that are stronger than any of their predecessors. We have tied our economies and societies more closely together with trade and interpersonal contact than ever before in history.

This chapter explores the leverage that we have in the pursuit of security and peace. The elaboration of realist and liberal worldviews in Chapter 4 suggested that there is considerable complexity in our efforts to attain both values. In some cases efforts to enhance security and peace appear compatible; in other cases there may be trade-offs. This discussion will investigate some of the causal linkages surrounding these issues but will leave the ultimate decisions with respect to policy choices to the reader.

CONTEMPORARY ISSUES

The Cold War is over. The armed forces of the former Soviet Union have abandoned their roles as occupiers (some said protectors) of Central

Europe. In fact, the Soviet Union has collapsed into fifteen independent republics and Russian forces have now departed from some of those—its forces remain as protectors (some say occupiers) of most. Defense spending throughout the former Soviet empire has collapsed precipitously. Moreover, nearly all political units of the former empire have denounced communism and officially instituted liberal democracy and opted for market economies. Obviously the reality of transformation will lag behind the official commitments to political and economic reforms, and some turmoil is inevitable, but the old bipolar world order, centered on the conflict between East and West, has collapsed.

There is now much discussion of a New World Political Order. What might be the character of that order? How should we bring it into being? In general terms, this chapter draws upon two competing visions. The first emphasizes the enduring nature of security concerns and the importance of giving them primary and active attention. The second stresses the opportunity for significantly advancing an emerging global community.

The breadth of support by Americans in 1991 of President Bush's call for action against Iraq after its invasion of Kuwait owed much to his creative fusing of these two disparate visions of the New World Order. On the one hand, the United States took strong military action in the name of preserving the balance of power in the Middle East and preventing one country from securing territory, oil resources, and nuclear weapons in an effort to upset that balance. On the other hand, a global coalition came together under the auspices of the United Nations to give military action the blessing of what appeared to be a newly unified global community.

The first vision stresses that important security threats remain. The former Soviet Union poses the most obvious and near-term threats to Western democracies. There are myriad difficulties associated with the breakdown of the country, including: the control by three republics of nuclear weapons; the possibility that some weapons will fall into the hands of other countries or even terrorist forces; and the danger of conflicts among and within the republics. In the somewhat longer run, a Russia liberated of costly external burdens could undergo still another political change and emerge as a revitalized threat. Threat perception depends, of course, on the perceiver. Russia, China, and even some Western democracies look at the overwhelming military superiority of the United States as a potential danger.

In addition, there is the growing military strength of many countries in the less developed world, especially China. As Figure 7.1 shows, military expenditures in the South have risen faster than those in the North for many years (the ratio has narrowed from 11:1 in 1960 to 4:1 in 1991). In addition, an increasing number of countries have one or both foundations of global nuclear capacity: an atomic bomb and missiles capable of launching satellites into orbit and therefore delivering atomic bombs. Table 7.1 documents the proliferation of the missile capabilities (Table 2.6 earlier presented information on the proliferation of nuclear capabilities). Many other countries, including Iraq, North Korea, and Pakistan, seek or have sought both capabilities.

Finally, there is always the possibility that one or more of the countries that the United States now considers allies could become a military adversary. Realists emphasize that the era of goodwill among countries in the early 1920s succumbed very quickly to intense rivalries. The economic pressures of the Great Depression pitted countries against each other in economic competition, and the rise of fascist and militaristic governments quickly squelched perceptions that World War I had made the world safe for democracy and therefore peaceful coexistence. In the

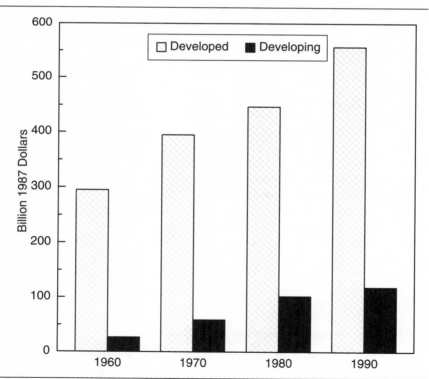

FIGURE 7.1 Military expenditures of developed and developing countries. *Source:* Ruth Leger Sivard, *World Military and Social Expenditures 1993* (Washington, D.C.: World Priorities, 1993), 42.

TABLE 7.1 Satellite Launch Capabilities

	Date of First Launch	Total Launches
USSR/CIS	October 1957	2,961
United States	February 1958	1,214
France	November 1965	32
Japan	February 1970	61
China	April 1970	38
Britain	October 1971	18
India	July 1980	17
Israel	September 1988	NA
European Space Agency		34
Germany		15
Canada		12

Sources: Christian Science Monitor, May 15, 1990, 13; World Almanac, *The World Almanac and Book of Facts 1996* (New York: World Almanac, 1995), 318; Leonard S. Spector with Jacqueline R. Smith, *Nuclear Ambitions* (Boulder: Westview Press, 1990).

post–Cold War era we could foresee similar economic desperation and comparable political changes.

The second contemporary vision emphasizes that global community is developing. The trend analysis of Chapter 2 traced the global spread of democracy and the rapid growth of intergovernmental and international nongovernmental organizations. Both have advanced quite steadily during this century and their cumulative growth is remarkable. Regional and global organizations, especially the European Union and the United Nations, have become stronger. Moreover, there is a grouping of countries that we increasingly call a "zone of peace." There has been no conflict since 1945 among the rich and democratic countries of the European Union, North America, and Asia (Japan, Australia, and New Zealand).

These two visions of a secure and peaceful future give rise to a number of more specific issues. We consider several of those in the rest of this chapter, as always looking for the leverage that we may have to influence events.

Military Spending and the Pursuit of Power

Memos leaked from the U.S. Department of Defense in 1992 suggested that the United States could and should actively pursue unilateralism— that it had the option of strengthening its position as the only superpower. Figure 7.2 shows the military outlays of today's four largest spenders since 1983 and confirms that dominant position. A subsequent

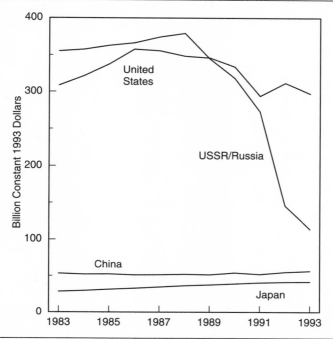

FIGURE 7.2   Military spending of great powers. *Source:* United States Arms Control and Disarmament Agency, *World Military Expenditures and Arms Transfers 1993* (Washington, D.C.: US ACDA, 1995).

statement of U.S. policy moved away from support for unilateralism. Yet the initial document highlighted one of the most important questions now facing decisionmakers around the world—namely, the optimal size of military spending. Do relatively higher military spending levels strengthen a country's security position and increase its power?

A first reaction might be that the answer is obviously yes. Yet even a little further reflection can quickly call that answer into doubt. For instance, some have argued that the real winner of the Cold War was not the United States, but Japan. Whereas the United States spent 5 percent or more of its GDP on defense for nearly forty years, Japan spent 1 percent or less. There are many reasons for the great economic success (and power) of Japan during the Cold War, but its lower military spending may well be an important one.

Japan's situation raises a fundamentally important definitional question: What exactly is power? How should one weight economic strength and military capability (or other factors, such as population size and technological prowess) in assessing it? One reason that analysis of security issues remains so difficult is that we have minimal consensus on a definition for the key concept in the discussion.

Chapter 4 outlined a second reason for caution about an assumption that higher military spending can enhance security. Arms spending imposes costs on other actors, as well as on the spending state, by threatening their security. That often gives rise to spending by the threatened states in a dynamic known as action-reaction. Although high military spending by a sole superpower could extend a security umbrella over some states that would dampen their own spending, it is hard to believe that the United States could long sustain high spending without engendering reactions elsewhere. By no means all arms races lead to war, but we know from history that many do.

Lewis Fry Richardson, a British meteorologist, devoted a substantial portion of his life to studying arms races. Early in this century he formulated a pair of equations that, with variations, analysts still rely upon to understand arms races (Richardson, 1960).[1]

$$XSPENDING_{t+1} = k \times YCAPABILITIES_t - a \times XCAPABILITIES_t + g$$

$$YSPENDING_{t+1} = l \times XCAPABILITIES_t - b \times YCAPABILITIES_t + h$$

The first equation says that military spending in country X at time $t + 1$ responds to capabilities of country Y in the last time period (dependent on a "reactivity" coefficient k), but is reduced by country X's own capability. Finally, a third coefficient (g) is called the "grievance" term and sets a basic level of spending independent of the dynamic terms. The second equation says that country Y sets its spending levels in the same fashion, although the parameters will normally differ.

The first term in the two equations, reactions to the capabilities of others, tends to set up the positive feedback loop of the security dilemma as we saw it in Figure 4.5. The second term of each equation, sometimes called the "burden" term, opens up the possibility that earlier spending will dampen arms races (it adds a negative feedback loop). Dampening will be especially probable if the parameter in the burden term is actually a variable that grows with the burden that arms spending can put on economic performance (consider the collapse of Soviet spending with the weakening of the country's economy).

This equation system suggests some points of leverage: Decrease reactivity to arms spending by others (for instance, alliances can substitute for reactive spending), increase the burden coefficient by fully recognizing the costs of spending, and resolve old grievances. Perhaps even more, however, the system emphasizes the tremendous uncertainty that surrounds the causal relationship between military spending and security. In even a bilateral relationship, the coefficients that bind two countries together are highly uncertain and subject to fairly rapid change (much more so than parameters in demographics or even in much of economics).

In addition, of course, security relationships are seldom strictly bilateral. The modern system includes many "great powers," minimally China, France, Germany, Great Britain, India, Japan, Russia, and the United States. And it is important in considering military spending not to focus only on the major powers of the contemporary system. The military spending of the global South has been growing at a considerably more rapid rate than that of the global North. Countries such as Iran, Iraq, Pakistan, Indonesia, South Korea, and Brazil have built powerful militaries in the past three decades. The Iran-Iraq war, which inevitably drew close attention from the oil-importing countries, and then the Iraqi invasion of Kuwait, which elicited an active response, indicate the importance of military developments, including ongoing nuclear proliferation throughout the world.

In short, the causal dynamics that link military spending to power are not simple ones. Similarly, the linkages between enhanced power and either security or peace are complex. Although it is common to argue that we have leverage with respect to our security and the avoidance of war, that leverage is highly uncertain.

Security Structures

An alternative to unilateralism for the United States and other major powers (and one that the revision of the Defense Department report subsequently supported) is military cooperation. One aspect of such cooperation since the end of the Cold War has been the maintenance of an active North Atlantic Treaty Organization (NATO), even though the mission for which it was created has vanished. In fact, the bombings of Serbian forces by NATO in 1994 and 1995 in retaliation for attacks on UN safe areas were the first "out of area" actions that NATO had ever undertaken.

NATO has to some considerable degree become an alliance of economically advanced democracies in collective defense against internal or external threats. NATO's support for democracy received added emphasis with the increased acceptance of one causal linkage that scholars verify repeatedly: Democracies do not fight with other democracies. Although there are some questionable possible exceptions, such as fighting between Peru and Ecuador, this tendency has become a near law of interstate politics. Both NATO and the European Union have increasingly built the consolidation and expansion of democracy into their missions.

During the Cold War, NATO consciously saw itself as having two pillars: the North American states (Canada and the United States) and the

Western European states (organized economically by the European Union and militarily by the Western European Union [WEU]). Since the Cold War's end NATO has reached out to the former communist countries of Central and Eastern Europe. The North Atlantic Cooperation Council (NACC) quickly brought all the members of the old Warsaw Pact together with those of NATO at the end of the Cold War in a forum for military co-operation. The smaller Partners for Peace (26 countries in 1995, including Russia) have agreed to significant openness and even coordination of military structures. And although the Organization for Security and Cooperation in Europe (OSCE) has an agenda that extends beyond military issues to human rights, it is a still more extensive element of the multilateral security structure of the post–Cold War period (see Figure 7.3).

Cooperation, or multilateralism, involves more than the development of formal security institutions. Even at the peak of the Cold War in the 1960s, the major powers and countries in the broader global system began to sign a wide range of arms control agreements limiting nuclear testing, the development and use of biological weapons, missile-defense systems, and the militarization of commons such as the Antarctic, the seabed, and space. Near the end of the Cold War, the superpowers agreed to reduce their nuclear arsenals, a process that accelerated after the Soviet collapse in 1991 even as internal debates on ratifications of treaties continued.

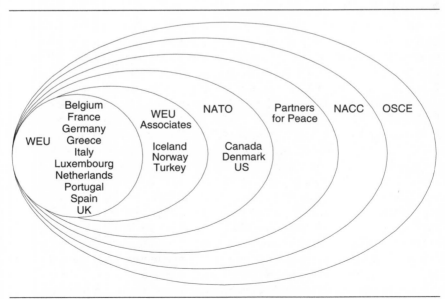

FIGURE 7.3   Multilateral security structures.

What implications do cooperative interaction on military structures and arms control have for security and peace? An immediate response might be that they will enhance both. Yet feverish and quite widespread efforts in the 1920s to cooperate militarily and control weaponry did not prevent global warfare in the 1930s. And in the 1990s both Russia and China harbor great uncertainties about the benefits of cooperation with the West. In short, with the seeming exception of the linkage between democracy and peace, the causal linkages underlying security and peace are highly complex and uncertain.

Energy Security

Although there are many specific issues that affect interstate relations, availability of energy must have a prominent place on any list. It is especially important in the modern fossil-fuel era because of the high dependence of large numbers of countries on the energy resources of a relatively small number of exporters. States have long sought guaranteed access to energy sources, and preferably long-term control of them. That impulse led, for instance, to the rivalries between Britain, France, and Germany over concessions for oil in the Middle East between the two world wars. The United States temporarily ended that rivalry after World War II by moving firmly into a dominant position within the region. Counterbalancing actions of the Soviet Union, coupled with nationalistic and religious forces within the region itself, gradually eroded U.S. dominance.

Today the countries of OPEC, especially those of the Middle East, potentially have great control over energy resources that have become essential to the economies of the Western developed world. The disruption that such control can cause became obvious when reductions in oil exports for political-economic reasons in 1973–1974 drove the world price of oil up by a factor of four. Oil-importing states face continuing choices as they decide how to minimize threats of supply disruption and dramatic price increases. We discussed the points of leverage that countries have with respect to energy in Chapter 5.

Nationalism, Security, and Peace

One of the great uncertainties of contemporary international politics concerns the set of causal linkages between nationalism and security or peace. Consider, for instance, the breakdown of Yugoslavia in the face of the nationalist fervor of Croats, Slovenians, Serbs, and other subgroupings of the former state. When Slovenia, Croatia, and the multiethnic republic of Bosnia declared their independence from Yugoslavia in 1991, a debate erupted within the European Union and beyond about whether to support such declarations. The debate was very sensitive to the issue of minimizing conflict among ethnic groups and to the possibility that such conflict would draw in additional states. Nationalistic conflict following the assassination in 1914 of the Austrian archduke by a Serbian nationalist in Sarajevo had spread into world war; that historical fact was very much on minds of leaders in 1991. Should the outside world act to recognize and support independence, or should it seek to maintain traditional state boundaries?

Europe fairly quickly decided to support independence declarations. Serbians, left in a rump Yugoslavia that controlled most of the former state's military capability, acted to deny independence of the newly declared states, especially of Croatia and Bosnia, where many Serbs also resided. The questions for the outside world then quickly became whether to intervene, and if so, how to intervene. Again, although there was widespread belief that the outside world had important leverage, there was great uncertainty concerning the consequences of any specific action. Over a period of several years the so-called Contact Group (Britain, France, Germany, Russia, and the United States), NATO, and the UN all struggled with this dilemma.

What future do we want with respect to international politics and what leverage do we have? Answers to those two questions depend not on extrapolation but on causal analysis and soul-searching value clarification. And it is clear that there are no easy answers. Scholars and politicians are divided. Obviously, everyone wants peace, but how to attain it, without jeopardizing security, is highly uncertain. You probably also are unsure about how it can be attained. Nonetheless, you will be asked to make decisions, minimally in the voting booth, and often in your own career and personal life. That is the dilemma you face. Inaction is, of course, simply acceptance of the choices that others make "on your behalf."

EXPLORATION OF INTERNATIONAL FUTURES

In this section we turn to the IFs computer simulation for help in extending our understandings of the issues surrounding security and peace. Use of that model will by no means resolve the dilemma of choice in the face of uncertain futures. In fact, because the causal linkages that underlie international politics appear more uncertain than those underlying international economics or the broader environment, the IFs model cannot represent them very confidently or fully. For instance, IFs includes no representation of nationalism or its consequences. You will need to involve yourself actively in thinking through missing or uncertain linkages.

You may need to return to Chapter 3 and review the use of the model. This discussion assumes that you know not only how to examine results from the base case of the model but also how to change parameters, run the model, and compare results with the base case (as discussed in the last section of Chapter 3).

As emphasized earlier, computer models are commonly built around scenarios—that is, alternative world futures. We begin by identifying some indicators we believe to be important, and then investigate our leverage with respect to them. Although we cannot measure security very directly, it is common to consider power a very important element of security. We therefore begin our analysis by looking at the long-term shifts of power within the global system (doing so will also allow you to refresh your memory on the display of the base case before plunging into scenario analysis).

We then move into a consideration of the action-reaction dynamics that so often characterize power relationships generally, and military spending specifically. We will illustrate such dynamics by considering possible Russian responses to continued increases in arms spending by China. We consider also the possibility that an arms race between these two countries could lead to war. We will then turn our attention to the flip side of arms races, namely, the prospects for arms control.

Finally, we look at energy issues in interstate politics. Specifically, we will investigate the threat that OPEC embargoes on the export of oil might pose to importing states.

Power in the Global System

The distribution of power among the largest countries of the world influences the interaction among those countries and between them and less powerful countries. After World War II, the United States and the former Soviet Union emerged as the most powerful states in the interstate system. They engaged in an intense rivalry that several times, especially in the Cuban Missile Crisis, came near to erupting in war. They also used their power to bind less powerful countries to themselves in military and economic relationships.

In the 1980s and 1990s the relative power of the two superpowers has declined (especially that of the former USSR). Although both have grown demographically, economically, and militarily, their rates of growth in all of these areas has lagged behind those of other countries. As other actors such as Japan, the European Union, China, and even India have emerged with comparable demographic and economic size, and with growing military capability, the superpowers have increasingly redirected the rapt attention that they long devoted to each other toward those other actors. And the ability of the United States and Russia to lead groupings of states in conflict with each other has declined. These consequences of shifting power balances became especially obvious in the last half of the 1980s, but the probability is that the global political structure will continue to change throughout the 1990s and the early twenty-first century.

How large are the populations, economies, and military capabilities of the United States and Russia relative to those of other countries? What are the trends over time? How fast is Japan surpassing Russia economically? How fast is the European Union overtaking the United States? What are the prospects of China and India? To begin answering such questions, call up from the base case tables, graphs, and pie charts of population (POP) and gross domestic product (GDP).

IFs also contains some indicators of absolute military power. It breaks that power into two types, conventional (CPOW) and strategic or nuclear (NPOW). In addition, you can look at an overall index of relative power (POWER) that summarizes the demographic, economic, and conventional and nuclear military positions of countries and regional groupings.

How does IFs compute these power measures? We discussed the computation of GDP and population size in Chapter 3; thus, here only the military and aggregate power measures will be addressed. Government spending is directed into five categories: military, education, health, foreign aid, and other. Military spending is split between conventional and nuclear spending (for most countries it is entirely conventional). Conventional military spending is converted to conventional military force units that augment existing strength (but gradually depreciate in value). Nuclear military spending is converted to warheads (these again gradually depreciate). The measure of relative aggregate power (POWER) computes a country's (or region's) portion of total world population, of total world GDP, of total world conventional power, and of total world nuclear power. It then weights those four portions (by PF1, PF2, PF3, and PF4), providing a crude guess at the country's share of world power. Where does the measure suggest aggregate power is rising and falling? Why?

You may want to explore relative power in the global system under a wide variety of alternative assumptions. In addition to investigating the impact of different weights, you may want to develop scenarios involving different assumptions about economic growth (using the parameter GDPM), population growth (using TFRM and/or MORTM), or military spending (using GK).

The Action-Reaction Dynamic: China and Russia

In a system characterized by the necessity of self-help, many actors strive to enhance their security through a buildup of arms. This is the case with China. Since most arms can be used either defensively or offensively, however, even honestly defensive actions can lessen the security of other states.

▶ Create a scenario for increased Chinese power based upon higher military spending (increase spending to 25 percent of total governmental spending over five years and then hold it there). The last section of Chapter 3 described how to create such a scenario using the parameter GK. The increase in power that China manages in your scenario comes at the expense of other countries and regions (to see this you could compare the power [POWER] of other actors in the "high-Chinese-military-expenditure" scenario with that of the base case). Under the conditions of the security dilemma, when defensive action is viewed as potentially threatening to other states because it reduces their relative power, those states react by attempting to improve their own defenses, setting in motion the "action-reaction" dynamic of arms races.

The nature of the action-reaction dynamic will vary over time and across groupings of states. For instance, significant increases in arms spending by Argentina would be unlikely to cause any reaction in Pakistan because Pakistani leaders would see no conflict of interest between the states and would doubt that Argentina could pose a credible threat, even after a major buildup. The leadership of Britain would take more notice; when Argentina used its military strength in 1982 temporarily to occupy the Falkland Islands (claimed by the Argentines as the Malvinas), Britain sent a naval task force to recapture them. Nonetheless, Britain's military strength is so much greater than that of Argentina that it might respond with a marginal increase in its own arms spending. In Brazil, the reaction could be proportionally much greater, especially if the buildup in Argentina ignored Argentine agreements with Brazil restricting spending on nuclear weapons programs. One can imagine circumstances under which Brazil would match every 1 percent of additional spending by Argentina with increases of 2 percent.

We can use IFs to examine such arms races and to investigate their consequences. Let us focus on the relationship between China and Russia (China and Japan would be another very interesting pair). There have been a few small military clashes between the two states since World War II. China has never fully accepted the loss of lands to Russia in "unequal treaties" during the late 1800s. A China that declared its antipathy to Russia while initiating a program of substantially increased military spending (as in the earlier scenario) might elicit a substantial reaction in Russia.

▶ Let us explore the implications for Russia of the military buildup in China. That military buildup increases the threat that China poses to Russia (THREAT$_{China,Russia}$). Threat in IFs rises with power depending on a reactivity parameter. The reactivity parameter (REACM) determines the change in threat from a specified actor to a specific target when the power of the actor changes relative to initial conditions.

In the base case of IFs, the reactivities of all countries to all others are set at 1.0, simply because we do not have a good data base for estimating them. With a reactivity of 1.0, the threat posed to Russia will rise in direct proportion to the Chinese power increase. See the equations in the Help system for full explanations of this and other causal linkages.

A state facing increased external threat will most likely respond in some way. IFs feeds increased threat through to increased military expenditures. Examine Russian expenditures to see how much they have increased in your scenario. Those increases may be less than you expect because Russia has been made sensitive to all actors in the system since all its reactivities have been set to 1.0. The impact of Chinese expenditure increases on Russia is muted because of this "diffusion" of its attention. Were you to make Russia sensitive only to China (by setting REACM for all actors toward Russia to 0.0 and then resetting REACM for China toward Russia to 1.0) and make China sensitive only to Russia (in the same way) you would see considerably greater impact. Make those changes to the scenario of increased Chinese military spending and rerun the model. Although the threat that China poses to Russia does not increase significantly, the fact that it is focused on Russia (and the Russian response is focused on China) changes the military expenditures of both. Look also at the loss in long-term economic performance that Russia must bear in order to react to the Chinese buildup. The best indicator of this loss will be GDP per capita (GDPPC).

Limits to Action-Reaction: The Burden of Arms

The basic action-reaction dynamic that we see in this arms race cannot go on without limit. When increases in military expenditure on either or both sides are sufficiently large, they will have a negative influence on economic growth. In this particular scenario, you have forced the Russians to increase military spending at the expense of other governmental spending (when they increased the allocation to the military, the model automatically decreased the spending on health and education—it uses a procedure called normalization to assure that total expenditures are unchanged). You can see that this scenario has a cost to both parties to the arms race in terms of slower growth in some aspects of quality of life that depend on other governmental expenditures. That slowdown has a secondary effect on economic growth, because in IFs quality of the work force affects its productivity. Were you to increase the tax rate (using the tax rate multiplier, TAXRAM) in order to augment total Russian governmental spending and protect spending on health and education in the face of higher military spending, the economic cost might be still greater, however, because you would begin to cut into the investment potential of the private economy. Within IFs the dynamic impact of arms spending on economic performance replaces the burden term in the simpler Richardson equation set.

The analysis in the next section will build upon what we have done so far. If you wish, you can Save the arms race scenario you have created with the name ARMSRACE.RUN. That will allow you any time later to pick up the analysis, which continues below, by reactivating that file. If you Quit IFs without saving your results, you will lose the working file and will need to reintroduce the parameter changes we have discussed (GK and REACM) before proceeding with the next section.

The Possibility of War

The preceding discussion of economic and noneconomic consequences of an arms race assumes that it does not end in a military conflict. If it does, the implications for other variables could be much greater. IFs treats warfare as an event that is by no means fully predictable. It computes a probability of conventional war (CWARPB) between any two model regions in each year and then lets a random number generator determine whether war actually occurs. More specifically, it increases or decreases the probability of war between two regions depending on a number of factors (threat levels between the two actors, military spending levels, and levels of democracy—see the Help system for a full specification). Thus, as threat increases, the probability of war increases. All such factors work as multipliers on a baseline probability of war (CWARBASE).

In the base case, however, all baseline probabilities are set to 0.0, because the author of the model makes no pretense of knowing the correct annual probability of war between Russia and China or between any other two regions.

▶ To examine the implications of increased Chinese military spending for warfare between China and Russia, first set the baseline probability for war (CWARBASE) initiated in both directions at some value like .01 (1 percent each year) or at .05 (5 percent) if you are quite pessimistic. Be aware that this value may generate warfare even with the military spending patterns of the base case. When a conventional war occurs, CWAR will switch from 0.0 to 1.0 for the dyad during the years of the war.

Now rebuild your scenario assuming high Chinese military spending and high Russian reactivity on top of this—or, more easily, build this change into that scenario if you saved it. You will generally see more wars as threat increases. Remember, however, that there is also a random element of warfare and you may not see more wars.

Casualties and economic damage usually depend on the conventional power of the two sides and the length of the war. Whenever either or both parties to a conventional conflict have nuclear weapons (as both China and Russia do), there is the constant danger of an escalation to nuclear war (the nuclear war probability during a conventional war is NWARPB, and when a nuclear war occurs NWAR switches from 0.0 to 1.0). Should that happen, both casualties and economic damage can increase dramatically.

In studying war it is useful to display the conventional war probability base (CWARBASE), which you set; the computed probability of conventional war (CWARPB); and the occurrence or absence of conventional and nuclear war (CWAR and NWAR). By the way, if you want to see what a global conventional war looks like, simply set CWARF to a value above 100 for any future year(s) in order to force warfare.

This is the only portion of the model that has a random (or stochastic) element and it makes the occurrence and length of conventional and nuclear wars unpredictable (although an intense arms race will almost always generate warfare eventually).[2] The sad reality is that we are incapable of foreseeing when potential conflicts will lead to war and when they will not. There is less predictability in international politics than in demographics.

There are many other dimensions of cleavage in the global system that could give rise to arms races. For instance, substantial militarization in Latin America could cause a reaction in the United States. So could a major buildup in some of the OPEC countries (like Iraq). If some of that increased spending were directed toward nuclear weaponry (the parameter that directs a portion of military spending into nuclear arms is NMILF), it might cause an especially large reaction. Another basis for an arms race would be increased spending by China and reaction by Japan. Still another would be increased spending by Russia and collective reaction by the United States, the European Union, and Japan.

Spend some time exploring possible arms races and the conflicts that might result from them. Use the Help system to examine both causal dynamics and equations from this section of the model. Never be afraid to change parameters and see what happens. For instance, increases that you posit in global community (GLOCOM) or in freedom (FREEDOM, where smaller numbers mean more free) will decrease the probability of war. Although extreme or nonsensical parameter changes can lead to nonsensical results (garbage in—garbage out), the model is not supposed to "blow up" regardless of what you do. If you do something that does cause the model to abort, please send me a description of what you did. Then simply start again—the model, base case, and any scenarios you have saved will always be unchanged.

The Promise of Arms Control

In the late 1980s the Soviet Union attempted to defuse or even reverse its arms race with the United States by unilaterally announcing some measures of restraint (including a ban on nuclear testing). How did the United States and its NATO allies in Europe respond? Initially with distrust and inaction. The reactivity parameter of the real world remained high with respect to conflict, but low with respect to cooperation. Eventually, however, NATO members began to perceive the efforts to be sincere, even while interpreting them as self-interested attempts to reduce strain on a weakening Soviet economy. Gradually NATO began to respond in kind and a certain amount of trust emerged. The Soviet Union announced that it wanted to rejoin the global community, and its actions gained it some access.

▶ Although there is much uncertainty with respect to the future of relations between Russia, as the principal successor state of the former Soviet Union, and the rest of the world, there is at least some reason to hope that, in spite of inevitable setbacks, the process it set in motion in the late 1980s will ultimately lead to a more peaceful world. Explore a scenario in which Russia's actions lead to a broadscale, even global process of arms reduction.

The base case actually constitutes such a scenario in its initial years. Return to the base case (by opening it as the working file from within Files). Display GK for military spending (the portion of government devoted to the military) for all regions of IFs. Note that it changes over time for many regions, because the base case has exogenously built in that particular manifestation of the end of the Cold War. Now look at THREAT from Russia to all other regions and see how it declines in the base case. By the time you read this, it is quite possible that one of two things will have happened: Either tensions between Russia and the countries of the NATO alliance will have grown, or Russia will have consolidated its democracy and come to view NATO's proposed expansion as nonthreatening. In the first case the reductions of military spending in the base case may appear too great; in the second case they may appear conservative. Adjust the spending of Russia, the United States, and the European Union accordingly. Consider also altering their reactivities to each other or toward other actors in the system.

Explore the degree to which your scenario affects economic performance and quality of life in these key actors.

Energy and Security

Although realists focus heavily on military power, states mobilize other forms of power to achieve objectives. For example, in 1973 a number of OPEC countries used their control over a significant fraction of global oil resources to drive up oil prices by limiting exports. You can introduce such limitations on energy exports by invoking the energy trade limit parameter (ENTL). That parameter is a switch; a value of 0 means that there is no trade limit. Positive values (like 3.5) turn on a limit and simultaneously specify the limit to annual energy exports in billions of barrels of oil equivalent. Negative values switch on and set a limit to imports. In addition to using this parameter for scenarios involving conscious and planned limitations to energy trade, one can also use them to represent the unplanned consequences of political or social instability.

▶ Reopen the base case (in Files). Look at OPEC energy exports (ENX) in the base case. Use ENTL to reduce those exports by more than one-half in the years 1995–2000. That is, change ENTL for OPEC to perhaps 3.5 for that period—if you leave its value at 0.0 for other years, the parameter will constrain OPEC exports (to 3.5 billion barrels per year) only between 1995 and 2000. Run the model.

Look at the results with special attention to the impact on major importers like the European Union. What does the OPEC restriction do to their GDPs? How does it affect energy prices (ENPRI) in those countries? Does the restriction help or hurt OPEC? In each case, compare the working file with the base case. The effect of this scenario on oil importers may be smaller than you expect. There are several reasons. First, your scenario has reduced global oil availability by less than 10 percent (see WENP). Second, importing regions have considerable stocks of energy (ENST) as they enter the period of restricted supply. Third and most important, IFs is a model constructed primarily for long-term analysis. The price elasticity of energy demand (ELASDE) is a long-term value and unfortunately exaggerates the conservation that Europeans and others might manage in the short run. Set its value for the European Union to –0.1 in the same years as your OPEC oil restriction and you will see a greater impact of the scenario.

Research Questions. For most effective research use of the model, it is best to begin with a specific question. What might be the U.S. reaction to renewed Russian military spending increases? How big would the economic growth penalty be were Japan to double military spending relative to the base case? How much damage would a war involving OPEC do to the economies of the oil-importing countries? How substantial would be the population losses in a war involving the European Union and Russia? It is also important to ask questions that are not so geographically specific: Do more or less powerful countries suffer most in wars? How often do arms races (of specified intensity) lead to war?

After you clearly identify a question, consider how to implement the scenario(s) needed to investigate (but not necessarily to answer) it. Always review your results carefully to be certain that the scenario you intended to implement is the one you actually generate. And perhaps most important, do not simply accept the results of the model as the answer to your question. Examine them carefully and try to explain why the model produced them. Do they make sense? Why or why not? Use the model as a "thinking tool," not as a crystal ball. Where might the model be inadequate?

CONCLUSION

In this chapter we investigated the pursuit of security and peace. We found that the pursuit is complicated by considerable uncertainty about many of the important causal linkages. Nonetheless, power is central to interstate politics and we have been able to explore possible developments in global power. We also identified the action-reaction dynamic as a well-established element of interstate politics and analyzed it.

There are many critical choices facing us with respect to global security and peace. Each country struggles with decisions about the appropriate level of military spending. Decisionmakers in each must ask themselves how involved the country should become in multilateral security structures and in cooperative relationships with other states. They must consider the nation's vulnerability with respect to energy availability and price and must make important decisions accordingly. Although the linkages between action in any of these areas and preservation of security and peace are uncertain, we must again act in the face of that uncertainty.

EIGHT

Preferred Futures

We began this book with the question, What will be the future of environmental, economic, and political-social systems? The obvious answer came quickly: No one knows. That simple answer creates a serious dilemma. Our actions, even decisions not to act, will affect the human future in potentially very significant ways. We cannot know the future, but we must act as if we can.

It therefore makes sense to improve our understanding of the future as much as possible. We have done so by decomposing the question into three somewhat more manageable ones: Where do current changes appear to be taking us? What kind of future would we like? How much leverage do we have in bringing about our preferred future? Chapters 2 and 3 explored contemporary long-term trends and used extrapolation to project them into the future. Subsequent chapters moved to causal analysis and explored both our values concerning the future and our leverage with respect to it. We examined alternative worldviews that emphasize somewhat different values and causal understandings, and we considered specific issues.

Having done all of this, we still obviously cannot know the future, and we still face the dilemma of needing to act in the face of that uncertainty. In this chapter we want to do four things. First, we will reiterate how important choices can be under conditions of uncertainty by considering the creation of the world order at the end of World War II. Second, we will review the character of our contemporary dilemma. Third, we will reintegrate the world—environmental, economic, and political systems do interact closely. Finally, we will put our improved understanding of trends, values, and leverage points to work by forcing ourselves to make some choices.

THE CREATION OF THE POSTWAR WORLD ORDER

In 1945, at the end of World War II, the old world order lay in ruins. Politically, that old world order centered on Europe and the balance of power that diplomats at the Congress of Vienna had consciously attempted to establish as long ago as 1815. The Eurocentric balance of power had faced many challenges, especially those presented by World War I, but it continued to function far into the twentieth century. At the end of World War II, however, the armies of two powers from the peripheries of Europe, the Soviet Union and the United States, sat astride the old Europe and made clear the irrelevance of the former intra-European balance.

The colonial empires of the Western and Central European powers had come by the turn of the century to dominate Africa and Asia. Only the Western Hemisphere had freed itself of direct political control. World War II disrupted the long-standing lines of authority between colonial center and colony. The future of those empires posed difficulties for those contemplating the postwar order. *Should they be reasserted or disbanded?*

At the end of World War I, states had made an attempt to create a security system that would supplement the balance of power that had failed in 1914. The principle of collective security, that all countries would assist any victim of aggression, stood at the heart of the League of Nations. Yet the League took limited action to help China against Japan in 1931 or Ethiopia against Italy in 1935. Although the League officially survived until 1946, it had ceased to be an important part of the world order long before then. *Should such efforts be abandoned or strengthened?*

The global economic system had also come apart. Its destruction was well under way before the beginning of the war and its disintegration was, in fact, an important cause of the spasm of global violence during the late 1930s and early 1940s. The old political-economic order had relied upon British economic leadership in maintaining relatively free trade throughout the globe and in providing a currency both linked to gold and in relatively plentiful supply. Mercantilist policies of states in pursuit of markets, including the protectionist orientation of the United States, put stress upon that system in the early part of the century. So, too, did the demands of victors for reparations and war repayments after World War I, which stymied the economic recovery of Germany and much of the rest of Europe. During the Great Depression, markets rapidly closed to imports, countries severed the links of currencies to precious metals, and world trade collapsed. *What kind of postwar economic order would serve the interests of global economic prosperity?*

Even during the war, the leaders of all the belligerents in World War II recognized the necessity of constructing a new world order once the fighting ended. After all, a world war is in substantial part a struggle over the character of such an order. Hitler's Germany and the emperor's Japan offered little but subjugation of defeated powers within political-economic empires in the aftermath of the destruction. In contrast, the leaders of the alliance called the "United Nations," bound together in opposition to the Axis powers by a declaration on January 1, 1942, began with less definition in their concepts of the postwar order. They worked seriously, however, to plan for that order.

Although the war did not end until late in 1945, China, Great Britain, the United States, and the Soviet Union declared already in 1943 the need for a new international organization to replace the League of Nations. They drafted a charter for the new entity at Dumbarton Oaks in late 1944. Fifty-one countries established the UN in early 1945, again enshrining the globalist principle of collective security at the institution's core. Recognizing that no collective action against an aggressor was possible without the participation of the Great Powers, however, they established a Security Council charged with maintaining global peace and security and gave the five dominant powers each a veto. Although a strong belief that traditional balance-of-power politics had failed too often and too catastrophically motivated many of the countries involved in establishing and structuring the UN, they would not ignore the reality of power.

In mid-1944 the United Nations Monetary and Financial Conference convened at Bretton Woods, New Hampshire. The Bretton Woods Conference, as most now call it, established the International Monetary Fund (IMF) and the International Bank for Reconstruction and Development (IBRD), better known as the World Bank. Founding countries charged the IMF with promoting international financial cooperation (including reestablishing a gold standard and maintaining relatively stable exchange rates for currencies) and the World Bank with rebuilding Europe. They also agreed upon the establishment of an International Trade Organization, which ultimately evolved into a weaker General Agreement on Tariffs and Trade (GATT). The purpose of GATT was to provide a negotiating forum for the reduction of tariffs and other barriers to trade. The efforts at Bretton Woods exhibited primarily liberal concerns with free markets and growth but did not entirely ignore new or existing gaps in economic conditions.

Thus even before the end of World War II (Japan surrendered on August 14, 1945), the outlines of a new world order had become visible. Countries acted with remarkable decisiveness in the face of great uncertainty. Multiple values and understandings motivated them. Yet the institutions that they created during that period remain fundamentally important in the current world order.

EARLY CHALLENGES TO THE WORLD ORDER

One hope of that period was that the UN alliance would continue to function cooperatively after the war. Another was that the institutions created at Bretton Woods would facilitate fairly rapid economic recovery in Europe. Both hopes were dashed before the end of the war. The alliance already showed signs of stress. The leaders of the United States, the Soviet Union, and the United Kingdom met at Yalta in early 1945 to consider the postwar shape of Eastern Europe, the pursuit of the war in Asia, the status of the new UN organization, and the treatment of Germany after defeat (McWilliams and Piotrowski, 1988: 29–38). The grudging acceptance by Roosevelt and Churchill of Stalin's military domination of Poland and other parts of Eastern Europe, which both saw as a fait accompli, would subsequently create problems. Churchill and Stalin accepted Roosevelt's suggestion of veto power in the UN for five Great Powers (France and China were included in the club), a power Roosevelt believed necessary to rally the American people behind the organization. The three leaders decided temporarily to divide Germany into occupation zones, reserving one also for France.

The seeds of disagreement planted at Yalta germinated rapidly. At Potsdam in mid-1945, after the defeat of Germany, U.S. and British leaders protested the quick establishment of communist governments in Eastern Europe and resisted Soviet demands for $20 billion in reparations from a devastated Germany. The division of Germany became more than temporary.

In early 1947 the ongoing civil war in Greece led President Truman to condemn the Soviets for intervention and to issue a statement, known as the Truman Doctrine, that it was "the policy of the United States to support free peoples who are resisting attempted subjugation by armed minorities or outside pressures" (DeConde, 1978: 219). Britain and the United States began to organize Europe into a coalition to resist the Soviets. In early 1948, Britain, France, Belgium, the Netherlands, and Luxembourg signed the Brussels Pact, with U.S. support. Britain, France, and the United States moved to coordinate policies in their zones of occupied Germany. In June 1948, the Soviets interrupted ground transportation to Berlin in protest of Western currency reform in their zones. The West responded with an airlift that broke the blockade. In April 1949 twelve countries established the North Atlantic Treaty Organization (NATO). The Soviet Union denounced it as hostile to them and incompatible with the UN Charter and intent.

One can interpret the events of 1942–1949 as a struggle between the values and causal understandings of competing worldviews. It appeared initially that the globalist liberal view, enshrined in the UN and other new institutions, might prevail. There was a widespread desire to break free of balance-of-power politics. Ultimately, the realist view, with its emphasis on balance of power, proved better able to describe the new world order that emerged from the chaos of World War II.[1] There remains some debate over whether the reemergence of politics based on balance of power was inevitable or a result of choices made by those who led the superpowers in that period. Nonetheless, the "Cold War" had begun and no phrase better describes the global political order of the next 40 years.

In addition, all was not completely well with the liberal postwar economic order envisioned at Bretton Woods. Although the USSR attended the Bretton Woods Conference, it opted not to join the institutions created there. More urgently, Western Europe was not recovering economically. In early 1947 the idea of an assistance program for Europe moved rapidly forward and emerged in the form of the European Recovery Program, or Marshall Plan. The United States began a pattern of unilateral economic leadership both within and outside of the framework of Bretton Woods.

More generally, the Bretton Woods system has always faced two challenges to its liberal character. The first is from the realists in the form of mercantilism. The United States itself maintained a pattern of subsidies and protection for its agricultural sector, the portion of its economy that had suffered earliest and most in the Great Depression and that continued to be weak. Since the early 1970s the mercantilist challenge has grown.

The second challenge comes from the less developed countries of the world and had a structuralist character. The Bretton Woods institutions, with their principles of open markets and trade reciprocity, became quickly identified with the economically developed countries of the Western world. LDCs believed, however, that they needed access to the markets of more developed countries while being able to protect their own. In 1964, the Group of 77 (G-77), consisting of 77 LDC members of the UN (now G-77 has about 120 members), supported the convening of a United Nations Conference on Trade and Development (UNCTAD). UNCTAD became institutionalized with a permanent secretariat and meetings every four years.

Although a "new world order" came into view at the end of World War II, it was never completely stable or free from challenge. Nor was it the order that the UN alliance members had planned during the war. Adjustments were made throughout the Cold War and tensions remained high. With the end of the Cold War, it was immediately obvious that another period of major transformation was imminent.

CONTEMPORARY WORLD ORDER TRANSFORMATION

The contemporary situation has much in common with the period at the end of World War II. The world order is almost certainly now going through the greatest and most rapid change it has experienced since the late 1940s. One important difference is that the Allies fighting Germany and Japan in World War II expected the war to end and had therefore planned a new order. Moreover, the Allies understood the war to be a failure of the prewar system, which they therefore believed to need significant change. In contrast, the end of the Cold War surprised the West, which had largely failed to plan for such an occurrence and was relatively more comfortable with existing structures.

On November 11, 1989, the Berlin Wall, the most vivid symbol of the Cold War since its construction in 1961, opened to movement of East and West Germans. On November 30 the Czechoslovakian Parliament voted to end the dominant role of communists and to hold free elections. During December the Romanian revolution toppled the communist government there and executed President Ceausescu. In February 1990, the Soviet communists gave up their complete hold on power. At the end of 1991 the USSR ceased to exist. The new year of 1992 dawned with a Russian flag flying above the Kremlin and Boris Yeltsin, democratically elected President of Russia, inside it.

Even in the absence of planning for the end of the Cold War, these domestic changes throughout most of the communist world reverberated quickly in international relations. In December 1990, the United States offered food and other aid to the USSR. The two countries signed an agreement in June 1991 limiting conventional forces in Europe and another in July reducing nuclear arsenals. The Warsaw Treaty Alliance, established in 1955 in formal reaction to the creation of NATO, ceased to exist in July. The Baltic Republics of Estonia, Latvia, and Lithuania joined the UN as independent states in September. Russia and 14 other newly independent states of the former Soviet Union joined the IMF and the World Bank in April 1992.

The changes have potentially revitalized the UN. In 1990–1991 all five states with veto power, including the Soviet Union and China, supported UN Security Council resolutions condemning the invasion of Kuwait by Iraq, imposing sanctions, and ultimately authorizing U.S.-led military action against Iraq. In its first 40 years of operation, the UN sponsored only 13 peacekeeping missions; during the 1991–1992 period alone it ran 12 simultaneously and in 1994 managed 18 missions deploying 70,000 troops.

Contrary to many predictions in 1991 and 1992, NATO did not collapse at the end of the Cold War. Instead it quickly began reconsidering both membership and mission. Already in 1991 the North Atlantic Cooperation Council (NACC) combined the membership of NATO and the former Warsaw Pact. In 1994 NATO issued an invitation to members of NACC to join a Partnership for Peace, implicitly a way-station for some countries toward membership in NATO itself. Russia and 25 other states had elected partnership status by 1995. With respect to mission, in 1995 NATO took over from the UN in former Yugoslavia, its first significant "out-of-area" mission.

The world therefore stands clearly on the cusp of great change with respect to political and security arrangements. On one hand, there appears to be the prospect of strengthened global community and even tighter community among democratic states. The surprising advances of Western democratic forms, not just in Central and Eastern Europe but in Latin America, Asia, and even Africa, give additional support to those who anticipate a new era of global political relations.

On the other hand, there is the possibility that this era is simply another interim period prior to the emergence of a redefined balance of power and a new action-reaction dynamic. Russia's concerns about both NATO membership expansion and out-of-area missions like that in Bosnia could be the first signs of a renewed East-West split. Russian suppression of the rebellion in Chechnya in 1994–1996 and its threat to unilaterally violate the Conventional Forces in Europe (CFE) treaty created similarly serious concerns in the West.

The West has also begun to worry a great deal about Chinese intentions. Chinese military spending increased in the early 1990s as that of NATO and former Warsaw Pact countries declined. China began to exert its influence in the South China Sea, acted through missile tests to make Taiwan nervous, and prepared for the 1997 reversion of Hong Kong to the People's Republic. Countries throughout Asia increased military spending in this period in reaction to China and to each other.

The global political economy is also in a state of transition and accompanying uncertainty. The Third World's demand for a new international economic order (NIEO) remains on the table. The economic success of a number of newly industrialized and export-oriented developing countries has, however, muted much of its force. The collapse of the Soviet Union, long a principal advocate of global economic restructuring, has similarly weakened the demands of structuralists for fundamental change in the order of Bretton Woods. Problems of Third World debt have lessened. It would, however, be foolish to dismiss the power of the gap between global rich and poor to mobilize the energies of the poor in mounting renewed challenges to the current order. A variety of economic problems, and a general discontent, could reemerge with force in the wake of economic downturn.

Nonetheless, the greatest contemporary challenge to the existing economic order appears to be from mercantilism. The United States ran trade deficits of more than $40 billion with Japan for each year from 1986 to 1995 ($65 billion in 1994). Japanese surpluses with Europe increased steadily in this period. Both the United States and Europe have responded to what they perceive as unfair trade practices by Japan with efforts to protect their own markets. Some of those efforts target Japanese goods specifically. Others have a more general protectionist character.

The United States has been somewhat concerned that movement in the European Union toward greater economic integration and some protection against Japanese goods is creating a "Fortress Europe." At the same time, Canada, the United States, and Mexico entered into a North American Free Trade Agreement. Argentina, Brazil, Paraguay, and Uruguay have largely eliminated tariffs among themselves in an association known as Mercosur. Observers of these free trade agreements debate whether the zones will provide building blocks for renewed attention to free trade within GATT or close themselves into trading blocs and thereby subvert the liberal principles of the Bretton Woods institutions.

In 1995 a new World Trade Organization (WTO) made its debut. It extended the interests and authority of GATT into services and intellectual property, and also included an extensive accord on reduction in protection of agriculture. Moreover, the WTO has a built-in dispute resolution mechanism. Potentially, the founding of the WTO could be the first step in another extended period of global trade liberalization.

At the end of World War II, environmental issues were essentially absent from the world's agenda. They began emerging in the 1970s. The United Nations Conference on the Human Environment in Stockholm during 1972 was the first major sign of this change. That conference created the United Nations Environment Program and set in motion a number of efforts that have continued to grow, including a program to protect the regional seas of the world. During the 1980s two global atmospheric issues added to the agenda. The world identified chlorofluorocarbons (CFCs) as a threat to the stratospheric ozone layer and then acted to reduce it with remarkable speed. Twenty-two countries signed an agreement in Montreal during 1987 and have continued to strengthen it since then. The extent of the threat to global temperatures and ocean levels from the buildup of atmospheric carbon dioxide has drawn more debate and less action.

The United Nations Conference on Environment and Development (UNCED) in 1992 signaled the arrival of a full range of environmental issues onto the global agenda. A host of issues now define an environmental agenda that is much broader than the quality of global oceans and air. They include the interaction between population growth and environmental quality, the ability of humanity to feed itself, and even the condition of forests within countries, a debate once confined solely to domestic politics.

Nonetheless, the future of domestic and international action on such environmental issues remains very uncertain. On one hand, the Montreal Protocol on CFCs could serve as an exemplar for cooperation on a wide range of issues. On the other hand, international tensions arising from the establishment of a new balance of power could undercut action on all such issues. For instance, China has insisted upon special treatment in the agreements on CFCs, arguing that it needs to satisfy the consumption needs of 1.2 billion people and does not have the resources or technology to do it without CFCs. Political tensions with China could easily spill over into this and other environmental areas.

THE INTERACTION OF CHOICES

The simultaneous consideration of environmental and development issues at Rio in 1992 suggests the increasing linkage between those issues on the world agenda, something that we have argued also extends to political or security issues. It might be reasonable to hypothesize that during periods of transformation in the world order, issues tend to become fused, much as they did during the building of the postwar economic and security arrangements. When and if power balances reestablish themselves as the dominant character of international politics, renewed global tensions may suppress the linkages and again relegate nonsecurity issues to the domain of "low politics." Do we now find ourselves in a period analogous to 1944–1946, when global resolution of many such issues appeared possible? In 1946 the United States even suggested the Baruch Plan, calling for international control of atomic power. Or are we perhaps about to move into a period like that of 1947–1948, when the two superpowers that dominated the victory of World War II acted to divide the world and consideration of all its security, economic, and environmental issues into two zones?

Up until this chapter, we have largely separated those issues centering on security and peace from those of growth and equality and, in turn, from those of progress and sustainability. In reality the issues interact closely, not least in our ability to devote time and financial resources to their attention. In this chapter we have begun to recognize that interaction.

It is therefore time for you to reflect on the interaction of these issues and to begin asking yourself about the comprehensive shape of the world order you wish to see evolve in the next decade. This book leaves you not with a vision but with an exercise. Take some time to describe the world you would like to see in place at the end of 10 years. Where do you believe changes are taking us? What do you value? How do you rank security, peace, growth, equality, progress, sustainability, and other values? What leverage do you think humans have in bringing about the world you envision? What specific actions need to be taken and what might be the costs of taking them?

In terms of security arrangements, do you anticipate multipolarity, a renewed bipolarity, or a period of U.S. hegemony? Do you prescribe strengthening the UN, NATO, or the defense of particular individual states? In terms of economics, do you anticipate a strengthening of free trade, perhaps led by the new World Trade Organization, a struggle simply to maintain the gains of GATT, or a movement toward trade blocs? In terms of the environment, do you foresee increased environmental destruction or the technological redress of multiple environmental problems? Do you prescribe substantial global environmental regulation, national approaches, or sponsorship of technological advance?

The assignment is a difficult one and you may hesitate to do it. Remember that whether or not you undertake it, others will. Do they share your values? Do they have the same understanding of trends and causal linkages that you have? Is it possible that they do not even fully recognize the significance of addressing the dilemma of choice in the face of uncertainty?

EXPLORATION OF INTERNATIONAL FUTURES

You can use the IFs simulation to help you undertake the exercise of this chapter. The model does not, however, allow you to introduce new global or regional institutions with respect to security, economics, or the environment. In that sense, it has a clear bias toward the continuing importance of the existing state system. The bias may not be a significant distortion of reality, since the existing state system appears unlikely to cede its dominant role in policymaking any time soon. Nonetheless, the reliance by IFs and other world models on states as the sole political actors may force you to be creative in your work with them.

What IFs does allow you to do, as we have seen in the preceding chapters, is to introduce a wide range of alternative policy choices and alternative assumptions about causal linkages (parameters). You may need to return to Chapters 4–6 to refresh your memory in each issue area. And you can once again turn to the Help system of IFs for a full list of key parameters.

Begin the exercise by assessing your own values. What features of the world you hope for in 10 years hold the greatest importance for you? The next step is to begin considering your leverage points. The easiest way to do the exercise might be to put together two extreme scenarios—the most pessimistic and the most optimistic scenarios about the future that you believe have any credibility. Identify clearly the policy changes and variations in causal understanding (possibly based in worldview differences) that differentiate the two scenarios. Your most optimistic scenario should help you identify policies that you would recommend; your most pessimistic scenario will help spot those to avoid.

By now, however, you should have a healthy distrust of all computer simulations or other bases for forecasts of the future. Because no one can know the future, the base case of IFs around which you have undertaken this and earlier analyses is almost certainly wrong. You might wish to map out a scenario with IFs that represents your own current "best guess" with respect to the developments of the next 20 years (or longer, if you wish). That is, you may wish to create your own base case.

Finally, it is time to evaluate IFs with respect to its ability to help you understand the world and represent it meaningfully. What are the major strengths of IFs? What are the major weaknesses? About what do you find yourself most uncertain? How might you gather additional information (facts or theoretical insights) in order to diminish that uncertainty? In short, how can you further develop your own mental model of the world? I would be very happy to see your suggestions for improvements of it.

CONCLUSION

This book began by defining a dilemma: *We cannot know the future; yet that future is terribly important to us, and we must therefore act in the face of uncertainty as if we did understand the consequences of our actions.* The first chapter suggested an approach to reducing (or perhaps more accurately, identifying) uncertainty via the examination of trends and through causal analysis. Ironically, you may actually now feel more uncertain about the future than you did before reading the book and therefore less able to act. If so, the book has probably added some complexity to your mental model and your most important need is time for absorption and personal analysis. It will never be easy to make choices in an uncertain world. No one can eliminate the uncertainty and simplify the task. We can only hope to define our values, identify important leverage points, and thereby make our choices somewhat more likely to achieve our goals. After all, we do have a world order to create.

APPENDIX

Where to Go Next

There are three directions you could pursue to build upon the ideas you have explored in this book and with the IFs simulation. First, you may want more information about the state of the world and major development trends. Second, you might wish to learn more about world modeling and forecasts made with world models. And third, you might want to explore IFs in more detail and even build upon it. This final discussion provides some suggestions in each case.

THE STATE OF THE WORLD

The best source of information about the world's physical and biological environment may be the series that the World Resources Institute publishes and titles *World Resources* (for the latest edition, see World Resources Institute, 1995). In addition, the Worldwatch Institute publishes an annual series with global data called *Vital Signs* (Brown, Lenssen, and Kane, 1995). Worldwatch has a second series that interprets the condition of the environment; it is called the *State of the World* (Brown et al., 1995) and has a distinctly eco-wholist viewpoint. See Bailey's (1995) *The True State of the Planet* for a modernist counterpoint.

For information on the state of the world's economy, the most useful single source is probably the World Bank's annual series called the *World Development Report* (World Bank, 1995), especially the tables included at the end. For a somewhat more structuralist counterpoint to the liberalism of the World Bank, see the United Nations Development Program's *Human Development Report* (UNDP, 1995). For additional information (and some short-term forecasts), turn to the International Monetary Fund's annual *World Economic Outlook* (IMF, 1995a). And for raw economic data look to the IMF's *International Financial Statistics* (IMF, 1995b).

Moving to political and social systems, Ruth Leger Sivard's biannual series on *World Military and Social Expenditures* (Sivard, 1993) summarizes some of the most important information on state interaction (including war), domestic priorities (including social expenditures), and quality of life. The CIA's annual *World Factbook* (CIA, 1995) is another very rich source of both political and economic information for states. There are, of course, many sources of data for more specialized interests, including the British Petroleum Company's *BP Statistical Review of World Energy* (British Petroleum Company, 1995), the Stockholm International Peace Research Institute's *SIPRI Yearbook* (SIPRI, 1994), the United States Arms Control and Disarmament Agency's *World Military*

Expenditures and Arms Transfers (US ACDA, 1995), and the United Nations Food and Agricultural Organization's *Production Yearbook* (UN FAO, 1992).

IFs has drawn heavily upon the data sources listed here. Perhaps 80 percent of its data comes from them.

MODELS AND FORECASTS

There have been many models of specific issues such as world population, the world economy, and the world climate. There are even more models of specific issues that have limited geographic scope (a country or region). Here we will focus only on those models that have global scope and treat the interaction of multiple issues.

The first world model to devote attention to both the environment and the economy was the one used to produce *The Limits to Growth* (Meadows et al., 1972), a clearly eco-wholist book that received worldwide recognition in the 1970s. The authors have revisited their analysis with *Beyond the Limits* (Meadows et al., 1992). In fact, no model since that time has elicited comparable public interest. The model looked at the world as a whole (no country or regional divisions) and was remarkably simple. Moreover, the documentation for that model (Meadows et al., 1974) is very complete and easy to read. The books thus provide a good place to continue your study of world models. Meadows and colleagues also used a technique called "systems dynamics" that facilitates translation of theoretical and commonsense understandings of the world into models even in the absence of complete data. The technique builds upon causal-loop diagrams of the kind we have used throughout this book. For more information on system dynamics, see Forrester (1968).

Several other teams released models in the 1970s. The Mesarovic-Pestel approach, or World Integrated Model (WIM), looked at the environment and the economy but broke the world into 12 regions, much like those of IFs (Mesarovic and Pestel, 1974; Hughes, 1980). In fact, IFs adapted some of the features of its energy and agriculture modules.

The British government sponsored a model called SARUM that improved the representation of economies relative to earlier models (SARU, 1977). The United Nations sponsored one that became known as the United Nations model, or the Leontief model, that used a technique called input-output matrices (Leontief, Carter, and Petri, 1977). IFs has drawn on both SARUM and the UN model in its representation of economics—combining the general equilibrium structure of the former and the I-O structure of the latter. The Argentine government sponsored a project at the Bariloche Foundation that produced a model taking the name of that foundation (Herrera et al., 1976). That model had a clearly structuralist bent and influenced the inclusion within IFs of basic human needs and of some structuralist logic.

At the end of the 1970s the U.S. government commissioned a study of the future that looked to some of these models as well as to models of particular issues and to a broad data base for an understanding of probable global developments through the end of the century. Gerald Barney directed that study and produced a three-volume study called *The Global 2000 Report to the President* (CEQ, 1981a). That study had a generally eco-wholist orientation and its volumes remain one of the best sources for insights into the U.S. government's capability for forecasting.

Although the models of the 1970s combined attention to the environment and the economy with increasing sophistication, they made little or no effort to represent political processes either within states or across them. Karl Deutsch recognized this weakness and initiated a project in Berlin under the leadership of Stuart Bremer that produced a model called GLOBUS (Bremer, 1987; Bremer and Gruhn, 1988). That model was the first to make states (countries) the basic unit of analysis and to represent both domestic and international political processes. In addition, it incorporates state-of-the-art representations of domestic and international economics, making it a unique political-economic world model. Bremer and Hughes (1990) used that model in a study of possible global arms control and global development efforts. IFs incorporates a much simplified political representation based roughly on GLOBUS. For strictly political models see Bremer (1977) and Cusack and Stoll (1990).

Few of these models are available to you—most were used in scientific studies and have not been developed further. The GLOBUS model is an exception (Bremer and Gruhn, 1988). It is, however, larger than IFs and proportionately more difficult to use. In addition, it lacks any treatment of the biological and physical environment (such as agriculture and energy submodels) and has only a rudimentary demographic module.

MORE INFORMATION ON IFs

You already know quite a bit about IFs. If you review the information presented about it throughout this book you should generally understand its structure. Yet this book has stressed several times that the structure and parameters of IFs constitute a complex if-statement that one should not accept uncritically, and you may not yet have studied the equations or even the causal diagrams of IFs, both of which are in the Help system. Obviously, not everyone will have the technical skills to understand the structure and equations of the model or even have an interest in them. Yet the causal diagrams should be fairly easy to grasp and you may find even the equations easier to understand than you think.

The equations of IFs are both more and less than a set of econometrically estimated equations developed to project the future. They are *more* so because they are system- and theory-oriented. IFs is concerned with long-term behavior of global development systems—that concern requires theory and structure, not just the best fit to data. The IFs equations are *less* so, however, because the resultant equation structures and decisions on variable inclusion make estimation of parameters very difficult. The overall structure of IFs is a hybrid in terms of modeling style. It maintains an orientation toward the overall system and its closure, even in the face of holes in theory and knowledge, that is characteristic of systems dynamics and that uses some of those techniques. At the same time, like econometric models, it directs attention to the data that are available.

World modeling and forecasting with world models began in the early 1970s and the techniques have advanced quite dramatically in the intervening years. As this book has stressed, one cannot rely upon world models for predictions of the future—they are thinking tools, not crystal balls. Nonetheless, the growing sophistication of the models indicates the degree to which our theoretical understandings of the world and the availability of data about it have grown. Moreover, the development of the models is itself now increasingly contributing to our comprehension of global development processes—to the elaboration of our own mental models. The next generation of world models will draw upon this record of success and will also utilize faster and more powerful computers. The next decade of world modeling should be an exciting one.

Notes

PREFACE

1. The National Science Foundation, the Cleveland Foundation, the Exxon Education Foundation, the Kettering Family Foundation, the Pacific Cultural Foundation, and the United States Institute of Peace provided much-appreciated financial support for earlier versions of IFs and thereby indirectly for this edition. None of these organizations bears any responsibility for the content or remaining failings of International Futures.

CHAPTER 2

1. *The Washington Post* (March 28, 1992: A16) reported that rate for 1991. The area deforested in that year constitutes about 0.3 percent of total Amazonian forest.

2. *The Economist* (December 21, 1991–January 3, 1992: 25–27) provides these and many other examples.

3. A large portion of that increase in life expectancy is a dramatic drop in infant mortality. The growth in life span of those who live through infancy is considerably less dramatic.

4. Cipolla (1962: 116) reported a rate of 56 percent literacy already in 1955.

CHAPTER 3

1. See, for example, Mesarovic and Pestel (1974); Herrera et al. (1976); SARU (1977); Leontief, Carter, and Petri (1977); Bremer (1987). Those models added geographic differentiation, coverage of additional global issues and forces (such as technological change and politics), and sometimes greater sophistication.

CHAPTER 4

1. Similarly, Gilpin developed a relatively formal but noncomputerized model of state behavior in which he assumed that "once an equilibrium between the costs and benefits of further change and expansion is reached, the tendency is for the economic costs of maintaining the status quo to rise faster than the economic capacity to support the status quo" (Gilpin, 1981: 156).

2. Bremer and I (Bremer and Hughes, 1990: 32–38) reviewed the literature that examines the linkage between arms races and warfare. We found that the empirical evidence is quite mixed.

3. James Lee Ray of Florida State University has tentatively identified an unpublished list of 22 potential exceptions, going back to the war between Athens and Syracuse in 415–413 B.C. He is skeptical that any of them truly violated the rule of nonbelligerence among democracies.

4. The eco-wholist and modernist worldviews also carry other names. For obvious reasons, Pirages (1983, 1989) calls them "inclusionist" and "exclusionist"; Grant (1982) prefers "Jeremiads" and "Cornucopians." Many others prefer "neo-Malthusians" and "technological enthusiasts."

5. IFs uses a "cohort-component" approach to representing population growth in which it tracks population in age categories grouped by five-year spans. It thus captures the momentum that population growth attains.

6. Bailey (1995) brought together a very useful collection of modernist articles. They tend to combine technological optimism with great support for markets and private ownership of property (that is, they combine modernism and liberalism).

7. This calculation is based on assorted issues of the World Bank's *Commodity Trade and Price Trends* and on CIA figures (CIA, 1991b: 42–43).

8. Ehrlich would probably argue that the 1980s were atypical in that poor global economic conditions (especially in Latin America and elsewhere in developing countries) suppressed demand.

9. In addition, this book may serve as a companion piece for my *Continuity and Change in World Politics*, 3rd ed. (Hughes, 1997). The discussion of theory in that book is organized according to worldviews.

CHAPTER 5

1. Although the treaty did not come officially into force until 1994, states began negotiating in 1973 and signed it in 1982.

CHAPTER 6

1. For nearly identical estimates in the 1970s and 1980s, see IMF (1990b: 123).

2. What we might call the global middle class, including the newly industrialized countries, has grown much faster than either the richest or poorest countries. Inclusion of them in the global South accounts for the stability of the overall income ratio of North to South.

3. The IMF does report, however, that the terms of trade for LDCs in manufacturing improved by an annual rate of 0.7 percent during the same decade (IMF, 1990b: 152).

4. The investment in agriculture scenario factor (IASF) and the investment in energy scenario factor (IESF) similarly allow one to increase or decrease investment in those two sectors (although shifts into or out of either are offset by changes in other investment, not in consumption).

CHAPTER 7

1. See the chapters in Zinnes and Gillespie (1976) for variations in presentation of the equations.

2. Each time you start IFs, the random number generator will produce the same sequence of numbers. Thus you can control the stochastic element by simply restarting IFs. But if you run the same scenario two or more times within the same session with IFs, the random numbers will change and you will see different results with respect to war.

CHAPTER 8

1. Hans Morgenthau published a new textbook on international politics in 1948 explicating realism for two generations of American students (Morgenthau, 1948).

References

Avery, Dennis. 1995. "Saving the Planet with Pesticides," in *The True State of the Planet*, ed. Ronald Bailey. New York: The Free Press, pp. 50–82.

Ayres, Robert U. 1969. *Technological Forecasting and Long-Range Planning.* New York: McGraw-Hill.

Bailey, Ronald, ed. 1995. *The True State of the Planet.* New York: The Free Press.

Bremer, Stuart A. 1977. *Simulated Worlds: A Computer Model of National Decision-Making.* Princeton: Princeton University Press.

———, ed. 1987. *The GLOBUS Model: Computer Simulation of World-wide Political and Economic Developments.* Boulder: Westview Press.

Bremer, Stuart A., and Walter Gruhn. 1988. *Micro GLOBUS: A Computer Model of Long-Term Global Political and Economic Processes.* Berlin: Edition sigma.

Bremer, Stuart A., and Barry B. Hughes. 1990. *Disarmament and Development: A Design for the Future?* Englewood Cliffs, N.J.: Prentice-Hall.

British Petroleum Company. 1991. *BP Statistical Review of World Energy.* London: British Petroleum Company.

———. 1992. *BP Statistical Review of World Energy.* London: British Petroleum Company.

———. 1994. *BP Statistical Review of World Energy.* London: British Petroleum Company.

———. 1995. *BP Statistical Review of World Energy.* London: British Petroleum Company.

Brown, Lester R. 1981. *Building a Sustainable Society.* New York: W. W. Norton.

———. 1988. "Analyzing the Demographic Trap," in *State of the World 1987*, eds. Lester R. Brown et al. New York: W. W. Norton, pp. 20–37.

Brown, Lester R., et al. 1992. *State of the World 1992.* New York: W. W. Norton.

Brown, Lester R., et al. 1995. *State of the World 1995.* New York: W. W. Norton.

Brown, Lester R., Nicholas Lenssen, and Hal Kane. 1995. *Vital Signs 1995.* New York: W. W. Norton.

Buchanan, William. 1974. *Understanding Political Variables*, 2nd ed. New York: Charles Scribner's Sons.

Central Intelligence Agency (CIA). 1990a. *The World Factbook 1990.* Washington, D.C.: Central Intelligence Agency.

———. 1990b. *Handbook of Economic Statistics, 1990.* Washington, D.C.: Central Intelligence Agency.

———. 1991a. *The World Factbook 1991.* Washington, D.C.: Central Intelligence Agency.

———. 1991b. *Handbook of Economic Statistics, 1991*. Washington, D.C.: Central Intelligence Agency.

———. 1994. *The World Factbook 1994*. Washington, D.C.: Central Intelligence Agency.

———. 1995. *The World Factbook 1995*. Washington, D.C.: Central Intelligence Agency.

Cipolla, Carlo M. 1962. *The Economic History of World Population*. Baltimore: Penguin.

Cook, Earl. 1976. *Man, Energy, Society*. San Francisco: W. H. Freeman.

Council on Environmental Quality (CEQ). 1981a. *The Global 2000 Report to the President*. Washington, D.C.: Government Printing Office.

———. 1981b. *Environmental Trends*. Washington, D.C.

———. 1991. *21st Annual Report*. Washington, D.C.: Government Printing Office.

Cusack, Thomas R., and Richard J. Stoll. 1990. *Exploring Realpolitik: Probing International Relations with Computer Simulation*. Boulder: Lynne Rienner Publishers.

DeConde, Alexander. 1978. *A History of American Foreign Policy*, 3rd ed. Volume 2: *Global Power*. New York: Charles Scribner's Sons.

Deutsch, Karl W. 1988. *The Analysis of International Relations*, 3rd ed. Englewood Cliffs, N.J.: Prentice-Hall.

Eberstadt, Nicholas. 1995. "Population, Food, and Income," in *The True State of the Planet*, ed. Ronald Bailey. New York: The Free Press, pp. 8–47.

Edwards, Stephen R. 1995. "Conserving Biodiversity," in *The True State of the Planet*, ed. Ronald Bailey. New York: The Free Press, pp. 212–265.

Ehrlich, Paul R., and Anne H. Ehrlich. 1972. *Population, Resources, Environment*. San Francisco: W. H. Freeman.

Forrester, Jay W. 1968. *Principles of Systems*. Cambridge, Mass.: Wright-Allen Press.

Gilpin, Robert. 1981. *War and Change in World Politics*. Cambridge: Cambridge University Press.

Grant, Lindsey. 1982. *The Cornucopian Fallacies*. Washington, D.C.: Environmental Fund.

Gurr, Ted Robert, Keith Jaggers, and Will H. Moore. 1990. "The Transformation of the Western State." *Studies in Comparative International Development* 25, no. 1 (Spring), p. 94.

Haas, Ernst B. 1990. *When Knowledge Is Power*. Berkeley: The University of California Press.

Herrera, Amilcar O., et al. 1976. *Catastrophe or New Society? A Latin American World Model*. Ottawa: International Development Research Centre.

Hopper, W. David. 1976. "The Development of Agriculture in Developing Countries," *Scientific American* 235 (September), p. 200.

Hughes, Barry B. 1980. *World Modeling*. Lexington, Mass.: Lexington Books.

———. 1982. *International Futures Simulation: User's Manual*. Iowa City: CONDUIT, University of Iowa.

———. 1985a. *International Futures Simulation*. Iowa City: CONDUIT, University of Iowa.

———. 1985b. "World Models: The Bases of Difference," *International Studies Quarterly* 29, pp. 77–101.

———. 1985c. *World Futures: A Critical Analysis of Alternatives*. Baltimore: Johns Hopkins University Press.

———. 1988. "International Futures: History and Status," *Social Science Microcomputer Review* 6, pp. 43–48.

———. 1991a. *Continuity and Change in World Politics*. Englewood Cliffs, N.J.: Prentice-Hall.

———. 1991b. "International Futures 1990 (IFs90): Equation Documentation." University of Denver: Graduate School of International Studies, unpublished.

Information Please Almanac. 1990. *The 1990 Information Please Almanac*. Boston: Houghton Mifflin Company.

———. 1992. *The 1992 Information Please Almanac*. Boston: Houghton Mifflin Company.

International Monetary Fund. 1990a. *International Financial Statistics*. Washington, D.C.: International Monetary Fund.

———. 1990b. *World Economic Outlook*. Washington, D.C.: International Monetary Fund.

———. 1991. *World Economic Outlook*. Washington, D.C.: International Monetary Fund.

———. 1992. *World Economic Outlook*. Washington, D.C.: International Monetary Fund.

———. 1995a. *World Economic Outlook*. Washington, D.C.: International Monetary Fund.

———. 1995b. *International Financial Statistics*. Washington, D.C.: International Monetary Fund.

Jansson, Kurt, Michael Harris, and Angela Penrose. 1987. *The Ethiopian Famine*. London: Zed Books Ltd.

Jeffreys, Kent. 1995. "Rescuing the Oceans," in *The True State of the Planet*, ed. Ronald Bailey. New York: The Free Press, pp. 296–338.

Kahn, Herman, William Brown, and Leon Martel. 1976. *The Next 200 Years*. New York: William Morrow.

Kennedy, Paul. 1987. *The Rise and Fall of the Great Powers*. New York: Random House.

Leontief, Wassily, Anne Carter, and Peter Petri. 1977. *The Future of the World Economy*. New York: Oxford University Press.

Liverman, Dianne. 1983. *The Use of Global Simulation Models in Assessing Climate Impacts on the World Food System*. Dissertation, University of California, Los Angeles.

McWilliams, Wayne C., and Harry Piotrowski. 1988. *The World Since 1945*. Boulder: Lynne Rienner Publishers.

Meadows, Dennis L., et al. 1974. *Dynamics of Growth in a Finite World*. Cambridge, Mass.: Wright-Allen Press.

Meadows, Donnela H., Dennis L. Meadows, and Jorgen Randers. 1992. *Beyond the Limits*. Post Mills, Vt.: Chelsea Green Publishing Company.

Meadows, Donnela H., Dennis L. Meadows, Jorgen Randers, and William K. Behrens III. 1972. *The Limits to Growth*. New York: Universe Books.

Mesarovic, Mihajlo D., and Eduard Pestel. 1974. *Mankind at the Turning Point*. New York: E. P. Dutton & Co.

Morgenthau, Hans. 1948. *Politics Among Nations*. New York: Alfred A. Knopf.

Pirages, Dennis. 1983. "The Ecological Perspective and the Social Sciences," *International Studies Quarterly* 27, no. 3 (September), pp. 243–255.

———. 1989. *Global Technopolitics*. Pacific Grove, Calif.: Brooks/Cole Publishing.

Population Reference Bureau. 1991. *World Population Data Sheet 1991*. Washington, D.C.: Population Reference Bureau.

———. 1995. *World Population Data Sheet 1995*. Washington, D.C.: Population Reference Bureau.

Richardson, Lewis Fry. 1960. *Arms and Insecurity*. Chicago: Quadrangle Books.

Sedjo, Roger A. 1995. "Forests: Conflicting Signals," in *The True State of the Planet*, ed. Ronald Bailey. New York: The Free Press, pp. 178–209.

Shane, Harold G., and Gary A. Sojka. 1990. "John Elfreth Watkins, Jr.: Forgotten Genius of Forecasting," in *The 1990s and Beyond*, ed. Edward Cornish. Bethesda, Md.: World Future Society, pp. 150–155.

Sinsheimer, Robert L. 1980. "The Presumptions of Science." In *Economics, Ecology, Ethics*, ed. Herman E. Daly. San Francisco: W. H. Freeman, pp. 146–161.

Sivard, Ruth Leger. 1991. *World Military and Social Expenditures 1991*. Washington, D.C.: World Priorities.

———. 1993. *World Military and Social Expenditures 1993*. Washington, D.C.: World Priorities.

Stockholm International Peace Research Institute (SIPRI). 1994. *SIPRI Yearbook*. New York: Oxford University Press.

Systems Analysis Research Unit (SARU). 1977. *SARUM 76 Global Modeling Project*. London: Departments of the Environment and Transport.

United Nations Development Program (UNDP). 1992. *Human Development Report*. New York: Oxford University Press.

———. 1994. *Human Development Report*. New York: Oxford University Press.

———. 1995. *Human Development Report*. New York: Oxford University Press.

United Nations Food and Agricultural Organization (FAO). 1992. *Production Yearbook*. Rome: FAO.

United States Arms Control and Disarmament Agency. 1992. *World Military Expenditures and Arms Transfers 1992*. Washington, D.C.: ACDA.

———. 1995. *World Military Expenditures and Arms Transfers 1995*. Washington, D.C.: ACDA.

The Universal Almanac 1995. 1994. Kansas City, Mo.: Andrews and McMeel.

Watkins, John Elfreth, Jr. 1990. "What May Happen in the Next Hundred Years," in *The 1990s and Beyond*, ed. Edward Cornish. Bethesda, Md.: World Future Society, pp. 150–155.

Wildavsky, Aaron, and Ellen Tenenbaum. 1981. *The Politics of Mistrust*. Beverly Hills, Calif.: Sage Publications.

World Almanac. 1992. *The World Almanac and Book of Facts 1993*. New York: World Almanac.

World Bank. 1985. *Commodity Trade and Price Trends*. Baltimore: Johns Hopkins University Press.

———. 1991a. *World Development Report 1991*. New York: Oxford University Press.

———. 1991b. *World Tables 1991*. New York: Johns Hopkins University Press.

————. 1992. *World Development Report 1992*. New York: Oxford University Press.

————. 1995. *World Development Report 1995*. New York: Oxford University Press.

World Resources Institute. 1988. *World Resources 1988–89*. New York: Basic Books.

————. 1990. *World Resources 1990–91*. New York: Basic Books.

————. 1992. *World Resources 1992–93*. New York: Oxford University Press.

————. 1994. *World Resources 1994–95*. New York: Oxford University Press.

————. 1995. *World Resources 1995–96*. New York: Oxford University Press.

Wortman, Sterling, and Ralph W. Cummings, Jr. 1978. *To Feed This World*. Baltimore: Johns Hopkins University Press.

Zinnes, Dina A., and John W. Gillespie, eds. 1976. *Mathematical Models in International Relations*. New York: Praeger.

□ □ □

About the Book and Author

Fully updated and including a new and expanded Windows computer simulation, this unique text/disk combination provides a survey of alternative futures in international relations. By manipulating a wide range of variables in
major countries and geographical regions, students can generate a limitless number of future scenarios in the areas of demographics, food, energy, the environment, economics, and international politics. This new edition of *International Futures* coherently defines and develops key concepts in global issues and allows
interactive development of alternative views of our global future. Complete with
tables, flowcharts, feedback loops, computer notes, and research suggestions, the
text and simulation allow students to transcend the usual level of speculation
about the future by moving to an empirically grounded, values-based consideration of issues, strategies, and outcomes. The broader environmental context of international politics is a special focus of the new edition, just as it has emerged as
one of the most important areas in international relations.

Barry B. Hughes is professor of international relations in the Graduate School of
International Studies at the University of Denver, as well as the vice provost for
graduate studies. He has written numerous articles and books, including *World
Futures* (1985) and *Continuity and Change in World Politics* (forthcoming).

BOOKS IN THIS SERIES

Kennth W. Grundy
South Africa: Domestic Crisis and Global Challenge

☐ ☐ ☐

Georg Sørensen
**Democracy and Democratization:
Processes and Prospects in a Changing World**

☐ ☐ ☐

Steve Chan
**East Asian Dynamism: Growth, Order, and
Security in the Pacific Region, Second Edition**

☐ ☐ ☐

Jack Donnelly
International Human Rights

☐ ☐ ☐

V. Spike Peterson and Anne Sisson Runyan
Global Gender Issues

☐ ☐ ☐

Sarah J. Tisch and Michael B. Wallace
**Dilemmas of Development Assistance:
The What, Why, and Who of Foreign Aid**

☐ ☐ ☐

Ted Robert Gurr and Barbara Harff
Ethnic Conflict in World Politics

☐ ☐ ☐

Frederic S. Pearson
**The Global Spread of Arms:
Political Economy of International Security**

☐ ☐ ☐

Deborah J. Gerner
**One Land, Two Peoples:
The Conflict over Palestine, Second Edition**

☐ ☐ ☐

Karen Mingst and Margaret P. Karns
The United Nations in the Post–Cold War Era

☐ ☐ ☐

Gareth Porter and Janet Welsh Brown
Global Environmental Politics, Second Edition

☐ ☐ ☐

Bruce E. Moon
Dilemmas of International Trade

Index

DISCARD

BY OPENING THE SEALED COMPUTER DISK PACKAGE IN THE BACK OF THIS BOOK, YOU FORFEIT YOUR OPTION TO RETURN THE BOOK FOR REFUND AND INDICATE YOUR ACCEPTANCE OF THE FOLLOWING LICENSE AGREEMENT:

(1) GRANT OF LICENSE. You are licensed to use IFs, the computer software program designed to accompany the book, *International Futures.* This software is provided as an educational tool to enhance learning rather than as a commercial software product. It has been carefully reviewed and classroom tested, but even so certain restrictions, warranty disclaimers, and limitations apply.

(2) OWNERSHIP OF SOFTWARE. As the Licensee, you own the disk(s) on which the software is recorded, but Barry B. Hughes retains title and ownership of the software itself. You may copy your disk(s), but you may not modify, adapt, translate, or create derivative works based on the software.

(3) COPYRIGHT. Both the software and the book are copyrighted. Copyright notice must appear on any copies of the disk(s) you make. You are not authorized to copy any portions of the book without written permission from Westview Press except for your own personal use.

(4) DISCLAIMER OF WARRANTY AND LIMITED WARRANTY. The software and book are provided "as is" without warranty as to performance, merchantability, fitness for a particular purpose, accuracy, reliability, currency, or otherwise. The entire risk as to the results and performance of the software is assumed by you. Westview Press warrants to the original Licensee that the disk(s) on which IFs is recorded is free from defects in materials and workmanship under normal use and service for a period of ninety (90) days from the date of delivery as evidenced by a copy of the receipt. Westview Press's entire liability and your exclusive remedy shall be replacement of defective disk(s) returned with a copy of the receipt.

The above are the only warranties of any kind, either express or implied, that are made by Barry B. Hughes or Westview Press regarding the software IFs. Neither Barry B. Hughes nor Westview Press shall be liable for any direct, indirect, consequential, or incidental damages arising out of the use or inability to use IFs software.

IF YOU DO NOT AGREE TO THESE TERMS, DO NOT OPEN THE SEALED DISK PACKAGE. PROMPTLY RETURN THE UNOPENED DISK PACKAGE AND BOOK TO THE PLACE WHERE YOU OBTAINED THEM FOR A REFUND IF AVAILABLE. BY OPENING THE SEALED DISK PACKAGE YOU FORFEIT YOUR OPTION TO RETURN THE BOOK FOR REFUND.